The Social Life of Numbers

The Social Life of Numbers

A Quechua Ontology of Numbers and Philosophy of Arithmetic

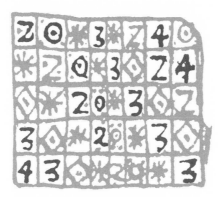

Gary Urton

With the collaboration of Primitivo Nina Llanos

University of Texas Press

Austin

Requests for permission to reproduce material from this work should be sent to Permissions, University of Texas Press, Box 7819, Austin, TX 78713-7819.

⊗ The paper used in this publication meets the minimum requirements of American National Standard for Information Sciences—Permanence of Paper for Printed Library Materials, ANSI Z39.48-1984.

Library of Congress Cataloging-in-Publication Data

Urton, Gary, 1946–
 The social life of numbers : a Quechua ontology of numbers and
philosophy of arithmetic / Gary Urton with the collaboration of
Primitivo Nina Llanos.—1st University of Texas Press ed.
  p. cm.
 Includes bibliographical references and index.
 ISBN 0-292-78533-X (cloth : alk. paper).—ISBN 0-292-78534-8
(paper : alk. paper)
 1. Quechua Indians—Mathematics. 2. Quechua language—Numerals.
3. Quechua philosophy. 4. Quipu. I. Nina Llanos, Primitivo. II. Title.
F2230.2.K4U791997
510′.98—dc21   97-598

For Primo and Noah

. . . mathematics makes subjective assertions—dubitable
and subject to revision—about entities that are time-bound
and culturally loaded.

B. ROTMAN

"Toward a Semiotics of Mathematics"

The genesis of counting systems, just as of any other cultural forms,
is at once a structural and historical process.

J. MIMICA

Intimations of Infinity

Contents

Figures

Tables

Acknowledgments

Many people have offered me invaluable advice, support, and encouragement during the two years (1993–1995) of research for, and writing of, this book. As always, my wife, Julia Meyerson, was the principal source of support and encouragement throughout the project. Julia read and commented on various drafts of several of the chapters, and she produced the drawings. Primitivo ("Primo") Nina Llanos was a remarkable friend, colleague, and teacher during the year (1993–1994) that my family and I spent in Sucre, Bolivia. Primo's patience, originality, and intelligence in the face of my obtuseness (mostly in Quechua) were extraordinary. I thank him also for his sincere affection for, and attention to, my sons, Mark, Jason, and Noah. This study would have been, quite literally, unthinkable without Primo's help and advice. I thank my son Mark, who provided me with the first critical reading of Chapter I, in Sucre, in 1995.

Other friends and colleagues also read and commented on different chapters in various stages of the metamorphoses they underwent to reach the point represented here. My Colgate colleague Anthony Aveni has been, as always, effusive in his support and critical and insightful in his commentary. Marcia Ascher provided important commentary and criticism early in the writing on what turned out to be about one-half of the text. I marvel now at her patient criticism following what must have been, for a professional mathematician, an excruciating reading of my early attempts to make sense of the data I had collected in the field. Elayne Zorn's reading of the same draft was invaluable, particularly in bringing to my attention a number of unrecognized problems in my discussion of Andean textiles and weaving. In Sucre, Antero Klemola, Colin Gomez, and Elka Weinstein raised important questions, especially with regard to Quechua linguistics, from the reading of several chapters in draft form. Tristan Platt offered comments and advice on certain theoretical and practical matters; I hope that I have successfully heeded his advice. I acknowledge with thanks the comments and suggestions that I received on the final manuscript from David Dearborn. Frank Salomon wrote extensive comments on the final draft, which aided me greatly in thinking through several unresolved (and some unrecognized) problems that remained. The final form that this work has assumed owes much to his thoughtful commentary and suggestions. Conversations with my long-time friends and colleagues Tom Zuidema and Richard Bielefeldt were critical in stimulating my thinking on several problems discussed herein. I also gratefully acknowledge the help of my research assistants at Colgate University, Dixie L. Henry (1996) and Tom Palmer (1997).

In May 1996 I presented an overview of the arguments made in this book in a month-long seminar that I taught at the École des Hautes Études en Sciences Sociales, in Paris, at the invitation of Nathan Wachtel, Gilles Rivière, and Carmen Salazár-Soler. I thank the participants in that seminar, who made many insightful and helpful comments on the data and arguments presented herein.

None of the people mentioned above is responsible for errors of fact, judgment, or logic that remain in this work; these are my responsibility alone.

My field research in and around Sucre benefited greatly from the support and advice of Verónica Cereceda and Gabriel Martínez. Verónica and Gabriel generously took me under their wing and made a place for me and my project in the conduct of their development work in the organization Antropólogos del Surandino (ASUR). Several staff members of ASUR—including Santiago Pórcel, Jaime, and Lalo—became good friends and field companions who helped me find my way in and around the villages of Candelaria and Marawa.

In Candelaria, I thank especially the family of Damián Flores and Santusa Quispe, who were my hosts. I also thank María Condori and her daughters, Irene and Benedicta, who, along with Valentina Flores, were my principal weaving teachers. Sixto Condori's help was invaluable in getting me settled into Candelaria. In Marawa, I thank the family of Cicilio Cruz and Amalia Mamani, who served as my hosts.

I express my profoundest gratitude to the following institutions, foundations, and organizations that provided the financial support that allowed me to take two years off from my teaching duties at Colgate University in order to pursue research and writing on this project. During my year (1993–1994) of ethnographic and linguistic research in Sucre, funds were provided by research grants from the National Science

Foundation (No. SBR 9221737) and the Social Science Research Council. Colgate University also provided me with a sabbatical leave. During the year (1994–1995) in which I wrote this book, support was provided by a fellowship from the National Endowment for the Humanities, as well as a Senior Faculty Leave from Colgate University.

As I also discuss in this book material that I collected concerning the Inka *khipus* (knotted-string records), I would like to express my appreciation to the German Academic Exchange Service (D.A.A.D.) for a study-visit grant that provided partial support for my research on *khipus* in the Museum für Völkerkunde, in Berlin, Germany (June 1993). The National Endowment for the Humanities summer stipend program provided a fellowship that further supported my research in Berlin, as well as one month's (July 1993) subsequent research in the Archivo General de Indias, Seville, Spain, on historical documents containing Spanish transcriptions of *khipu* accounts. I also express my appreciation to the Sloane Foundation, which provided a faculty development grant that allowed me to purchase and copy research materials pertaining to ethnomathematics.

The Social Life of Numbers

Anthropology and the Philosophy of Arithmetic

Why Study Quechua Numbers and Mathematics?

I expect that some (if not many) who pick up this book will ask themselves the question posed in the heading to this section. The question is certainly not without merit, as I asked it of myself many times during the early days and months of research and writing on this book, which concerns the numerical knowledge and arithmetic practices of the Quechua-speaking peoples of the Bolivian and Peruvian Andes. The perceptive reader will of course recognize a confession buried in the previous sentence. That is, I must admit that I did not take up this study from a profound, single-minded interest in numbers and mathematics. Behind this confession lies another, decidedly more embarrassing one, which is that while I have always had a great interest in science and mathematics, I am not a math whiz—the type of person who seeks out mathematical problems and puzzles against which to test their mathematical acumen. So, the question in the section heading now becomes both more urgent *and* personal: Why would someone who is not an expert in the art of mathematics take up the study of numbers, arithmetic, and mathematics? There are two answers to this question, which, I am quick to point out, have undergone a complete reversal in terms of their priority in motivating my work on this topic. The first has a historical focus, the second an ethnographic one.

Initially, I came to the study of contemporary Quechua numerical knowledge and arithmetic and mathematical practice as what I saw early on to be an essential first step in pursuing my primary interest at the time, which was the analysis of the Inka *khipus*. *Khipus* are the knotted-string devices that were used by the Inkas to record both quantitative data (such as census accounts and tribute records) and information that was said to have been used in the recording and retrieval—or "reading"—of Inka histories, genealogies, and myths. We know with some certainty that many of the *khipus* preserved today in museum and private collections contain quantitative data (see Ascher and Ascher 1981; Locke 1923; Radicati di Primeglio 1979). Since the beginning of this century, scholars have succeeded in "cracking" the code, or organization, of the numerical information in the *khipus,* thus allowing us a glimpse into the numerical knowledge and—indirectly at least—the mathematical practices of the Inkas.

There is, however, a fundamental methodological problem in the way that all previous studies of the numerical information recorded on the *khipus* have been carried out. That is, the numbers have in all cases been translated using Hindu-Arabic numerals or the language of numbers of the investigator, especially English and Spanish. Such approaches to the *khipu* numbers inevitably mask, and eliminate from analysis, any values and meanings that may have been attached to these numbers by the Quechua-speaking bureaucrats of the Inka empire who recorded the information. Such symbolic, metaphorical, and other meanings that may have been associated with these numbers (or number groupings, patterns, etc.) could be of great importance in our continuing efforts to understand Inka numerical and mathematical concepts and practices. But, in addition, we might find that such values could provide us with a basis for approaching the task of "deciphering" the narratives recorded on the *khipus*—a challenge which we have not addressed in a serious way to the present day (Urton, n.d.).

It was this set of interests and objectives that most directly and profoundly motivated my study of contemporary Quechua numerical knowledge and mathematical practices initially; that is, I was seeking a body of knowledge and practice in the present that could help direct and inform my investigations of the past. In this regard, I should note that such historically motivated and, frankly, superficially "romantic" investigations of contemporary Quechua society and culture as that outlined here are often viewed with uneasiness, if not with outright disdain, especially by some who insist on seeing Andean peoples today solely as the victims of poverty and as either the perpetrators or the victims of violence (see, for example, Starn 1991). According to this view, Andean peoples have nothing to add to the human record other than the misfortunes of their material conditions of life. However, I (and others) continue to insist on seeing Andean peoples as bearers and manipulators of bodies of knowledge and practice—from animal husbandry and agriculture (see Van der Ploeg 1993) to astronomy (Urton 1988)—that are profoundly important for us to understand in historical and comparative terms. To ignore, and thereby undervalue, the complex traditions and systems of knowledge that have been maintained and continually rethought and reformulated by Andean peoples through history strikes me not only as pernicious, but, more importantly, as performing a disservice to people who have been regarded over the past five hundred years as too culturally and intellectually debilitated to offer anything of interest to the record of human accomplishments.

The second reason that I embarked on a study of Quechua numerical knowledge and arithmetic and mathematical practice was because this is an almost totally unstudied domain of knowledge and practice in Andean studies.[1] Having earlier investigated the astronomical knowledge and cosmological beliefs of people in a community near Cusco, Peru (Urton 1988), and having found there beliefs, ideas, and traditions that are of considerable complexity and (I think) of great comparative interest and importance, it seemed to me that the same might prove to be true of numbers and mathematics. I admit here that this second motivation for undertaking the present study was initially far less compelling than the first—my interest in the Inka *khipus*. Therefore, I was quite unprepared for, if not for some time actually resistant to, what I would find in this study. For what I found as my research proceeded, especially during a year of linguistic study and ethnographic research carried out in and around Sucre, Bolivia, in 1993–1994, was a complex and well-articulated set of ideas and practices that represent a new (to us) and arguably unique ontology of numbers and philosophy of arithmetic and mathematics. I hope to show that the ontology and philosophy to be elaborated herein provide us with a new perspective—perhaps a new paradigm—with which to reexamine and rethink well-known bodies of ethnographic and historical data pertaining to Andean societies and cultures, past and present.

This is a broad and immodest claim for such a slim book. It is therefore imperative that I inform the reader from the beginning about the basic arguments to be presented in the following chapters. However, in order for this summary to be meaningful, I must first make clear exactly what the intended topic of study is here and who the people are whom I have been referring to as the "Quechua-speaking people of the Andes."

The Topic of Study: Is It Ethnomathematics or Ethnoarithmetic?

As will soon become apparent, my principal concern in this study is with understanding the cultural significance of numbers and arithmetic among Quechua-speaking peoples in the Andes. Given that the primary focus here will be on the positive integers (1, 2 , 3, 4 , 5, . . .) and the arithmetic procedures for manipulating relations among them (i.e., addition, subtraction, multiplication, and division), this study falls comfortably under the heading of the "anthropology of numbers" (Crump 1990) or the more common, but somewhat more problematic, label "ethnomathematics" (Ascher 1991). Identified either way, the field of studies we are concerned with is new and little developed to date; thus, there remain several problems in the definition of terms, as well as in the conceptualization of topics to be addressed, assumptions made, and approaches used, by researchers in the field. To get straight to some of these problems, we may begin by defining the two principal fields of study in Western academic practice most closely connected with our topic of study—arithmetic and mathematics—and then move on to discuss the meaning and significance of attaching the prefix "ethno-" to one or the other (or both) of these terms.

In James and James's *Mathematics Dictionary* (1976), "arithmetic" is defined as: "The study of the positive integers, 1, 2, 3, 4, 5, . . . under the operations of addition, subtraction, multiplication, and division, and the use of the results of these studies in everyday life." This definition encompasses the great majority of topics and practices that I will be concerned with in this work. However, there are certain equally important topics discussed here that fall outside the boundaries of the above definition of arithmetic. These include such questions as the ontology of numbers generally; the logical foundation, motivation, and symbolic and metaphorical meanings of the cardinal and ordinal numeral sequences in Quechua; and the relationship between shape and quantity (as in the geometrical designs of Andean weavings). Certain of these matters fall more naturally within the domain of what we know in the West as mathematics.

As many authors have noted, it is virtually impossible to define mathematics in any concise way, thus producing a notable resistance on the part of scholars who have written on comparative and historical mathematics to provide anything but the most general characterization of this subject (e.g., Ascher 1991: 2–3, and Joseph 1991: 3). Nonetheless, we have to begin *somewhere,* especially if we propose later to attach to this undefinable-something the even more ambiguous "ethno-" prefix! Citing James and James's work again, mathematics can be defined as:

> *The logical study of shape, arrangement, quantity and many related concepts. Mathematics often is divided into three fields:* algebra, analysis, *and* geometry. *However, no clear divisions can be made, since these branches have become thoroughly intermingled. Roughly, algebra involves numbers and their abstractions, analysis involves continuity and limits, and geometry is concerned with space and related concepts. (1976: 239)*

It is also relevant (especially in relation to topics discussed later in this introduction) to take note of James and James's definition of *pure mathematics* as "the study and development of the principles of mathematics for their own sake and possible future usefulness, rather than for their immediate usefulness in other fields of science or knowledge. The study of mathematics independently of experience in other scholarly disciplines" (1976: 239).

Before taking stock of the relevance of the terms arithmetic and/or mathematics for our interests here, we should consider the significance of the prefix "ethno-." Ascher argues that the appropriate object of study in "ethnomathematics" is mathematical *ideas* not "mathematics" *per se,* the latter of which, she argues, is a Western category and thus is not even to be found in traditional cultures. Among the mathematical ideas that Ascher proposes as appropriate for, and accessible to, study are "those involving number, logic, spatial configuration, and, even more significant, the combination or organization of these into systems or structures" (1991: 2).

"Ethno-" is, of course, used today quite liberally to indicate that the investigation of a particular field of study (such as biology or astronomy) is being discussed from the perspective, and on the basis of the knowledge, of the people of some non-Western, "traditional" society. In such contexts, "traditional" is used to denote a society that, at least as characterized in the "ethnographic present" of the published anthropological literature, is largely nonliterate, nonindustrialized, and overwhelmingly rural and agriculturally based. Now, as has been recognized in the anthropological literature for some time, the designation of any particular society as "traditional" is highly problematic, especially when this category is considered to stand in some meaningful opposition to a "modern" society. For our purposes here, the point that I want to stress regarding this dual classification is that "modern" societies are generally assumed to be so partially in relation to their possession of *science,* whereas "traditional" societies are considered not to have science. The questions for us to consider in this regard are: How does the science/nonscience dualism characterizing the split between modern and traditional societies condition the pursuit of the investigation of numbers, arithmetic, and mathematics in a particular non-Western society? And, more to the point, why has the field of studies we are engaged in here come to be known as "ethnomathematics" and not, for instance, "ethnoarithmetic?"

There are two observations that will direct us on our way to finding answers to the questions raised above. The first observation, which has not been addressed specifically in any previous ethnomathematical studies that I am aware of, is this: In the classification of societies according to the traditional/modern dualism, there has been at least an implicit recognition that traditional societies possess, *to varying degrees,* numbers and arithmetic, while modern societies possess numbers (*to the nth degree*), arithmetic, *and* mathematics. It is important to note that the collection of knowledge and practices referred to as mathematics is often accorded to a handful of earlier, literate societies, such as China, India, Greece, and Rome, as well as to the schools of Islamic scholars who were directly responsible for preserving, and innovating on, both Greco-Roman and Eastern mathematical traditions (see Joseph 1991).

According to the above characterization, *numbers* and *arithmetic* are not only considered to be knowable and doable by people in all societies, but there is also the presumption (suggested by the fact that there is no talk in this body of literature about either "ethnonumbers" or "ethnoarithmetic") that the concept of numbers and the procedures of arithmetic are unaffected by cultural differences. Before I comment on this point, let me raise a second related point, which is that, while it is common to discuss the philosophy of mathematics, there is not a comparable body of literature dealing with the "philosophy of arithmetic." The conclusion that I draw from these two observations is that when scholars talk about "ethnomathematics," they generally do not by the use of that label mean to suggest that culture can affect the nature and meaning of numbers, nor the procedures of arithmetic or mathematics. That is, no one seems to be suggesting that, in some other culture, two plus two might equal anything other than four, or that transfinite numbers might be imagined in some cultural tradition in such a way as to possess characteristics other than those assigned to them in Western mathematics. Rather, it is clear that by the use of the label *ethno*mathematics, what is considered to be susceptible to cultural influence are the *conceptions* of numbers and the *philosophy* of mathematics. In other words, to my mind at least, ethnomathematics is actually concerned with *ethnophilosophy*. The elision of "philosophy" in the word ethnomathematics masks the idea, firmly held by most practitioners of ethnomathematics, that while philosophy may be influenced by culture, mathematics is not.

Now, I think it *has* been clearly demonstrated that the *philosophy* of mathematics is indeed subject to different cultural, linguistic, and perhaps even *national* formulations. This is evident from any survey of the Western history and philosophy of mathematics, in which we find a record of a few significantly different traditions of mathematical philosophy, such as Platonism, Intuitionism, and Formalism.[2] The question for us to consider here, however, is: Where does this leave us in defining what it is we are (or ought to be) concerned with in an anthropological study of numbers, arithmetic, and mathematics? While I will have more to say later in this chapter on the question of the intersection of anthropology and mathematics, the position that I will adopt here is to place everything on the table—numbers, arithmetic, philosophy, and mathematics—not privileging any particular form of human knowledge and practice as being above either language or culture. That is, I assume that to some degree and in varying ways (linguistic, logical, metaphorical, etc.), all of these forms of knowledge and practice are susceptible to formulations reflecting the differing customs, values, and ways of constructing and pursuing logical arguments among cultures worldwide. Whether or not that susceptibility is realized, and what its consequences might be, are matters to be determined on the basis of intensive ethnographic and linguistic research on number theory and ethnomathematics in different cultures. For instance, while we find that the Hindu-Arabic numerals 1, 2, 3, . . . are used to sign the same quantities in all cultures that have adopted these symbols, nonetheless, we will find in this study that the *relations* between any two adjacent numbers are conceptualized quite differently in Quechua numerical ontology than they are in Western number theory. At this level, then, I will argue that there are "ethnonumbers" and that there can be (and is) such a thing as "ethnoarithmetic." As far as I am aware from the published literature, we have barely even begun comparative investigation of numbers at the level outlined above (one of the few such studies is that carried out by Mimica [1992]).

In summary, while I will not be overly concerned with using a particular label (such as "ethnomathematics") for what it is I am investigating here, I will try to label the different topics that I address below (for example, the ontology of numbers, the philosophy of arithmetic and/or mathematics) consistently so that the reader will be clear about what concept or practice is at issue, at least as it is to be understood on the basis of the normal English usage of the terms involved. Before turning to discuss more general problems in the anthropological study of numbers, arithmetic, and mathematics, I will clarify the particular language and culture that we will focus on in this study.

Defining the Language of Study

"Quechua" refers to a widespread language family, the numerous variants of which are spoken by some six to ten million people (Crystal 1987: 442) primarily in the Andean nations of Peru, Bolivia, Ecuador, Colombia, and Argentina. The language family has its present, widespread distribution as a result of a long and complex history of language dispersal, contact, and attempts at cultural unification that occurred both before and after the Spanish conquest of the Andes, beginning in 1532. The Quechua language is thought to have had its origins in central or coastal Peru. From its origins, there developed two main branches: Central Quechua and Peripheral Quechua, the latter of which was divided primarily between two sub-branches, one to the north and the other to the south of Central Quechua (Parker 1963; Torero 1964, 1974; Mannheim 1991). We will be concerned in this study with two varieties of the southern sub-branch of Peripheral Quechua: Southern Peruvian and Bolivian Quechua.

The present distribution of Southern Peruvian and Bolivian Quechua is intimately related to the history of the Inka empire and its conquest and colonization by Europeans. Beginning several centuries before the European invasion, populations from central Ecuador southward to central Chile were under at least the nominal, if not actual, control of the Inkas, whose empire was centered in Cusco, located in what is today south-central Peru. While there were many different languages spoken throughout the territory of *Tawantinsuyu* ("the four united quarters/parts")—the name that was used by the Inkas to refer to their empire—the Southern Peruvian variety of Quechua spoken in the heartland of the empire, the southern highlands of Peru, had the status of a *lingua franca,* partially because this was the language of administration in the Inka empire. Provincial nobility throughout the empire were required to send their heirs (their sons and/or brothers) to Cusco for training in Quechua. As Damián de la Bandera noted in ca. 1557, "All the caciques and chief persons of the whole kingdom who held any office or position in the state were obliged to know the general language [Quechua] in order to be able to give whatever information was necessary to their superiors" (cited in Rowe 1982: 96). However, the Inkas seem not to have been particularly disturbed by the myriad other languages that were spoken within the empire. In addition, through such institutions as that of the *mitmaq*—the relocation of populations within the empire for purposes of pacification, or the resettling of people where their particular skills were needed—the discontinuities in the distribution of languages became, if anything, more pronounced during imperial times. The relocation of Southern Peruvian Quechua–speaking *mitmaq* to the Cochabamba valley and elsewhere in central Bolivia (see, for example, Wachtel 1982) may at least partially account for the development of Bolivian

Quechua, a variety of southern Peripheral Quechua that is mutually intelligible with the Southern Peruvian, the Inka *lingua franca*.

Following the Spanish conquest of the Andes, the European colonizers were faced with an exceptionally complex linguistic picture. This included the myriad minor languages spoken in different locales; a few languages—such as Aymara, Puquina, and Yunga—that had a fairly widespread distribution and which were (initially at least) encouraged over local languages by the Spaniards; and the Inka *lingua franca*— Southern Peruvian Quechua. As a part of their strategy of administering to the native population in both civil and ecclesiastical terms, the Spaniards increasingly promoted the use of Quechua over other languages. In addition, from early colonial times, the Spaniards were responsible for the publication in Quechua of certain works, especially ecclesiastical items such as catechisms and confessional manuals (see Barnes 1992; Mannheim 1991: 34). Thus, as has been made clear by a number of students of Quechua over the past few decades, the present widespread distribution of the Quechua language throughout the Andes is primarily a result of Spanish initiatives at language standardization, rather than a reflection of an attempt by the Inkas to eliminate linguistic diversity within the empire (Mannheim 1991; Torero 1974).

What is important for our purposes about the above observations is, first, that the people who speak Quechua today throughout the Andes do so as a consequence not of descent, in some pure manner, from the Inka nobility in Cusco or from their provincial administrators throughout the empire, but rather as a result of the project of linguistic homogenization that was carried out by the Spaniards during the colonial era. Nonetheless, and this is the second point of interest, the Southern Peruvian and Bolivian varieties of Quechua spoken today in southern Peru and central Bolivia are the historical descendants of the language spoken by the Inkas in Cusco (Mannheim 1991: 11). While many changes in phonetics, vocabulary, and, to a lesser degree, grammar have occurred in Southern Peruvian and Bolivian Quechua since the European invasion (see Mannheim 1991: 113 ff), it is clear—for example, from dictionaries and other early colonial sources in Quechua—that there are far more similarities than differences between the Quechua spoken today and that spoken in late pre-Hispanic and early colonial times throughout southern Peru and central Bolivia. In other words, there would be mutual comprehension between and among the speakers of these two varieties of Quechua at the two end points of the historical continuum from late pre-Hispanic times to the present day.

The question that is raised for us by these observations is: What is the status, in terms of continuities from colonial times, in the lexicon, syntax, and semantics of the language of numbers and arithmetic operations (the terms and phrases used for addition, subtraction, etc.) in the varieties of Quechua spoken today in southern Peru and central Bolivia? While I will address different aspects of this question in each of the following chapters, the short answer to this question is that the language of numbers, arithmetic, and mathematics does not appear to have undergone significant changes, either in terms of the vocabularies involved or in the ways terms are strung together syntactically in phrases denoting compound numbers and arithmetic operations.

One thing that may account for the persistence of Quechua numbers to the present day is that, like the numbering system of the conquering Europeans, Quechua utilizes a base-10, or decimal, system of numeration. Thus, there are no fundamental structural discontinuities in the two numbering systems as we might expect would arise, for example, were the number system of the conquering society to have been based on a binary, quinary, or vigesimal principle. This means that values expressed in one of the two languages (Quechua or Spanish) can be easily translated using the number names and grammatical constructions of the other. This is not to say, however, that even in predominately Quechua-speaking villages Quechua numbers are utilized on all occasions, for not only do Spanish number words predominate in certain settings (such as marketing and telling time), but also Quechua and Spanish number names and constructions are freely mixed by certain types of people in certain settings. This will be clear, for instance, to anyone who becomes attuned to the number words and phrases used in urban and provincial markets throughout the Andes today. I will return in Chapter 6 to the discussion of a number of issues concerning uses of, and conflicts over, Quechua and Spanish numbers in the Andes during the colonial era.

To return to the question of linguistic continuities in Southern Peruvian and Bolivian Quechua, wherever and whenever Quechua number names and phrases are used today, there are few differences from colonial times in such features as, for instance, the grammatical entailments of combining "minor" units (1–9) with "major" units (10, 100, and 1,000) to form compound numbers—those combining two or more primary lexemes in the decimal system of numeration, as English "seventeen" (7 10). Therefore, generally speaking, we can use the material on numbers and arithmetic from one era (for example, the colonial dictionaries of Quechua) to enlarge, enrich, and in some cases contextualize data collected in another era (such as contemporary ethnographic data from Quechua-speaking communities in southern Peru and Bolivia).

With this brief overview of the Quechua language in the Andes as background, we now turn to a summary of the principal arguments to be made in the following chapters concerning the ontology of numbers and the philosophy of arithmetic and mathematics among contemporary Quechua-speakers of southern Peru and Bolivia. This summary will also inform the discussion, to be taken up later in this introduction, of the question: What contribution can anthropology make to the science of mathematics?

Outline of a Quechua Ontology of Numbers and Philosophy of Mathematics

When I speak of an "ontology" of numbers, I am referring to ideas about the origin and nature of numbers. That is: Where do numbers come from? What kind(s) of thing(s) are they? And how is one number related to another, or the next, number? These are questions that have been of central concern to philosophers of mathematics in the West for several centuries (Boyer 1968; Dummett 1991; Wittgenstein 1978). In this work, I will show that the characteristics and identities of numbers as conceived of and formulated in Quechua language and culture are predicated in terms of relations and identities constituting and governing social life in Quechua communities. More concretely, family relations and kinship roles and statuses represent the principal types of relations—such as hierarchy, descent, succession—in terms of which numbers are conceptualized, organized, and talked about. Any given sequence of natural numbers (as four, five, six, . . .) or ordinal numerals (as fourth, fifth, sixth, . . .) is motivated, and finds its rationale in, the social and biological relations uniting and organizing a descent group. The rules, or organizing principles, underlying *succession*, which is one of the cen-

TABLE 1.1

The Prototype of Cardinal and Ordinal Sequences

Cardinal Sequence	Ordinal Sequence	Prototype
1	first	mother
2	second	first-born
3	third	second-born
4	fourth	third-born
5	fifth	fourth, or last, born

tral processes that must be accounted for in any ontology of numbers, are identified on two levels in Quechua ideology; the first is that between a mother and her offspring, with the former as the prior number (usually "one") and the latter as her successor(s); the second is that of age-grading among siblings, with an older sibling as a prior number and a younger sibling as its successor. Thus, kinship and social relations will be shown to form the matrix for thinking about, and talking with, numbers.

Following from these observations, the prototype of a sequence of cardinal numbers or ordinal numerals combines the two principles of succession described above in the group formed by a mother and her several offspring born successively over time (see Table 1.1). I will explain later (Chapters 3 and 4) why the prototype, or model, of number/numeral sequences contains five elements.

Thus, numbers are not conceived of in Quechua ideology as abstractions whose nature and relations to each other rely on the predications of pure logic, as in the West. Rather, numbers are conceptualized in terms of social—especially family and kinship—roles and relations. One consequence of their participation in social life is that all of the linguistic formulations and grammatical constructions that are used to talk about inheritance, succession, dependence, and interdependence within a kin group (such as the Andean *ayllu*) can be applied as well to number identities and numerical relations. I would note that the metaphorical links between kinship and numerical relations outlined here are consistent with what Turner (1987) has so cogently identified as the central role of kinship relations in the construction of metaphors more generally.

With this stark outline of the ontology of numbers as background, we now turn to a summary of the philosophy of arithmetic and mathematics to be encountered herein (see especially Chapter 5). By a "philosophy" of arithmetic, I am referring to ideas, discourse, and practices concerning when and why, or under what conditions, certain manipulations of numbers, or mathematical operations, are both called for and are considered to be appropriate. The operations that we will examine include the arithmetic operations of addition, subtraction, multiplication, and division. The fundamental notion on which the performance of any one of these operations is premised is the idea that the desired and proper state of affairs in the world is one in which resources, labor, behavior, and all other objects, relations, and attitudes are in a state of balance, equilibrium, and harmony. If and when a state of imbalance or disequilibrium emerges (as through an inappropriate distribution of resources, or inappropriate behavior), then the imbalance and disequilibrium must be rectified. The arithmetic operations of addition, subtraction, multiplication, and division represent several of the principal forms of rectification that may be carried out. That is, for example, if resources are distributed inappropriately (*note:* "inappropriate" is not necessarily synonymous with "unequal"), then the situation must be rectified, perhaps by taking something from one part (subtraction) and applying it to another (addition).

In Chapter 5, I will refer to the *philosophical* principles outlined above as constituting an arithmetic and a mathematics of "rectification." It will be seen that these notions of the nature, logic, and purpose of arithmetic practice are radically different from those encountered in the West, while potentially yielding the same results, at least insofar as numbers are manipulated in Quechua practice. That is, in Western mathematics, one need have no purpose or justification for manipulating numbers, nor are arithmetic and mathematics to be justified solely on the grounds of their "utility." In particular, pure mathematics undertakes its manipulations of numbers for the purpose of exploring the properties of numbers, shapes, spatial relations, etc. If the properties that are discovered result in having some use value, so much the better; however, the search for such values (that is, "applications") is not the driving force behind mathematical explorations in their purest form (see Hardy 1993; see also above, in this chapter).

When we consider the Quechua ontology of numbers and philosophy of mathematics summarized above, we can appreciate the uniqueness of these concepts as well as the potential value to Andean studies, conceived of broadly, of the investigation of these numerical, arithmetic, and mathematical forms of reasoning. As I noted, these issues have received virtually no attention to date. These observations also provide an appropriate point of departure for a consideration of the broader question of the potential contribution that anthropology can make to the study of number theory, arithmetic, and mathematics. Before taking up the latter question, let me clarify the ethnographic status of the two terms used above (and in the subtitle to this work) to refer to the general topics of inquiry here—"ontology" and "philosophy."

Except in the case of my principal teacher and informant, Primitivo Nina Llanos, the Quechua-speaking people with whom I discussed numbers, arithmetic, and related matters (such as "sets" of objects; correlations between one quantity and another) in villages in Peru and Bolivia did not use either one of these metalinguistic terms (ontology and philosophy) to describe, in an abstract sense, what general category of knowledge their comments referred to. Primitivo Nina, who is a literate, highly analytical professor of Quechua, easily makes the transition and connections between individual acts and such abstract, analytical categories of knowledge as "ontology." My other informants also were entirely capable of using abstract, analytical terms for types of people, forms of behavior, and categories of kinship and other social relations. Thus, for example, people in Candelaria would daily use a term such as *mama* to refer equally to "mother," the "thumb," the first "ear of corn" sprouting on a cornstalk, and the first color to appear in a rainbow (see Chapter 3). However, the people in this community (or in any other that I am familiar with) have no interest in, or need for, a set of analytical terms for talking about their thinking and speech (see below, Chapter 4). Out of such general uses of terms and correlations of phenomena and actions as those given above for *mama,* I have grouped together speech acts, objects of reference, etc., as indicative of the subject matter of a Quechua "ontology" of numbers. I have done the same for what I call herein the "philosophy" of arithmetic (in a manner similar to Isbell and Roncalla Fernandez's [1977] discussion of the "ontogenesis" of metaphor in

Quechua). My hope is that by the end of this study, I will have successfully explained and interpreted the linguistic and ethnographic materials
to the point that I will have justified my use of the particular metalinguistic labels "ontology" (of numbers) and "philosophy" (of arithmetic).

Anthropology's Potential Contribution to Mathematics

What can anthropology contribute to the study of numerical and mathematical systems? While the literature relevant for addressing this question is not extensive, it is not my intention to summarize or review that
material here. Two very good summaries or overviews of mathematical
and numerical traditions in non-Western societies have appeared in recent years (Ascher 1991; Crump 1990). The reader is referred to those
works, and others (e.g., Gillings 1978; Hallpike 1979; Joseph 1991; Menninger 1969; Mimica 1992; Nakayama 1978; Needham 1959; van der
Waerden 1978; Zaslavsky 1990) for comparative descriptions and analyses of the nature, typologies, and evolutionary significance of the varieties of arithmetic, mathematical, numbering, and counting systems encountered worldwide.

In arriving at a statement of what I see as perhaps the most valuable
contribution that anthropology can offer to mathematics, I will begin
by questioning the degree to which our comparative studies of mathematical knowledge and practice in non-Western cultures have added
anything fundamentally new or challenging to the prevailing, Western-
oriented view of the nature and meaning of mathematics. What I mean
by this is the following. The dominant view among Western philosophers and mathematicians concerning the nature of mathematical
propositions and "truths" is embodied in the theory referred to as "Platonism." This theory posits that mathematics "discovers" and validates
logical truths which exist in a timeless, ideal state. As the case for Platonism (as opposed to Intuitionism and Formalism) was stated by G. H.
Hardy: "I believe that mathematical reality lies outside us, and that our
function is to discover or observe it, and that the theorems which we
prove, and which we describe grandiloquently as our 'creations' are simply our notes of our observations" (cited in Barrow 1992: 261).

Since, in the Platonist view, mathematicians observe and describe a reality that exists beyond the human realm—that is, beyond the realm of experience, change, and language—this reality ought to be describable in the same terms regardless of cultural and/or linguistic differences that distinguish one society from another. In fact, the view that mathematical truths do not—*cannot*—differ cross-culturally is a central tenet of the Platonist vision of the reality of numbers, shapes, sets, etc. (Barrow 1992: 263; Rotman 1988: 5). It is important to stress that for Frege, whose work is the principal source of twentieth-century Platonism, numbers are a part of this non-sensible, objective reality; that is, number is neither spatial nor physical, nor (unlike ideas) subjective. Dummett (1991: 81) characterizes Frege's notion of "objectivity" as "independence from our experience, intuition and imagination and from the delineation of inner images from the memory of earlier experiences."

Now, Frege himself pointedly stressed that, in investigating the fundamental principles of mathematics, it may be of some use to examine ideas and changes of ideas that occur during the practice of mathematics. Nonetheless, he notes, "psychology should not imagine that it can contribute anything to the foundation of arithmetic" (cited in Dummett 1991: 18). The question for us at this point, obviously, is: Should anthropology imagine that it can make such a contribution? As a prelude to answering this question and, in the process, of returning to explain why I have questioned whether or not previous ethnomathematical studies have added anything fundamentally new to the corpus of mathematical truths or have challenged the prevailing Western (i.e., Platonist) view on the nature of mathematical truths, we first have to answer the question of what type(s) of contributions anthropological data might possibly make to the comparative study of mathematics.

I would suggest that there are basically two types of data that would have one or the other of the effects noted above. The first would be at the level of the mathematical truths that might be apprehended by the people of some "other," non-Western tradition. That is, if we were to find, in the mathematics of society X, a recognition of some fundamental property of numbers and their relations that had not been recognized in the West, such knowledge could indeed represent a unique contribution to world mathematics. Now, in my reading of the anthropologically oriented studies that have been published to date, it is primarily at this first level that they seek to make a contribution to the mathematical literature. While these studies have presented a host of unusual, challenging, and novel mathematical formulations from cultures around the world (such as puzzles and unusual number matrices incorporated in weavings, metalwork, architecture, and games), none has identified mathematical truths or properties and relations of numbers that have not been recognized, or are not entirely consistent with, the properties of numbers identified in Western mathematics. This is the case, I would argue, despite the fact that many of the properties and relations that have been identified in such contexts are of a quite sophisticated nature (see, for example, Ascher's analysis [1991: 74 f.] of Walpiri kinship terms and relations, which, she shows, are organized according to what mathematicians call "the dihedral group of order 8"). Nor have these comparative data challenged the ideas about the nature and location of mathematical truths as conceived of in Western Platonist philosophy.

The second way that anthropology can potentially contribute to the mathematical literature is at—what I see as—the more fundamental level of a challenge to the philosophical and logical foundations of Platonism. In the characterization of some of the principal tenets of Platonism given above, we learned that mathematical truths are conceived of as existing in a reality "out there," apart from human ideas, actions, language, and experiences. What humans may do is attempt to discover, examine, and formulate theorems identifying and validating these objective truths. But just who says—that is, how and from whom do we know—that this notion of the location of mathematical truths is, in fact, true? If we find, for instance, that the Quechua conceive of numbers as grounded in family relations and kinship statuses and numerical relations as premised on social relations, both of which are not only apprehended but experienced and talked about (in Quechua) daily, how can we deny the truth of these views—*providing that they do not produce numerical values and mathematical formulations that are at odds with those recognized in other mathematical traditions?*

Now, the skeptical, cynical, or plain anthropologically *disinterested* reader might give the tag-on at the end of the last sentence the following significance: If the Quechua view does not produce a mathematics contrary to generally accepted mathematical truths based on Platonism, then why should we not *dis*regard Quechua ontology and philosophy, since it comes loaded down with a lot of cultural baggage, such as kinship and social organization, that can potentially complicate matters, as well as vary significantly from one society to the next? However, the anthropologically *interested* interpretation of the above tag-on would argue that, if we *do* identify a philosophy that does not disturb mathematical truths as formulated in our (Western) theorems but does allow us to link mathematics, cultural values, and social organization, then why not pursue that philosophy to its ends in order to discover what we can learn. For instance, we may find that the Cartesian split between the real and the ideal, which underlies the modern philosophical formulation of Western Platonism, represents an unnecessary sacrifice in our pursuit of the truth of mathematics. That is, might we find in this way that it is, in fact, possible to effect a convergence of the interests and objectives of anthropology and those of mathematics, at least at a certain level of analysis? The level of analysis that I am referring to is that of the investigation and articulation of the ontological and philosophical foundations of the description and analysis of objects, sets, collections, and the principles and forces organizing relations among them. If mathematical philosophies can be shown to vary in a fundamental way cross-culturally, then does anthropology not hold out to mathematics the offer of expanding and clarifying its philosophical grounding, thereby enriching both mathematics and anthropology?

It is in terms of the ideas laid out in the previous paragraph that I think anthropology *can* make a unique and significant contribution to mathematics. It is in these terms that I hope the present work will be of interest, both to anthropologists and philosophers. It is important to discuss here two works that have already begun, in different but complementary ways, the task of bringing together anthropology and mathematics. One work, Jadran Mimica's *Intimations of Infinity* (1992), was produced by an anthropologist; the other, Brian Rotman's "Toward a Semiotics of Mathematics" (1988), by a mathematician.

Mimica's book is a study of the numbering system and the ontology of numbers among the Iqwaye, of Papua New Guinea. The Iqwaye formulate their ideas about the nature and organization of numbers on the basis of complex symbols and metaphors relating fingers, toes, and genitalia to basic units, sets, and numerical relations (such as even and odd) of their numbering and counting systems. In addition, the organization of numbers, especially in terms of principles of hierarchy and succession found in sequences of cardinal numbers and ordinal numerals, is also formulated in terms of kinship relations and age-grading. For example, in Iqwaye numerical ontology,

> *Humans are permanently metaphorised as fingers. But they are not metaphorical fingers in some indefinite sense. Birth order is the order in the realm of substantial consanguineal relatedness. Children emerge from the genetrix's womb as a consequence of the procreative process engendered by genitor's semen and genetrix's blood and milk. Therefore, the metaphorical significance of the birth order suffixes [which are also assigned to fingers] is not simply—humans as fingers—but brothers and sisters as fingers which, as such, represent the hand(s) of a higher whole, their male genitor, father. (Mimica 1992: 61)*

In short, Mimica's presentation and analysis of the Iqwaye numbering system and ontology of numbers inform us of an ideology of numbers and mathematics that challenges the Platonist philosophy of a separation between the reality of numerical and mathematical truths, on the one hand, and the human body, culture, and the experience of social life, on the other (for another study showing the merging of these domains of experience in Papua New Guinea, see Biersack 1982). More specifically, Mimica (1992: 107–120) uses his analysis of Iqwaye concepts of number as the basis for, and as an entry into, an analysis of the philosophical principles motivating Cantor's formulation of the concept of transfinite numbers. This discussion leads, in turn, to Mimica's critique of Western philosophical, psychological, and mathematical conceptions of number and the concept of infinity.

An especially important and informative part of Mimica's study is his decidedly scathing evaluation of certain earlier works, both by anthropologists (such as Hallpike and Lévi-Strauss) and psychologists (Piaget), who have articulated—not always on the basis of compelling ethnographic materials, such as those offered by Mimica for the Iqwaye—unfavorable evaluations and over-generalized commentaries on the evolutionary significance of "primitive" numbering systems and precise knowledge in general. For instance, in making a transition between Piaget's notion of "primitive" counting and conceptions of number as indicative of "pre-operatory" thought and the use to which Hallpike put such a notion in his evaluation of the foundations of primitive thought, Mimica notes that

> *there is no need to assume that the structures constitutive of the category of number in its everyday and primordial sense of 'the number of things' or simply as 'number qua counting' are somehow less real or true than those formulated in logic and mathematics. One has to understand that the latter developed and exists in relation to the former and not the other way around.* . . . *Piaget's emphasis on the formal operatory stage in human development reflects the biases of a specific trend in Western metaphysics which, having become a historically and culturally developed mode of self-understanding, is* projected *upon humanity as a whole, and is usable for a wholesale self-aggrandisement. (1992: 151–152; my emphasis)*

I will return in Chapter 4 to a discussion of certain issues raised by Piaget's (and later Hallpike's) views on pre-operatory and analytical conceptions of numbers.

Brian Rotman's study of the semiotics of mathematics is more difficult to summarize, both because of its brevity and because of the large task it sets for itself, which is essentially that of "unmasking" the elaborate fiction propping up Platonist philosophy and language concerning the nature of mathematical truths.[3] Rotman argues that the development of mathematics in the West (as elsewhere) must ultimately be understood as the product of historical, cultural, and linguistic forces and processes (see also Kitcher 1984; Hurford 1987: viii, 69–71, 184–185). This may seem to be obvious to some readers, but if so, such an understanding will most likely be based on philosophical or political inclinations. This is because mathematicians have consistently and *purposely* written themselves as individuals—as subjects and agents of history and culture—out of the mathematical operations they perform. Therefore, since mathematical manipulations are formulated discursively as though they were objective and independent of the hand that scribbles them, the only way to confidently assert that mathematics is indeed a historical and cultural activity is to *expose* the nature of, and any weaknesses in, the linguistic, semantic, and ideological—that is, the semiological—constructions that prop up and perpetuate the proposition that mathematical truths are objective and timeless. This is Rotman's objective in the article cited.

For instance, why, Rotman asks, should one *not* believe that mathematics is about some timeless, ideal world full of unchanging objects—the mathematical truths—that are independent of human language and consciousness, and that theorems express what is eternally true about these objects? One response, Rotman suggests, is to question the semiotic coherence of the notion of *pre*-linguistic referents that is required in such a formulation. If the relationship between signs and signifiers *were* what it is purported to be in the Platonist view, then language—as cultural mediation—would be inextricable from the process of referring.

> *This will mean that the supposedly distinct and opposing categories of reference and sense interpenetrate each other, and that the object referred to can neither be separated from nor antedate the descriptions given of it. Such a referent will be a social historical construct; . . . it will be no more timeless, spaceless or subjectless than any other social artefact. (Rotman 1988: 25–26)*

In addition to raising questions about the status of the signs and referents of mathematical theorems, Rotman questions the various identities and epistemological statuses engaged in the performance of a mathematical theorem. These include: the *Mathematician,* who imagines the imperatives of the theorem ("consider all . . . "; "let $x = y$ . . . "); the *Agent,* who executes the actions within the fabricated world of the theorem; and the *Person,* the one whom the mathematician imagines would become convinced of the mathematician's proofs were the Agent to perform the operations demanded of him by the Mathematician. Platonism, in fact, occludes the identity and role of the Mathematician by flattening this trichotomy into an opposition between the subjective, changeable, mortal *Person* and the idealized, infinitary *Agent,* the supposed source of objective, eternal "thoughts." As Rotman notes: "it is precisely about the middle term [the Mathematician], which provides the epistemological link between the two [i.e., the Agent and the Person], that platonism is silent" (Rotman 1988: 29). This all-too-common obfuscation of the identity and activity of the Mathematician is as well one of the foci of Kitcher's critique of mathematical thinking and practice, a critique that guides his attempt to "dissolve the mysteries" which

Platonism spawns by "viewing Platonism as a convenient *façon de parler,* a position which errs by adopting a picture of mathematical reality without recognizing the route through which the picture emerged" (cited in Hurford 1987: 184).

I do not know whether Frege was right when he suggested that psychology has nothing to contribute to mathematics; I *do* know, however, that anthropology *ought* to have something to say about practitioners in a society who construct and elide *their* various identities in a cultural production (like mathematics) in the manner Rotman argues is done by Western mathematicians.

Finally, we should take note of Rotman's comments concerning the nature of numbers. He argues that the mathematician's conviction to the effect that the integers are not social, cultural, historical artifacts, but *natural* objects, is to be explained partially by the same processes of social alienation that Marx identified whereby, in order to be bought and sold, commodities must be "fetishized." That is:

> *human products [e.g., commodities or numbers] frequently appear to their producers as strange, unfamiliar, and surprising; that what is created may bear no obvious or transparent markers of its human (social, cultural, historical, psychological) agency, but on the contrary can, and for the most part does, present itself as alien and prior to its creator. (Rotman 1988: 30)*

This brief summary does not do justice to Rotman's masterful probing of the philosophical, linguistic, and ideological foundations of mathematical Platonism. It does, however, help us understand and appreciate (intellectually and historically) mathematical philosophies, like those of the Quechua and Iqwaye, in which the producers of the artifacts we call "numbers" do *not* systematically alienate those products from the social and cultural environments and processes in which they are produced. This brings up a final point regarding Rotman's work.

In his recent book *Ad Infinitum* (1993), Rotman further develops his critique of Platonism in the context of a larger questioning of the semiological and philosophical issues raised by the mathematical sign (. . .), the sign used for the injunction to "carry on counting to infinity" (e.g., 1, 2, 3, . . .). Rotman's goal in this work, aside from an analysis of the relationship between Platonism and the *ad infinitum* principle as used in mathematics, is to establish the logic of a corporeal, non-Euclidean science of numbers (roughly: a science of large, but finite, numbers). While I find Rotman's book extremely thought-provoking, I do not think he entirely succeeds in the challenge he sets for himself, particularly with respect to non-Euclidean numbers. The reason for this, in my view, is because Rotman seems not to recognize that a *corporeal* science of numbers is, in fact, an "anthropology of numbers." What is called for, then, is the development of a theory of numbers and infinity informed by anthropological data, theories, and insights. Mimica, in his book *Intimations of Infinity* (1992), has begun such a project with his analyses of Iqwaye numbers and the perspective that we gain from these data on such Western philosophical mathematical topics as Cantor's transfinite numbers (see esp. Mimica 1992: 107–125). The more general goal of this study of Quechua numbers and arithmetic is to contribute in some small way to this larger project initiated by Mimica and Rotman.

The main point that I want to leave the reader with at this point is similar to that which Hurford articulates at the beginning of his masterful and stimulating work, *Language and Number* (1987: 185): "it seems in most cases unobjectionable to treat numbers (as opposed to collections) as real, but abstract, objects created through an interaction of people, language, and the world." It will be the task of this book as a whole to attempt to elucidate how the Quechua ontology of numbers and philosophy of mathematics construct—grammatically and through symbols and metaphors—a concept of numbers and procedures for their manipulation (addition, subtraction, etc.) premised on values, institutions, and practices of Quechua society and culture more generally.

Aristotle and the American Indians—Revisited

We cannot leave the above discussion, in which I have urged an accommodation between anthropology and mathematics, without recognizing that such a proposal flies directly in the face of historical forces and ideological and philosophical traditions that have been at work for centuries in the West in an effort to rationalize and thereby maintain a division between precisely the forms of knowledge and practice represented in these two disciplines. That is, to the degree that anthropology today maintains an interest in the study of preliterate or largely nonliterate and nonindustrialized or only recently industrialized societies (which is certainly less a focus of anthropology today than it was even twenty years ago), the societies and systems of knowledge studied by anthropologists are those in opposition to which mathematics and the whole logico-empirical tradition in the West has defined itself. This point has been made clearly and forcefully in Goody and Watt's interesting and provocative essay, "The Consequences of Literacy" (1968).

Goody and Watt have been criticized, fairly I think, from the time of the publication of their article (see, for example, Gough 1968) down to the present day (for example, Halverson 1992) for attempting to draw too strict a causal connection between the widespread adoption of alphabetic writing in Greece, beginning around 700–500 B.C., and the emergence of logic (as expressed in syllogisms), as well as such Western institutions and traditions as history (versus myth), natural history, democracy, and a number of other philosophical attitudes and approaches to knowledge that are often found in literate societies (in opposition to societies based on oral communication). While I agree with most of the criticisms leveled at Goody and Watt's formulation of a causal link between alphabetic literacy and the institutions and practices mentioned above, the contrasts that they draw between literate and nonliterate societies will serve us usefully in providing the point of departure for considering the relationship between so-called "traditional" and "modern" societies and the systems of knowledge pertaining to each, not only with respect to literacy, but also numeracy. In particular, I want to consider two of the distinctions that Goody and Watt draw between oral and literate societies and systems of communication; one concerns the emergence of a new method of analysis based on logic; the second concerns the division of knowledge into different categories.

To take first the question of logic, Goody and Watt argue that in societies based on oral communication, changes are often made in stories, legends, and interpretations of the past from one recitation or narration to the next. However, such differences and changes will generally not be recognized by the listeners as "inconsistencies," precisely because there are no fixed records or texts against which the later versions can be compared. This situation changes with the introduction of writing and the gradual accumulation of texts that can be systematically compared. With the ability to compare texts comes the possibility of recognizing different and conflicting versions of a myth, or different interpretations given to a historical event; the inconsistencies thus noted, Goody and Watt argue, will eventually lead to a recognition of the fact that the cultural inheritance in a society is a patchwork of different ideas and beliefs composed of basically two types of material: "fiction, error and superstition on the one hand; and, on the other, elements of truth which can provide the basis for some more reliable and coherent explanations of the gods, the human past and the physical world" (Goody and Watt 1968: 49).

Now, we must ask, how are these "elements of truth" to be identified? According to Goody and Watt (1968: 53), the procedure used in classical Greece, as formulated especially in the works of Plato and Aristotle on the basis of the existing corpus of texts containing accounts of earlier beliefs and ideas about a variety of matters, was through the application of logical, systematic rules of thinking leading to the development of unified, analytical arguments whereby "truth" (*episteme*) could be sorted out from "current opinion" (*doxa*). It is important to recall that these procedures will be set in motion—at least insofar as they concern such matters as accounts of the past, explanations of the qualities and characteristics of the deities, the nature of forces controlling and affecting human destiny, etc.—by the recognition of "inconsistencies" in the recorded accounts.

Goody and Watt give a perfectly logical sounding account of the processes outlined above, yet we are left with a number of questions. Not the least of these is just how all of this is supposed to lead to the "truth" and why any such truths that do emerge could not be (or could not have been) formulated in oral argumentation (see Halverson 1992, on this point). In addition, what are we to make of an argument in which the authors present without reflection or criticism the view that the elimination of inconsistencies and the resolution of different versions or interpretations of events into a single, consistent account are not only central, but presumably positive and unproblematic, elements of the development of logical thinking in the West? But where do we—or more to the point, where did the Greeks—get the idea that all "inconsistencies" can or even should be resolved? Is it not possible that differences in interpretation may represent legitimately different points of view on such matters as what happened in some past event, or the interpretation of the causes and consequences of events? In other words, is it not precisely with the emergence of philosophical traditions, especially in the works of Plato and Aristotle, wedded to the notions of single causes of events and the existence of a single "true" version of the truth, that the West began to move ideologically and philosophically in a direction that we are still struggling to overcome to the present day? This is not to deny the fact that the rise of logic and of analytical modes of reasoning have been the foundations upon which the West has achieved virtually unparalleled advances in mathematics and the natural sciences. But has it ever been essential to the advance of logico-empirical reasoning not only to reject other modes of reasoning but to pointedly disregard potentially valuable insights into the nature of the physical and social worlds that might be contained in "other" ways of formulating and organizing knowledge?

The relevance of this discussion for our purposes here, obviously, concerns such questions as the evaluations that we give to the existence of differences and even "inconsistencies" in, for instance, the Quechua version of the ontology of numbers as opposed to explanations of the nature of numbers as formulated on purely logical grounds in Western philosophy. Do such radically different systems of explanation have to be resolved to the one true version? What is the cost to each society of concluding that one explanation may be valid for one cultural tradition while another is valid for another cultural tradition, that the two explanations have merit in their particular social and cultural contexts, and that both are therefore worthy of study?

It is, of course, questions like those raised above that often lie behind the challenge of "multiculturalism" to the natural sciences in Western academics today. However, whereas some may see the proper goal of a multicultural critique of accounts of the principles underlying Western logic as the attack on the political power and prestige of Western science, this at least is not my goal here. My interest in raising such questions is not to attack science but rather to argue for the value of investigating other systems of knowledge and ways of formulating the "truth." That is, I argue that in an accommodation between the West and the "rest," each side ought to be able to contribute something of interest and value to the other.

The second topic raised in Goody and Watt's article that I want to discuss concerns another example of what they see as a consequence of the rise of alphabetic literacy in early Greece; this is the division of knowledge into separate fields of study and practice. This process, which began with Plato's separation of theology—knowledge about the divine—as a special field of knowledge apart from concerns of the natural world and human affairs, was brought to completion by Aristotle and his school, the *lyceum* (Goody and Watt 1968: 54–55). Again, what Goody and Watt's account of the early phases of this process begs is some reflective commentary not just on the cause (which they identify as the rise of literacy) of such a historically momentous process, but of the sense, value, and finally the "social-logic" of such a project. The long-term consequences of such a division of labor in the study of problems concerning different and (supposedly) unrelated topics is, of course, represented in one setting in the discrete disciplines found in most modern academic institutions. Attempts to bridge the compartmentalization of academic knowledge and practice that Goody and Watt believe were set in motion in early Western societies by alphabetic literacy are the objective of the many multi- and interdisciplinary programs that have sprung up over the past few decades in Euro-American academic institutions.

The nearest that Goody and Watt come to raising questions that might prompt one to reflect not on the cause but rather on the value and the sense of this tradition of fragmentation in Western epistemology comes in their conclusions; however, their comments there are exceedingly diffuse and have little relevance for the questions I have raised above. For instance, in talking specifically about anthropology's reaction to the Aristotelian classification and division of knowledge into different categories, they note that the progress of anthropology since the nineteenth century derives from "an awareness of . . . the extent to which, in the culture of oral societies, non-Aristotelian models are implicit in the language, the reasoning, and the kinds of connection established between the various spheres of knowledge" (Goody and Watt 1968: 64).

However, the only implications for anthropological theory and practice they take note of deriving from the "awareness" noted above are analytical trends in contrasting lineal and nonlineal modes of thought and the study of the relationship between the mechanistic ways of thinking in European societies and the segmentary grammars of European languages. But surely the awareness of the differences between Aristotelian and non-Aristotelian modes of thought has had more significance for the practice of anthropology than providing us with a few interesting contrasts that we can analyze. For it is precisely the recognition of the differences in these modes of thought in the West, and the reification of these differences in social philosophies and political stances, that have systematically excluded from serious consideration the systems of knowledge and values of societies that anthropologists have traditionally been concerned with—and which many have found reason to respect.

These comments lead us back to the question of the general interest of, for instance, the Quechua and Iqwaye ontology of numbers, based as they both are on a non-Aristotelian insistence on seeing one body of knowledge (such as numbers) as relevant for others (such as the body, kinship, and social relations). Surely the significance of such systems of knowledge is not exhausted in the observation that they are consistent with thought in nonliterate, non-Aristotelian societies. As I suggested in the previous section, such systems of knowledge are valuable to analyze because of the insights they may give us into alternative principles for formulating ideas about the origin, nature, and relationships among numbers. We may find, in fact, that such formulations offer not only perfectly adequate accounts of the ontology of numbers (and other related matters), but that they do so without paying the price of the fragmentation and disarticulation of knowledge, as well as the social and intellectual alienation, that have so often been associated with the development and spread of the literate, Aristotelian intellectual and cultural tradition.

Literacy and Numeracy

Before leaving the discussion of Goody and Watt's article, I want to make it clear that although I have emphasized above only what I take issue with in their study, the central problems they address in this important and stimulating article—the effects of literacy on the organization of knowledge and society—are of exceptional importance for general anthropological theory as well as for the specific problems we are concerned with here. Regarding anthropological theory in general, earlier studies of literacy (see, for example, the classic study by Gelb [1963]) failed to address the question of what impact the evolution or acquisition of writing might have had on social institutions, ideology, and cognition more generally. That the occurrence of alphabetic literacy *does* seem to be associated in many cases with many of the institutions and practices that Goody and Watt see as consequences of literacy make it essential that we consider carefully any outright rejection of their thesis (although Goody himself has retreated from almost all of its original, core elements; see Halverson 1992). In addition, this issue is of particular interest in considering those cases in which alphabetic literacy was introduced, often through conquest, into previously alphabetically non-literate societies. To a certain extent, the latter can be said to characterize the circumstances of the introduction of writing into the Andes.

I would argue that the Andes represents a site of particular importance insofar as we are concerned with the question of the nature and consequences of literacy. This importance results from the fact that, while such highly complex, state-level pre-Columbian Andean societies as that of the Inka empire did not develop a system of alphabetic literacy, nonetheless, the *khipu* did represent some form and level of "writing." The questions that arise in the Andean/Inka case are, first: What kind of writing, or system of literacy, did the *khipu* represent? In order to address this question (which I intend to do in a future study), we will need to take account of recent, more highly nuanced approaches to the definition and investigation of literacy, such as those contained in Boone and Mignolo's *Writing Without Words* (1994; see especially the articles by Cummins and Rappaport; see also Mignolo 1995). I would note that the Andean case presents a particular set of complications for studies of literacy. For example, although we have no evidence to suggest that there was a high level of alphabetic literacy in the colonial Andes, Rappaport (1994) has made it abundantly clear that there was an extremely high level of awareness of the existence of written documents and the importance of their manipulation for political and ritual ends—both in terms of their contents and their status as objects (as items to be displayed, stored, etc.).

The second question that we need to consider with regard to pre-Columbian Andean literacy concerns many of the same issues raised by Goody and Watt in the article discussed above—but with a twist. That is, what are the consequences for social and epistemological organization of the development of a complex, but *nonalphabetic* system of record-keeping? How are the supposed effects of alphabetic literacy modified, or otherwise transformed, when the type of literacy involved is based on relatively simple and highly personalized mnemonic schemes (as some argue was the case with the *khipus*), or on ideographic or logographic schemes? We are just beginning to address such questions as these in a comparative mode; however, as such studies advance, the investigation of the *khipu* recording system and its relationship to Inka and early colonial Quechua social and cognitive organization ought to be pursued aggressively (for example, see Zuidema's [1982] discussion of the *khipu* in reaction to Goody's arguments concerning the consequences of literacy).

The last point that I want to raise—and this will bring us back to the problems we are concerned with in this work—involves the question of the relationship between literacy and numeracy. That there were close historical and cognitive relations between these two types of knowledge and practice is evident from a number of studies of the development of recording systems worldwide. For instance, as has been amply documented, the majority of early cuneiform tablets from Middle Eastern sites contain records of temple accounts. As Green (1991: 54) has noted for the city of Uruk, some 90 percent of the Archaic period tablets were clerical records. These records contained formulaic verbal phrases combined with numerical signs. For example, Green (1991: 52) notes that in the cuneiform script, the semantic form for "dead" or "die" evolved from the sign for the numeral *one* with a wedge drawn through it. This pattern is found in other ancient scripts as well; for example, Chadwick (1958: 44) notes that in Linear B, numerals often accompany syllabic signs and ideograms.

Schmandt-Besserat (1991: 27–30), in her studies of the pre-Sumerian evolution of recording systems in the Middle East, has shown how writing evolved from systems of record-keeping based on the use of two types of clay tokens, plain and complex. The appearance of plain tokens coincided with the rise of agriculture; complex tokens proliferated (but did not replace plain tokens) with the emergence of cities (see also Schmandt-Besserat 1978). Both types of tokens were used to organize and store economic data. Sets of plain tokens were often grouped together and enclosed in clay envelopes that bore seal impressions. Complex tokens, on the other hand, were often strung together and attached to oblong clay *bullae,* which were also impressed with seals. Schmandt-Besserat (1991: 33–35) argues—and is able to demonstrate in some cases—that the signs used in cuneiform writing evolved from the shapes of the plain and complex tokens.

Of even greater importance for our interests here are Schmandt-

Besserat's observations on the invention of numerals in relation to the two types of tokens. That is, she notes first that the duality of the token system gave rise to two different types of signs in the Sumerian script; plain tokens were replaced by impressed markings, whereas complex tokens were replaced by pictographic signs incised with a stylus (Schmandt-Besserat 1991: 36). From this difference, there then appeared two different types and ways of signing numerals: impressed signs expressed plurality by making marks, or tallies, in a one-to-one system of correspondences; incised signs began to use signs denoting abstract numbers. As she notes concerning the significance of these developments,

> *The extraordinary invention of abstract numerals amounted to a revolution in accounting and communication, since it provided, for the first time, a reckoning system applicable to any and every item under the sun. Each numeral stood for the concept of oneness, twoness, threeness, and so on, abstracted from the item counted.*
>
> *This put an end to the cumbersome system necessitating particular symbols for counting different goods. (Schmandt-Besserat 1991: 39).*

Now, I have given this rather extended discussion of the coevolution of Sumerian numeracy and literacy because, whereas such questions as the "rise of literacy" and "alternative forms of literacy" have received an enormous amount of attention in the past decade, relatively little direct attention has been devoted to the question of the "rise of numeracy." For instance, although the text of Goody's book *The Domestication of the Savage Mind* (1978) contains an extraordinary number of references to numbers as well as to the discussion of various topics touching on the relationship between literacy and numeracy, Goody cites only one reference to "number" in his index; "numeracy" does not even appear as an entry in the index. Similarly, the word "number" does not appear in the index of Mignolo's recently published book (1995) on literacy and writing during pre-Columbian and colonial times in the Americas—this *despite* the fact that the Mayas and the Inkas could both rightly be accused, if anything, of having had an absolute obsession with signing numbers.

From the evidence available to us, it is clear that literacy and numeracy are complementary processes and forms of knowledge. Hurford's study *Language and Number* (1987) makes clear the inseparability of the syntactical structures and semantics of number words and phrases and the more general (non-numerical) syntax and semantics of the languages of which they are a part. This being the case, I suggest that the high level of attention given in recent years to the investigation of the nature and consequences of literacy is like straining to hear the sound of one hand clapping. Only by bringing together the two hands of literacy and numeracy will we hear the true, complete repercussion that we seek in investigating how different societies have achieved meaningful schemes for signing meaning.

The present study represents a beginning of the investigation of numeracy in the Andes. That is, this is the "one hand" (of numeracy), which I plan to bring together—I hope in the semblance of a clap—with the "other hand" (of literacy) in a future study.

Fieldwork and Research Methods

Most of the materials on which I build my arguments in Chapters 2 through 6 are drawn from ethnographic and linguistic materials that I collected during the course of several different sessions of fieldwork. In addition, as will be seen from a perusal of the bibliography, I have made use of relevant ethnographic and historical studies on other communities and regions in the Andes, and elsewhere in the world. I will provide below a description of the circumstances and the methods of study used in collecting linguistic and ethnographic data in my own fieldwork.

The ethnographic materials discussed in this work derive principally from two fieldwork experiences. The first of these was an extended fieldwork project carried out over some two and one-half years, between 1980 and 1988, in the community of Pacariqtambo, Peru (Province of Paruro, Department of Cusco).[4] I have published elsewhere on a number of other, non-numerical and nonmathematical, aspects of that research (see Urton 1984, 1986, 1988, 1990, 1992, 1993). While my research in Pacariqtambo focused primarily on the study of sociopolitical, economic, and ritual organization, I have found that certain data collected and observations recorded in the course of that fieldwork are relevant to the topics addressed in this study. While virtually every person born in Pacariqtambo comes to know (Southern Peruvian) Quechua as a first language, bilingualism is fairly common; that is, about one-half (with a greater proportion of men than women) of the approximately one thousand people in this town possess a reasonable facility in speaking Spanish. Ethnographic data were collected in Pacariqtambo in the course of both formal and informal interviews (in both Quechua and Spanish). Most of the informal interviews took place as I helped different men in the village do agricultural work in their fields.[5]

The second fieldwork experience was aimed directly at investigating Quechua numbers, arithmetic, and mathematics. This research was carried out in and around the city of Sucre, in south-central Bolivia, from August 1993 through mid-July 1994.[6] The research in Sucre was divided between two types of studies—linguistic and ethnographic. For a period of some four months, beginning in August 1993, I worked intensively with Primitivo Nina Llanos, a professor of Quechua in the Department of Languages at the Universidad Mayor, Real y Pontificia de San Francisco Xavier, in Sucre (or Chuquisaca). Nina is a native speaker of Bolivian Quechua who is from the town of Betanzos, located between Sucre and Potosí. He has often served as a private tutor of Quechua for anthropologists working in and around Sucre, and he has collaborated with the historian-anthropologist Tristan Platt on two formal research projects in the Norte de Potosí. Nina has also taught Quechua on two separate occasions in the Latin American Studies program at the University of St. Andrews, Scotland.

I have introduced Primitivo Nina to a rather extensive degree because he was my principal source for probing beneath the everyday speech involving numbers and arithmetic and mathematical concepts (which I encountered in my ethnographic fieldwork) to try to help me understand the complex grammatical structures, linguistic principles, and semantic meanings of the Bolivian Quechua language of numbers. My work with Nina produced hours of taped conversations in which we discussed, primarily in Quechua, such topics as: the verbs to count, add, subtract, multiply, and divide; each number from 1 through 10 (for example, I recorded four and a half hours of conversation and analysis of Quechua terms, and their uses, for "one" and "first"); terms for quantitative comparisons and evaluations (such as more than, less than, equal to, too much, too little); and a host of other topics that touched—sometimes remotely—on the language of numbers, arithmetic, and mathematics used in a variety of settings (such as farming, weaving, and marketing) in Quechua. As a competent, native speaker of Bolivian Quechua, who both understands what anthropology is about and who maintains a deep commitment to Quechua society and culture as lived and experienced in villages around Sucre, Nina was an invaluable informant and collaborator on this project.

Following this period of intensive linguistic research, which continued intermittently throughout the rest of the year during my returns to Sucre from the field, I carried out fieldwork in two villages. The first was a four-month stint in the community of Candelaria, located some sixty kilometers southeast of Sucre, in the province/region of Tarabuco. A town of about three hundred people, Candelaria is the site of the Hacienda Candelaria, which was a dominant economic and political force in this region from the early decades of this century until the Agrarian Reform of 1952 (Langer 1989). Candelaria is today the location of one of the principal weaving *talleres* ("workshops") sponsored by the development project known as ASUR (Antropólogos del Sur-Andino). With the cooperation of the directors—Verónica Cereceda and Gabriel Martínez—and staff of ASUR, I was able to move into the household of Damián Flores and Santusa Quispe in Candelaria and set to work immediately on my research.

The focus of my research in Candelaria was talking to, working with, and apprenticing myself out to weavers. As I explain in more detail in Chapter 5, warping and weaving textiles are arts intimately concerned with counting and manipulating sets of threads in complex patterns and routines. Talking to weavers and learning to weave several simple designs represented perhaps the best and most direct ways not only of talking with and about numbers in Quechua, but also of practicing the manipulation of sets of threads to produce designs that are considered to be beautiful, because of their shape, proportions, colors, etc., by weavers throughout the Andes. This research allowed me to collect information on patterns and procedures for counting threads in warping and weaving a variety of textile designs.

I attempted to continue with the basic research orientation outlined above during some three months of fieldwork in the village of Marawa, which is located about twenty kilometers west of Sucre. While in Marawa, I lived in the household of Cicilio Cruz and Amalia Mamani, and I again received the support of ASUR, in the form of transportation to and from the village and introductions to the village authorities and the officers of the weavers' workshop. The weavers of Marawa produce textiles bearing Potolo-style motifs (Femenias 1987); the town of Potolo is located a few hours' walk west of Marawa. While I was able to do some work with the women who weave for the ASUR project, there was actually little weaving going on during the period of my stay there, in April–June 1994. This was the harvest season, and both the men and women were busy with the various tasks of harvesting wheat, barley, and corn. Thus, I spent most of my time in Marawa working with people in their fields.

The most valuable information I gained in Marawa from the point of view of my project on numbers and mathematics concerned everyday, especially agricultural, uses of the wide range of terms having to do with arithmetic operations (addition, subtraction, etc.); units of land measurement and various ways of dividing land and apportioning labor; and the numerical terms and metaphorical expressions (in both Quechua and Spanish) for the weights, measures, and units of currency used in marketing.

Before ending this discussion of the ethnographic materials from my own fieldwork that have been useful to me in writing this book, I should mention that I have also gone back to my notes from my earliest fieldwork in the Andes, which was carried out for a little less than two years (in 1974–1976) in the village of Misminay, Peru, located some thirty kilometers northwest of Cusco.[7] This research focused on the study of astronomy and the organization of time in scheduling agricultural activities (see Urton 1988). Certain data from the research in Misminay have been useful in clarifying ideas and topics discussed herein.

An Overview

To assist the reader, an overview of the organization of this book and the main topics addressed in each of the following chapters is presented here.

Chapter 2 takes up the description and analysis of the cardinal numbers in the Quechua language. I also examine syntactical and semantic elements of the construction of compound numbers, as well as ways of talking about certain classes, types, and groupings of numbers (such as pairs and even and odd numbers), that are similar to discourse and other forms of interaction involving kinship and social relations. These data allow us to begin to identify some of the central grammatical and ideological elements of the Quechua ontology of numbers, which is developed in detail in the next chapter.

Chapter 3 is concerned with the ordinal numerals and the nature of the principles motivating and organizing ordinal sequences (including reproduction, hierarchy, and succession). It is in this chapter that I elaborate most clearly the Quechua ontology of numbers. This is done through the examination of several examples of numeral—or ordinal—sequences, as well as non-numeral ordinal-like series, whose various elements are classified and organized in terms of kinship and social relations.

Chapter 4, which concerns the language of "counting" (*yupay*), is a bridge between the elaboration of the ontology of numbers (in Chapters 2 and 3) and the description of the philosophy of arithmetic and mathematics (in Chapter 5). Chapter 4 is a "bridge" because it is in counting—especially with higher, compound numbers—that one first learns and gains practice in certain of the arithmetic operations (especially addition and multiplication) that are used to construct compound numbers. The most explicit examples of counting discussed in Chapter 4 involve routines and "recipes" for warping and weaving textiles.

Chapter 5 begins with a discussion of the mathematical status of arithmetic terms (add, subtract, etc.), as well as a statement of the methodology to be used in analyzing such terms in Quechua. I then take up the description and analysis of the Quechua philosophy of arithmetic and mathematics, which I refer to as the "art of rectification" (see discussion above). The argument in Chapter 5 develops through analyses of terms, concepts, and practices relating to the arithmetic operations of addition, subtraction, multiplication, and division. I also provide an overview of the language of comparison and evaluation, which motivates the arithmetic and mathematics of rectification.

Chapter 6 provides a historical perspective on the material discussed in Chapters 2 through 5 by considering changing ideas about numbers and arithmetical and mathematical practices over the period from late pre-Hispanic through early colonial times. I am particularly concerned with the recording of numerical data (especially pertaining to Inka tribute) on the *khipus* in the pre-Hispanic Andes and with the transformations of numbers and record-keeping with the introduction of new systems of state administration and tribute in early colonial times.

Chapter 7, the conclusion, brings into a unified view the implications of the analyses of the Quechua ontology of numbers and the arithmetic and mathematics of rectification discussed in the previous chapters. The principal substantive contribution of the conclusions is the articulation of a hypothesis for the logical principles and semantic categories (in Quechua) underlying and motivating decimal organization and numeration in the Andes, past and present.

The Cardinal Numbers
and Their Social Relations

Introduction

Number names form a distinct, though not isolated, lexical domain in the Quechua language.[1] That is, when one speaks or hears, for example, the words *iskay* ("two"), *phishqa* ("five"), or *chunka* ("ten"), the primary referents are to collections having the quantities of units indicated by the English translations of the respective terms. However, number names as well as numerical concepts are not isolated from the more general syntactical rules and semantic processes that govern everyday communication between Quechua-speakers within any given community. That is, in their production in everyday speech, number names undergo many of the same syntactical changes that occur in non-numerical words. Such modifications are seen—or, more appropriately, heard—most clearly in the addition to number words of the full range of suffixes typical of Quechua syntax in general.

At the semantic level, Quechua number names are commonly employed in figures of speech, puns, and metaphorical constructions, thus exposing them to the wider operations of the production of meaning in Quechua discourse in general. The use of numbers in metaphorical constructions lends to number words and numerical concepts meanings drawn from the semantic domains to which they are compared, while at the same time, such metaphorical constructions extend to those other domains an added dimension of meaning and relevance through the influence of their (primarily) quantitative meanings. For example, in

Quechua number symbolism, "seven" (*qanchis*) is considered to be some-thing of a rascally character; it is the very image of excess, compulsive-ness and, by extension, of loutish behavior. The numerical explanation of the nature of *qanchis* begins from the fact that "three" (*kinsa*) is con-sidered to be the number of wholeness and completeness (for example, events often happen in cycles of three repetitions). The number "six" (*suqta*) constitutes two full units or cycles of three; however, seven is now exposed as "excessive," for seven is one number/unit in excess of what is considered to be sufficient, whole, and (doubly) complete. It is not sur-prising, then, to find that the braying of a burro is often likened to the loud repetition of the word for seven: *"qanchis, qanchis, qanchis!"* The excessiveness of seven is here attuned perfectly to the insistent braying of a foolish animal, the burro.[2]

It is because of their "exposure" through metaphors, puns, etc., to virtually the full range of Quechua semantic activity, a large chunk of which is drawn from and refers to the world of everyday social (espe-cially kinship) relations, that I have indicated in the title to this work that what we are concerned with here is the "social life" of numbers. Such an anthropomorphizing of numbers emphasizes the idea that numbers cannot be separated from the wider linguistic, social, and cul-tural universe in which they are daily (re-)conceptualized and spoken.

I note that an important characteristic of the larger linguistic uni-verse in which numbers are reproduced today is the alternative to the use of Quechua numbers that is offered by Spanish number names and the potential replacement of Quechua statements describing arithmetic operations (addition, subtraction, etc.) by Spanish ones. Not surprisingly, at least not for anyone who has a nodding acquaintance with the litera-ture on class and ethnicity in the Andes, the use of the number vocabu-lary of either Quechua or Spanish is closely linked, while not being en-tirely determined by, the social context in which the number words are produced. For example, Quechua is used primarily in the household and within the village, while Spanish is used more in the city, in market-ing and in the presence of *mestizos*. In general, Spanish tends to replace Quechua in those settings in which money, with its fixed units and (rel-atively stable) values, is the primary focus of communication.

In order to arrive at a point from which we can discuss meaningfully the social and cultural characteristics of Quechua numbers, as well as to begin to develop an understanding that will lead us to an articulation of a Quechua ontology of numbers, we begin with a discussion of the basic vocabulary of number words in Quechua and of the ways these primary lexemes are combined and transformed to produce compound numbers.

The Primary Lexemes of Cardinal Numbers

The primary lexemes of cardinal number names are given in Table 2.1. These terms constitute what is known in Quechua as *yupana*, or *yupaykuna*. The term *yupay*, which I will examine in some detail in Chapter 4, has the basic meaning, "to count, account." *-Na* is a nominalizer, and *-kuna* is a pluralizer. Numbers, then, are "counting things," or "counters." In this regard, Quechua etymology and ontology endorse Hurford's general conclusion that "numbers are abstractions from conclusions reached by counting" (1987: 174).

The practical limit of counting in everyday Quechua in communities

TABLE 2.1
The Primary Lexemes for Numbers in Quechua

Primary Lexemes	Translation
uj	one
iskay	two
kinsa	three
tawa	four
phishqa	five
suqta	six
qanchis	seven
pusaq	eight
jisqon	nine
chunka	ten
pachaq	one hundred
waranqa	one thousand

that I am familiar with is the phrase denoting "one million," which is identified in the construction *waranqa waranqa* (1,000 × 1,000). This phrase also carries the sense of an uncountable or "infinite" number. As for the other end of the continuum—that is, "zero"—I will discuss this matter later in this chapter. I would note that although the term *hunu* is the ethnohistorically well-attested primary lexeme for the number 10,000 (see below, Chapter 6), I did not hear this term used by people during my research in villages in Peru or Bolivia.

From the dozen terms that form the lexical basis of the Quechua decimal system of numeration given in Table 2.1, and from combinations of these that are performed to produce compound numbers, the Quechua order, name, and compare the units, aggregates, and collections of things that make up their world. However, number names do not exhaust the categories employed in such activities as we will see later when we examine the terms that are used for certain types of collections, such as "pairs." The tasks of organizing and comparing categories are also performed using ordinal numbers, a topic to which I turn in Chapter 3.

As we see in Table 2.1, Quechua has distinctive terms for the numbers from one to ten. The terms are "distinctive" in the sense that none is formed as the result of the recombination of two or more terms within the sequence. This point can be made more clearly if we compare Quechua names for the numbers from 1 to 10 with those of Aymara, another (unrelated) Andean language that is widely spoken in the southern part of Quechua-speaking territory (on the relationship between Quechua and Aymara, see Hardman-de-Bautista 1985).[3] The Aymara names for numbers from 1 to 10 are given in Table 2.2.

In Aymara, there are distinctive primary lexemes for the numbers from one to six, as well as ten. However, the terms for numbers from seven to nine are formed from words (or roots of words) that precede and/or follow them; that is:

$$
\begin{array}{ccccc}
 & pa & / & qallqu & \\
7 & = & 2 & + & (5?) \\
 & kimsa & / & qallqu & \\
8 & = & 3 & + & (5?) \\
 & lla* & / & tunka & \\
9 & = & (1) & - & 10 \ (\text{i.e., } 10 - 1)
\end{array}
$$

*Bertonio (1984 [1612]) calls "9" *llallatunca,* and glosses *llalla* as "almost, a little less."

TABLE 2.2

Number Names in Aymara

Number Name	Translation
maya	one
paya	two
kimsa	three
pusi	four
pisq'a	five
suxta	six
paqallqu	seven
kimsaqallqu	eight
llatunka	nine
tunka	ten

SOURCES: Forbes 1870: 273–274; Briggs 1993: 95–96.

Thus, unlike Quechua, whose numbers appear to be based purely on the decimal (base-10) principle, and which, therefore, has distinct primary lexemes for the numbers from 1 to 10, Aymara shows evidence of both a quinary (base-5; i.e., 2 + 5 = 7 and 3 + 5 = 8) as well as a decimal principle in the formation of number names. It is interesting to note in passing the use of a *subtractive* principle in the number word formation of Aymara primary lexemes (for example, 9 = 10 – 1). The use of this principle is unusual not only in comparison to Quechua but in more global comparative terms (Hurford 1987: 240).

As has been amply demonstrated in comparative studies of number names in a variety of languages (see, for example, Ascher 1991; Crump 1990; Menninger 1969; Mimica 1992; Zaslavsky 1990), base-5, -10, and -20 (vigesimal) number systems often display a derivation of number names for these incremental units from the natural divisions and collections of fingers and toes. One of the best examples of the analysis of such a system of nomenclature is Mimica's study of the counting and number system of the Iqwaye, of Papua New Guinea (1992; see also Zaslavsky 1990: 238–254). In South America, Karsten reported in 1935 the following number names from the Upano tribes of Jivaroan-speakers of eastern Ecuador (Table 2.3):

TABLE 2.3
Jivaroan Names for Quinary Number Groupings

Number Group	Jivaroan Name	Translation
1 =	*chikichi*	counting one finger
5 =	*wéhe amukei*	I have finished the [one] hand
10 =	*mai wéhe amúkahei*	I have finished both hands
15 =	*huini náwi amúkahei*	here I have finished one foot
20 =	*mai náwi amúkahei*	I have finished both feet

SOURCE: Karsten 1935:548.

Neither Aymara (despite its suggestion of both base-5 and base-10 number principles) nor Quechua displays an origin of number names in collections of fingers or toes. This is not to say, however, that there is nothing to be learned about the nature, conception, and meaning of Quechua numbers from the naming of the digits. I will return to this question in Chapter 3.

Number Symbols and Metaphors

As is true in languages worldwide, certain numbers have particular symbolic or metaphorical significance in Quechua thought. These ideological attachments serve to expand the fields of meaning of specific numbers and, once again, to position them within a variety of semantic domains in Quechua language and culture. I have assembled the information on number symbols and metaphors in the Appendix (see also Mendizábal Losack's discussion of Inka number symbols based on data recorded in the Spanish chronicles [1989: 75–91]). While I have chosen not to place this material in the text, there are two points that should be made here concerning the nature of the information in the Appendix that have to do with matters of more general theoretical or method-ological importance for this study. First, I should like to make it clear from the outset that my principal informant for the information pre-sented in the Appendix was a bilingual (Quechua and Spanish) man, Primitivo Nina. I have also gleaned bits of information concerning this topic over the years in talking to, and working with, various men, both in Peru and Bolivia. While I have collected some information on this topic from women (especially from weavers in Bolivia), I nonetheless lack detailed, in-depth, and reflective accounts of number symbols and metaphors from women. The reason that this is of concern and, there-fore, why I feel it is both necessary and important to be explicit about the sex of my informants is that some of the number symbols included in the Appendix refer to sexual matters, such as metaphorical compar-isons between numbers and the genitalia.

Now, my principal informant, Primitivo Nina, stated that he was aware that women have their own number symbols and metaphors and that many of these are of an explicitly sexual nature; however, he did not feel sufficiently knowledgeable about women's number symbols to try to characterize them for me. Certain of the women's symbols are shared with men, but many are "private symbols," known only to women, and a woman does not discuss them with a man—and certainly not with a *gringo* anthropologist!—with whom she is not intimately ac-quainted. Therefore, I have reported in the Appendix only what I know and have experienced regarding number symbols and metaphors. I ex-tend a hearty invitation to my female colleagues to take up the study of the symbolism of numbers and the Hindu-Arabic numerals among Quechua women.

The second note of explanation that should accompany a reading of the Appendix concerns the fact that, while some of the number symbols are posited on the basis of a nonmaterial relationship between signifier and signified—that is, they are of a purely ideological and linguistic na-ture—others have as their objects of reference the written numeral signs (1, 2, 3, . . .). For example, the sign "2" is easily transformed into the figure of a "duck" (*pili*); thus, "two" (*iskay*) is often referred to as *pili*. Similarly, the bumps along the right-hand side of the numeral "3" are said to look like a buttock, so "three" (*kinsa*) can be called *uhete* ("anus"); and "8" is likened to a pair of testicles (*runtu*, "egg[s]"), and so on (see Appendix). I should note that the recognition of symbols based on the written numerals is not necessarily a mark of "literacy." People of all ages and educational backgrounds are exposed to the number signs in a variety of contexts, such as in school or in the market place, and they make what they will of the wealth of straight and curved lines that compose these signs. What is generally crucial in motivating symbols with respect to Hindu-Arabic numeral signs is their shape and conformation, not the read and spoken names of the signs—although the latter are *also* used by literate and "numerate" individuals in the construction of symbols and metaphors.

The Formation of Compound Numbers

As stated earlier, the Quechua construct names for compound numbers by combining the twelve terms given in Table 2.1. We will look at a representative sample of such number constructions in this section. Our objectives here will be not only to understand the basic rules of the formation of compound numbers, but also to attempt to understand, on the basis of the syntactical rules and patterns in their production, how numbers are conceived of and manipulated *as cultural products*.

Above the number "ten" (*chunka*), Quechua adheres strictly to the *decimal* principle in the formation of complex numbers. That is, given the two primary sets of building blocks of the base-10 system of numeration—the units, 1–9, and the decimal units 10 (*chunka*), 100 (*pachaq*), and 1,000 (*waranqa*)—compound numbers are formed by the application, either separately or jointly, of two basic strategies: *yapay* ("to add") and *miray* ("to multiply").

Yapay involves the *addition* of a unit (1–9) to any one of the three decimal units, and/or the addition of a lower decimal unit to a higher one. In this operation, the higher value number precedes (or is spoken before) the lower (for example, 13 = *chunka kinsayuq*, "ten, possessor of three"). It is important to note that this ordering of units in number names is not universal. For instance, in Tehuelche, a now-extinct language of Tierra del Fuego, "thirteen" was spoken in the order: "three - ten" (Musters 1873: 339). But of course, we do not have to resort to such an exotic language as Tehuelche to find an example of such an "inverted" word order—for "three - ten" is, of course, the order of the units in the spoken (but not written) number 13 in English as well.

To return to Quechua, in a compound number ending in a unit, the unit number name always carries the possessive suffix -*yuq* (e.g., *kinsa-yuq*). When the number word ends in a consonant or a semiconsonant, the connector -*ni* precedes -*yuq* (e.g., *pusaq-ni-yuq*). When the terminal number word in a compound number is either of the decimal units *chunka* or *pachaq*, it carries the third-person singular possessive ending -*n* (e.g., *chunka-n*); the ending -*n* is preceded by the connector -*ni* when added to *pachaq* (i.e., *pachaqnin*). This usage should be clarified as follows. *Chunka* (10) carries the possessive ending when the number in question is a part of a full 100 (*pachaq*) unit (e.g., 130 = *pachaq kinsa chunkan* = 100 + 3 × 10). Similarly, the possessive ending is added to *pachaq* when the number in question is a part of a full 1,000 (*waranqa*) unit (e.g., 1,300 = *waranqa kinsa pachaqnin* = 1,000 + 3 × 100). Examples of the application of the *yapay* principle are given below:

a) *chunka kinsayuq:* 10 + 3 = 13
b) *chunka ujniyuq:* 10 + 1 = 11
c) *pachaq pusaqniyuq:* 100 + 8 = 108
d) *pachaq chunkan:* 100 + 10 = 110
e) *pachaq chunka iskayniyuq:* 100 + 10 + 2 = 112
f) *waranqa tawayuq:* 1,000 + 4 = 1,004
g) *waranqa pachaqnin:* 1,000 + 100 = 1,100
h) *waranqa pachaq chunkan:* 1,000 + 100 + 10 = 1,110
i) *waranqa pachaq chunka jisqoniyuq:* 1,000 + 100 + 10 + 9 = 1,119

In the *miray,* "multiplication," principle of compound number word formation, a decimal unit may be multiplied by a unit (e.g., 2 × 10) or by another decimal unit (e.g., 10 × 100). In speaking the formula for this operation, the lower number (the multiplier) precedes the higher (the multiplicand). Examples of the application of the multiplication principle are given below:

a) *iskay chunka:* 2 × 10 = 20
b) *qanchis pachaq:* 7 × 100 = 700
c) *jisqon waranqa:* 9 × 1,000 = 9,000
d) *chunka waranqa:* 10 × 1,000 = 10,000
e) *kinsa chunka waranqa:* (3 × 10) × 1,000 = 30,000
f) *waranqa waranqa:* 1,000 × 1,000 = 1,000,000

One question that often arises in the comparative study of numbering and mathematical systems is whether or not true multiplication, as opposed to repeated addition, exists. The use of the *miray* ("to multiply") operation in the formation of compound numbers is a first indication that true multiplication does, indeed, exist in Quechua number theory. It is interesting to note for comparative purposes that the Uru language of northern and western Bolivia contains similar explicit uses of multiplication in the formation of compound numbers (LaBarre 1941: 498). For example, in Uru, 10 is *kalo*; 100 is *kalo kalo* (10 10), or *pac*; and 1,000 is *kalo-pac* (10 100).

The two principles and operations discussed above—addition and multiplication—may also be combined in a third type of operation in the formation of compound numbers. When the two principles are combined, the application of the multiplication (*miray*) principle precedes that of the addition (*yapay*) principle; thereafter, the two operations are applied in alternation. Examples of the joint application of the multiplication and addition principles are given below:

a) *iskay chunka ujniyuq:* $(2 \times 10) + 1 = 21$
b) *kinsa pachaq chunka pusaqniyuq:* $(3 \times 100) + 10 + 8 = 318$
c) *tawa pachaq suqta chunka jisqonniyuq:* $(4 \times 100) + (6 \times 10) + 9 = 469$
d) *iskay waranqa iskay pachaq iskay chunka ujniyuq:* $(2 \times 1,000) + (2 \times 100) + (2 \times 10) + 1 = 2,221$
e) *tawa chunka tawayuq waranqa tawa pachaq tawa chunka tawayuq:* $[(4 \times 10 + 4) \times 1,000] + (4 \times 100) + (4 \times 10) + 4 = 44,444$

Some Problems in Quechua Numbers: Nothingness and Possession

Having now examined how number names are formed in Quechua, we will turn to two problems that arise from this presentation; one concerns the status of "zero" in Quechua; the other involves the question of the nature and meaning of the linguistic markers of possession that are utilized in the formation of compound numbers.

The Status of "0" in the Quechua Number Naming System

It will be noted that a number name for "zero" does not appear in Table 2.1. The number zero is not, in fact, spoken in the formation of compound number names, nor is there (to the best of my knowledge) a well-attested name or word "zero" in Quechua. When I have asked informants the name of the number sign "0," I have on a few occasions been given the term *muyu* ("circle"). However, I have never heard the number zero referred to by this term in everyday speech. As *muyu* is not given the gloss "zero" (Sp. *cero*) in any of the older Quechua dictionaries, it seems fairly clear that the term is a label that was devised, or invented (perhaps in answer to my question) for the purpose of describing the written sign "0." Having said this, it is also nonetheless true that the knowledge of this symbol would have entered Quechua consciousness, at least at some level, with the introduction of written mathematical notations in record keeping soon after the Spanish conquest. Today, if one wants to indicate the absence of a quantity or unit, this can be done either by using one of a number of terms signifying "nothing"—e.g., *q'ala, qhasi, ch'usaq,* or *saqisqa*—or by means of a descriptive construction, most commonly *mana kanchu* ("there is nothing").

The question that arises, then, is: Does the absence of a number name for "zero" mean that the numerical concept of zero, as distinct from a descriptive qualifier such as *mana kanchu*, is (and was) unknown to Quechua-speakers? Given what we know about the incorporation and representation of zero in the knot records of the Inka *khipus,* in which the absence of a knot in a position as part of a compound number = 0 (or of *any* knots for zero itself), we clearly cannot deny to the Quechua the knowledge of the "empty set" (see Ascher 1991: 23–24). What we *can* question, however, is the existence of a cardinal number name in Quechua for that condition. Perhaps the explanation for the absence of a number name for zero in Quechua is related to the fact that (as we will discuss in more detail in the following section) a fundamental feature of numbers is their capacity for "possession"; since "nothing" cannot possess anything, it cannot, by definition, be a number—that is, it cannot be named.

The absence of a name for zero in Quechua is of considerable significance precisely because of the status zero occupies in those counting and mathematical systems in which it *is* named. As Rotman has argued, the introduction of the Hindu-Arabic numeral *zero* into Europe beginning in the tenth century met with considerable resistance over the following several centuries. Resistance to a symbol signifying nothing came from a variety of sources, the principal ones of which were based on philosophical and theological objections to, and abhorrence of, the naming and reification in the counting and number naming systems—two of the basic sources and representations of order in the world—of the concept of "nothingness" (Rotman 1987).

To the degree that the introduction into European mathematics of the Hindu-Arabic numeral for zero precipitated a philosophical and theological crisis, at the same time that it allowed (if not sparked) tremendous advances in abstract mathematics, it appears that the Quechua do not today, nor did they in the past, present themselves with the conditions for such a crisis by *naming* the empty set with a cardinal number. We are no doubt also confronted here with one of the implications of the absence of a system of written numerals in the Andes—that is, of *making* a mark to indicate nothingness in a system of writing signs on a two-dimensional surface, as opposed to *not making* any knots in a piece of string to indicate the same (absence of) value.

As a fundamentally linguistic (rather than graphic) phenomenon, a decimal unit number name such as *pachaq* ("one-hundred") is clearly not conceived of by Quechua-speakers as the juxtaposition of the number signs: 1 0 0; rather, *pachaq* is the linguistic signal of a complete unit in the base-10 system of *spoken* numeration, and the iteration of *one* one hundred times. Therefore, while "zero" is subsumed within and incorporated by the *written signs* for the decimal unit names *chunka* (10), *pachaq* (100), and *waranqa* (1,000), it does not appear to have an independent existence as a marker or sign of (the absence of) value in Quechua.

The Possessiveness of Numbers

Let us begin by reviewing the grammatical constructions that give rise to the question of markers of possession in Quechua number words. We saw above that if the terminal word of a compound number name is a unit (1–9), it will carry the possessive suffix *-yuq*. If the terminal word is either *chunka* (10) or *pachaq* (100), and if the number indicated is a part of a full 100 (*pachaq*) unit in the case of 10, or a part of a full 1,000 (*waranqa*) unit in the case of 100, then *chunka* or *pachaq* will be given the third-person singular possessive ending: *-n* (*pachaq* also carries the connector *-ni*). Thus, we can summarize the circumstances that require the use of one or the other of the possessive markers as follows:

a) *-yuq:* indicator of a part of a whole unit of 10
b) *-n:* indicator of a part of a whole unit of 100
c) *-ni-n:* indicator of a part of a whole unit of 1,000

Now, possessive markers are rare in number naming systems; it is, therefore, important that we try to understand what its semantic significance is in the Quechua system of naming numbers. The questions that arise in this regard are: Who or what is "possessed" in a number word? And by whom or what is it "possessed"? Before addressing these questions, we should look more closely at the modifications of meanings precipitated by the addition of *-yuq* and *-n*.

When added to a noun, the suffix *-yuq* deforms the meaning of that word in one of four ways. First, it can denote possession by a named or implied subject:

Hayk'a watayuqtaq kankiri? "How old are you?" (literally: How many year-'possessor' [*-yuq*] are you?)

Second, it may indicate place of origin; i.e., the place (town, region, nation) from which an individual comes, or to which he or she belongs:

May llaqtayuqtaq kankiri? "Where are you from?" (literally: Where town/place 'of' [*-yuq*] are you?)

Third, it may denote the owner of some form of property, or a person who has a particular skill:

Tumás wasiyuq. "Thomas is a homeowner." (literally: Thomas, house-'possessor' [*-yuq*])

And fourth, added to a noun, *-yuq* creates an adjective denoting a characteristic of a named or implied subject:

Warmiyuqmi chay runaqa "That man is married." (literally: woman-'possessor' [*-yuq*] that man). (Cusihuamán 1976: 228–229)

This same general explanation (that is, an indication of possession) holds for the significance of the third-person singular possessive form *-n* when added to an incomplete (i.e., below 100) collection of 10s and to an incomplete (i.e., below 1,000) collection of 100s.

We can now return to the question of the meaning of possessive suffixes in compound number names. In formulations such as *chunka kinsayuq* (= 13), *-yuq* indicates possession of the value 3 (*kinsa*) by the named subject 10 (*chunka*). Stated another way, *chunka kinsayuq* reflects the linguistic proposition that a characteristic of *this* ten is its possession of three. The numeral phrase is syntactically equivalent to a phrase such as: *Carlos warmiyuq*, "Carlos is married" (literally: "Carlos [the] woman possessor"). In numerical constructions of the type *chunka kinsayuq*, there is an asymmetrical relationship between the two types of number values (i.e., the unit and the decimal unit) in terms of which number unit has the capacity to incorporate, or "possess," the other. That is, as a complete unit, 10 (*chunka*) has the capacity to possess an incomplete collection of units, such as 3. However, apparently because of its incompleteness, three cannot possess ten. The qualities of completeness and the ability to possess something, or the capacity to incorporate "outsiders," that characterize *chunka* outlined here accord well with the metaphorical uses of the full decimal units *chunka* (10) and *pachaq* (100) in a social context; that is, these units are both likened to, and can be used as synonyms for, the social groups called *"ayllus."* Ayllus are the territorial, communal labor, ritual, and kinship groupings commonly found in Andean communities (González Holguín 1952 [1608]; P. Nina, personal communication, 1994; see also below, Chapters 3 and 6).

Another factor to be taken into account in understanding the consistent use of possessive markers in Quechua number names is related to what is considered to be an inherent property of numbers, especially as they are used in the act of counting; that is, numbers are considered, by their nature, to *separate* things—to isolate one unit from another (or the next). The practical implication of this feature of numbers is the existence of prohibitions on counting things that are considered to be inseparable; this prohibition applies especially to reproductive groups, such as herd animals (see the discussion of *yupay*, "to count," in Chapter 4). For instance, checking up on the number of animals in one's herd is done by identifying the animals one-by-one by their *names* (all animals in a herd have individual names). Thus, while admitting—through naming—the individuality of the various members of a herd, naming is not considered to carry with it the divisive force associated with counting the animals by cardinal number names.

These observations provide us with an approach to understanding the use of possessive markers in the formation of compound number names in Quechua. While numbers are considered to create or emphasize the separateness of the things that are numbered (i.e., counted), the linguistic markers of possession used in the formation of number words have the effect of counteracting the inherent divisiveness of numbers. That is, the syntactical constructions indicating possession in number names represent cohesive forces counteracting, or counterbalancing, the *ideological* notion that numbers and the act of counting constitute divisive forces. Thus, the syntactical markers of possession maintain the unity of collections—or collections of collections—otherwise known as numbers.

I should state explicitly the perhaps obvious point that all decimal systems are not created equal, at least not with respect to the syntactic and semantic features of the construction of number names discussed above. For instance, in the formation of compound number words in the decimal-based systems of numeration in English and Spanish, the complete and incomplete units (as defined above) are joined together solely by juxtaposition (e.g., 17 = E. "seventeen" and Sp. *"diez y siete"*; and 110 = E. "one hundred ten" and Sp. *"ciento diez"*). There are no syntactical markers of possession in either language holding together the complete and incomplete decimal units in compound numbers. Thus, I argue that, in comparison, there is a deeply social foundation to the ontology of numbers in Quechua language, culture, and ideology. As I will discuss in more detail in Chapter 3, the focal group of this ontological tradition is that composed of a woman—a *mother*—and her age-graded offspring.

Finally, it must be stressed, lest one think that numerical terms are marginal elements in everyday spoken Quechua and that, therefore, the interpretation of the significance of possession in number names given here is overblown, that number words incorporating these syntactical forms are produced by Quechua-speakers countless times every day in a variety of contexts (such as warping and weaving textiles, farming, marketing, game playing, and storytelling). Therefore, such linguistic constructions represent a crucial arena for the formulation and expression of collective values and cohesive relations in Quechua social life. I will argue in Chapter 5 that these and other linguistic constructions underlie the notion of Quechua arithmetic and mathematics as an "art of rectification"; that is, a conceptual understanding in which the arithmetical operations of addition, subtraction, multiplication, and division are assigned the tasks of maintaining and/or restoring social, political, and economic harmony and equilibrium. A first approximation of certain key principles in this philosophy of arithmetic will be elaborated in the following section.

Odd and Even in the Logic of Prognostication

Having outlined several basic features of the cardinal numbers in Quechua, we face the task of identifying some of the semantic domains and symbolic constructions in which numbers play a role. If numbers were to have significance only as names of quantities, collections, aggregates, etc., then their analysis would be quite straightforward. However, it is because, as I mentioned earlier, these primarily quantitative entities regularly become entangled with non-quantitative kinds of meaning that their study is both interesting and has the potential for shedding light into other areas of Quechua life. In the remainder of this chapter, we will look at two interrelated problems concerning the classification and meaning of numbers. These concern, first, the classification of numbers as "odd" and "even," and second, the closely related problem of the nature and meaning of "pairs" in Quechua culture. That these problems are, as I will explain below, interrelated is suggested by the meanings assigned to certain types of numbers and collections (i.e., odd and even) in agricultural prognostications.

The beginning of the planting season is an exciting and anxious time of the year in farming communities throughout the Andes. It is exciting because the preparations for planting require a great deal of work in making or repairing tools as well as scheduling household labor and planning inter-household labor exchanges. It is an anxious time because there are so many uncertainties involved in planting the crops for the coming year. For instance, when should one actually take up tools and seeds and begin to plant? What will the weather conditions be like over the coming agricultural season? How good will the crops be? Now, barring catastrophes, such questions are for the most part eliminated as major concerns in Western, scientific farming in which the availability of chemical fertilizers and pesticides minimize to a large degree the adverse effects of vagaries of climate, soil conditions, pests, etc. (see Van der Ploeg 1993). However, in most farming communities in the high Andes, where the crops are much more directly exposed to environmental perturbations, and where there are few if any "safety nets" that one can rely on in the event of a significant crop failure, the level of anxiety and concern over the welfare and progress of the crops is high. In the face of such uncertainties in the essentially subsistence-based farming systems of the Andes, the questions that arise are: Is there any way to know the future? To get a fix on your luck? Perhaps even to exert a bit of influence in the great game of chance known as "subsistence agriculture"?

When we answer these questions below by describing the common practice of crop prognostications based on the random selection of even or odd numbers of corn kernels, it should not mystify either the intentions of these activities or the interpretations of these "data" on the part of the Andean farmers who engage in such prognostications. All in all, Quechua farmers are extremely pragmatic people who know well the vagaries of a life lived depending on one's own physical skills and wits. But the point is . . . who knows? Perhaps there *is* something to be learned or some vague form of force or influence that can be redirected to one's benefit by an innocent play with numbers. In my opinion, such an attitude is probably borne from the impression that numbers possess a cleanness, a certitude, and a quality of absoluteness whose source—as hidden and ultimately perplexing to them as to us—may be induced or perhaps "tricked" into participating beneficially in one's affairs. The question that becomes relevant in these circumstances is: What "kinds" of numbers, and arrangements or collections of units, are *taken to signify* a good and/or a bad prognostication for the crops? What we will find concerning such matters in the following discussion is a reiteration of some of the properties and values associated with numbers that were elaborated earlier in this chapter. These involve an ideology of numbers, and of other types of named collections, grounded in family (especially mother-child) relations reinforced by the values of complementarity and reciprocity.

The principal type of crop prognostication that I have watched and participated in in Andean farming practices takes place at the beginning of the planting of corn (Q. *sara*, Sp. *maíz*). The following two passages are taken from entries in my fieldnotes made at the times of the planting of corn in the community of Pacariqtambo (Department of Cusco), in south-central Peru, in 1980 and 1981.

August 9, 1980

We were offered cups of chicha *[fermented corn beer]. Everyone in turn had a couple of horns (*astas*) of chicha and then two copitas of* trago; *this was repeated a couple of times. The man with whom I came to the field was then invited to bless the corn kernels before planting began. We were all sitting in a line, facing west, with the* chicha *and a* misa *[spread out carrying-cloth] of corn between us. The man dipped an ear of corn in the chicha and sprinkled the seed corn with the chicha. He did this four times, making a cross on the seed corn each time. He then knelt and said a prayer.*

After finishing off the chicha, he dipped the drinking horn into the sack of seed corn and drew out about 8–12 kernels. He then poured these out of his horn onto the left side of the cloth. Everyone then counted the kernels one-by-one, *and one of the kernels was left to the side. The other kernels were returned to the sack.*

They then asked me to bless the corn, and I repeated the above procedure. However, when I dipped the horn into the sack of kernels and laid them on the left side of the cloth, they all instructed me to count them by pairs. I did so, counting out 13 pairs, and everyone began shouting "wank'a! wank'a!" All but one pair of my kernels were returned to the sack of seed corn. (I did not notice what became of my pair of kernels or of the other man's one kernel after we started working again.)

September 21, 1981

Spent the day helping Don Andrés and a few other men plant Sra. Pascuala's corn field. After plowing and planting some 5–8 rows, we stopped for the first round of chicha. *Everyone in turn was given an* asta *(horn) of* chicha. *The seed corn had been placed inside the circle formed by the four of us seated in a U-shaped arrangement. Each person took his horn of chicha and propped it up on the east side of the bag of seed corn and said a short prayer in Quechua. T'inkasqas ("libations") were then made on the seed corn (some 4–6 by each person); a bit of chicha was poured on the ground in front of the corn and then the person stood up and made t'inkas to the various apus (sacred mountains).*

The asta was then drained and the person took the empty horn and scooped up a few kernels of the seed corn. These kernels were dumped out on the left side of the bag, and they were then counted by pairs. When one's bunch of kernels turned out to be composed of an even number (i.e., when all the kernels could be matched in pairs), this was called wank'a *and was taken to be a good prognostication for the crops. When there was one kernel left over from the pairing, this was called* qhespi(n) *and was taken to be a bad sign for the crops. Most of our counts were* qhespin. *Not much was said about the prognostication; it was shrugged off, and we went back to work.*

I must point out to begin with that, while I am familiar with the literal meanings of the terms *wank'a* ("rock; outcrop") and *qhespi* ("crystal"), I never learned in what specific, or technical, sense these terms were being glossed in relation to prognostication on the occasions described above. What *was* clear, however, was that *wank'a* was associated with an even number (i.e., a complete pairing) of corn kernels, whereas *qhespi* was associated with an odd number; that is, *qhespi* described the condition in which there was one corn kernel left over after the process of counting-by-pairs was completed.

From these observations, we can draw two tentative conclusions. First, in order to arrive at the final prognostication, one can either count the kernels one-by-one, or by pairs. In either case, what is crucial in the prognostication is whether one ends up with a complete pairing of the kernels, and therefore with an even number as the product, or if there is one kernel left over. This suggests that in investigating the categories of "even" and "odd," what may be at issue is not the actual number in question, but its potential reduction to a state of either a final pair (= "even") or a single, remaining kernel (= "odd"). The second observation concerns the fact that the condition of "one/odd" represents a negative, problematic, and unfortunate state of affairs, whereas "two/pair/even" represents a positive, fortunate, and ultimately *productive* state of affairs.

The particular evaluations given to these contrasting conditions and number values represent, I would argue, important values in Quechua life, ones grounded in a deeply *social,* especially family-based, ontology that are entirely consistent with the principles of Quechua number relations and arithmetic as an art of "rectification" (the latter of which I have outlined in Chapter 1 and will develop more fully in Chapter 5). As we proceed, we will explore and elaborate further the particular characteristics of these ideological principles and their application to the domain of numbers.

Before leaving the topic of crop prognostications, I should stress that the methods and principles of prognostication noted above are not unique to the community of Pacariqtambo. Similar practices have been noted in numerous Quechua- and Aymara-speaking communities throughout the Andes. For instance, Tschopik described two such prognostications among the Aymara of Chucuito, Peru. One method, which took place during potato planting, involved removing seed potatoes from a sack by twos. If an even number remained in the bottom of the sack, good fortune was indicated; a single (i.e., odd) remaining potato was a bad augury. Later, at what was presumably the harvest of potatoes, a perfect plant would be uprooted and the potatoes counted off by twos to divine the outcome of the crop (Tschopik 1951: 518, 563). And finally, LaBarre (1948: 178) noted the Aymara custom at the time of corn planting whereby a diviner—called *toqueni hacchiri*—would take a handful of maize and count the grains out by twos to see if the count ended in a pair or a single seed corn; an even count (i.e., a final pair) indicated good fortune, while a single, odd grain remaining indicated bad luck.

It is important to note that, with only one consistent exception, even numbers are considered to be a good sign, odd numbers are a bad sign. The exception is with the number, and collection of, *three.* That is, three of something or repeating some act three times is often taken to indicate good fortune (see, for example, Hickman 1963: 81; Parsons 1945: 115). The distinctiveness of three in classifications of the qualities of even and odd numbers or collections may reflect a similar principle to that mentioned at the beginning of this chapter; that is, that three is reckoned to be the—or at least *a*—number signifying wholeness and completion. Three may also have the special status that it does because it represents the combination of the two values, or types of sets, that are crucial to the classification of numbers: 1 (odd) + 2 (even) = 3.

Even and Odd Numbers and the Relatedness of Pairs

As I hope to have made clear above, the distinction between odd and even in Quechua is made primarily at the level of the contrast between "one" (*uj*) and "two" (*iskay*). I would note that *uj* may also indicate "another," or "the other." *Iskay* may also be given the additional gloss, "pair." Let us look at how these relations and values are formulated and expressed in the names and descriptive labels for certain of the lower-level odd numbers in Quechua (Table 2.4).

TABLE 2.4

The Semiotics of Odd Numbers

Odd Numbers 1 to 7	Explanation
uj (1):	
a) *uj maki*	something you can hold in one hand; can also indicate five of something (i.e., a natural set of fingers)
b) *ujninta*	one of a number of groups of things
kinsa (3):	
a) *uj yunta ch'ullayuq*	one *yunta* ("pair") together with one alone
phishqa (5):	
a) *tawaq ujnin*	four together with one
b) *tawaq ñawpaqnin*	the one after, or following, four
c) *ujpa tawan*	the one of, or belonging to, four
d) *suqtaq sullk'an*	the younger one of six
qanchis (7):	
a) *pusaqpa qhipan*	the one before eight
b) *iskay kinsaqpaq kuraqnin, millay*	the elder of six [literally: of two times three], [is] the ugly, excessive one (see chapter 2)

The consistent trait that emerges from the various examples of naming and referring to odd numbers shown in Table 2.4 is that, except in the case of "one," they are all identified as composed of a certain number of *pairs* (or twos) *plus or minus one*. Thus, the issue in understanding odd numbers is the relationship between one and two—or one and a variable number of pairs. We will return shortly to take up the question of the nature of "pairs" and "pairing" in Quechua grammar.

As is true in the case of the examples cited above, higher-level numbers such as 15 and 16 will *often* be evaluated, with respect to the distinction between odd and even, on the basis of their potential reduction to the primary opposition between one and two.[4] I emphasize the qualification "often," because some expressions or formulations of the odd/even relationship are not only *not* reducible to the opposition between one and two, but actually appear to contradict the normal assignment of the values of "odd" and "even" to specific numbers (i.e., that 1, 3, 5, . . . = odd, and 2, 4, 6, . . . = even). For instance, if one were to set out to group a collection of (what turns out to be) fourteen objects by sets of five, one would soon come to the realization that this operation produces two complete sets of five with an incomplete set of four remaining. The incomplete set of four—a *number* which is otherwise classifiable as "even"—will be referred to by one of the terms indicating an "uneven" value (e.g., *ch'ulla*, or *khallu;* see below). *This* four will be classified as uneven, of course, because it is a remainder left over from the operation of selecting groups of five; that is, the number of units in this remaining set (of four) does not contain the full value of the standard set-size used for grouping in this hypothetical case.

From the above example, we are warned against making uncritical generalizations or absolute statements about the specific numbers that might be classified as either "odd" or "even." Rather, we need to take into account a range of lexical items and grammatical constructions, as well as specific contexts in which numbers and collections are actually classed according to the contrast odd/even, in order to arrive at culturally meaningful generalizations of the significance of these values and concepts in the organization and theory of numbers in Quechua ideology. But, before taking up this task, we should be clear on why such an undertaking is important and worthwhile.

In the Western system of numeration and manipulation of numbers with which most readers are familiar, the distinction between odd and even is fundamental to the organization and conceptualization of numbers. All numbers can be assigned to one or the other of these categories. In this sense, the odd/even distinction is one of the few classificatory principles operating universally within the domain of numbers. The assignment of a number to one or the other of these two values reflects how that number behaves in arithmetic operations, especially in subtraction and division. In addition to this fact, and *linked to it causally,* the symbolic and metaphorical values attached to numbers will often be determined by their assignment to one or the other of these number "classes"—that is, to either the "odd" or the "even." These observations are consistent with the classification and manipulation of numbers in Western arithmetic, mathematics, and number symbolism. The question is: Do the same rules and generalizations hold true for Quechua-speakers? And if they do, how are these values and principles described both in relation to specific numbers and in their extension, metaphorically and otherwise, into other semantic domains?

A Lexicon and Grammar of "Odd" and "Even"

The first and perhaps most important observation to make in regard to the categories of odd and even numbers in Quechua is that terms for even numbers are primarily (although not exclusively) constructed grammatically as syntactical modifications of terms for odd numbers. This principle is seen in the following examples (see Table 2.5).

As we see in Table 2.5, there is a curious and interesting paradox contained in the Quechua terminology for odd and even. For while many of the terms denoting "even"—a concept that is most commonly glossed as "pair"—are constructed by the syntactical modification of terms for odd, the terms for odd are themselves formulated semantically as expressions identifying "one member of a natural or potential *pair*." This is seen, for instance, in the relationship between the terms *ch'ulla* ("odd; half of a pair") and *ch'ullantin* ("the one [or half; part] together with its pair"). Thus, "odd" is the *lexically* primary or marked category, whereas *conceptually* "even" is the primary category.

We will see a similar principle expressed in a different way in Chapter 3 (see Table 3.3). There, we will find in the terms for the fingers provided by Santo Tomás (1992 [1560]) that the first, third, and fifth fingers (the thumb, middle, and little fingers, respectively) are given individual

TABLE 2.5

The Terminology for Odd and Even

Terms for Odd Numbers	Terms for Even Numbers
ch'ulla:	*ch'ullantin:*
a) odd (Sp. *impar*)	a) the two together that make a pair
b) unequal, uneven	b) a pair of similar persons or things
ch'ullan:	
a) its (one's) pair, partner (but not spouse)	
khallu:	*khalluntin:*
a) one alone (e.g., one half)	a) the one together with its mate/pair (e.g., the two halves of a textile sewn together)
khallun:	
a) its (one's) pair (i.e., when the two are separate)	
uj:	*ujnintin:*
a) one	a) two (i.e., in reference to one thing that is divided into two parts)*
ñuk'ua:	
a) "odd" (Sp. *impar*); said in relation to the hands or arms (e.g., a one-armed person = "*ñuk'u*")	

iskaynintin = two things that are separate, each of which is a complete unit.

names, whereas the second and fourth fingers (the index and ring fingers, respectively) are referred to simply as "following, accompanying (*katiq*) finger" (cited in Zuidema 1964: 214, n. 5). Thus, the odd numbered fingers "one" and "three" are accompanied, or made a complete pair, by the following even numbered fingers "two" and "four" (the little finger is termed "youngest finger"). Here again, then, "odd" is the marked (named) category. What these various data suggest is that we need to analyze the concept of "pair" as a basis for identifying and understanding the semantic domain within which odd and even operate and from which they draw their meaning.

In addition to the terms denoting pairs that are identified in Table 2.5, there are a few others that we should take note of. These include:

> *yanantin*—two opposite but complementary things intimately bound together; *examples*: the two hands joined together, or a husband and wife joined as a couple.
>
> *yuntantin*—pair; two separate things bound intimately together (especially for purposes of work); *examples:* two bulls yoked together for plowing.
>
> *apañayuq*—pair (literally: "the one possessing [-*yuq*] a consanguineal successor); twins (i.e., the birth of two in succession).

I will return in Chapter 3 to look more closely at the last term— *apañayuq*. This is an interesting and important term, which denotes the event, or action, of two things being born from one source (as twins born from their mother). The term can be repeated in combination with the natural sequence of cardinal numbers to indicate a line of descendants organized by birth order—one being born after the other.

Now, aside from the "special" term *apaña*, it is clear from the terms given above, as well as from those listed under the "even" heading in Table 2.5, that the formulation of the concept of "pair(s)" is closely linked to the suffix -*ntin* (see Platt 1986b). I should point out here that González Holguín (1952 [1608]) formulates the distinction between even and odd numbers, especially as they are used in divination, in the contrast between *yanantincuna* ("evens") and *chullacuna* ("odds"). Anyone familiar with Andean culture history will already be alerted to the possible significance of the suffix -*ntin* in grammatical constructions denoting a grouping of things, as this suffix was central to the formation of the name by which the Inkas referred to the political unity of the "four" (*tawa*) quarters, or "parts" (*suyu*), of the Inka empire; that is, the Inka empire was called *tawantinsuyu* ("the four quarters/parts intimately bound together"). The question for us here, in our attempt to understand the underlying principles and concepts associated with pairs as conceived of in relation to odd and even numbers, is: What does *-ntin* signify? But, more specifically, what is the nature of the "binding force" that is exerted syntactically and semantically by the use of the suffix *-ntin* as the principal marker for a "pair"?

In his Quechua grammar of the early seventeenth century, González Holguín provides us with a range of glosses for the suffix *-ntin* and, therefore, of the semantic influence of the addition of this suffix in transforming the meaning of terms to which it is attached. González Holguín (1975 [1607]: 109) notes that *-ntin* has the following uses:

a) When added to a kinship term, *-ntin* signifies the connection between the named kinship status and a relative; e.g., *yayantin* ("the father with his son"); *huaoquentin* ("the brothers"); and *ñañantin* ("the sisters"). The force that binds these individuals together into the various, named groupings is that of consanguineal, family relations.

b) When added to temporal nouns, *-ntin* signifies the wholeness or completion of that unit of time; e.g., *huatantin* ("every year," or "all the years"); *quillantin,* or *quillantincuna* ("every month," or "all the months").

c) When added to a phrase containing terms denoting two periods, or units of time, *-ntin* unites them into a single, inclusive unit; e.g., *tuta punchaunintin* ("the nights and days").

d) When indicating the adverbial construction "a day later," or "several days later," one specifies a unit of time and adds *kayantin* ("to be together with"); e.g., *pasqua kayantin* ("one day, or several days, after Easter").

e) When added to nouns having a part-to-whole relationship to each other, or to circumstances or conditions that are characteristic of, or possessed by, the principal noun, *-ntin* indicates the thing or member that is possessed in the relationship; e.g., *runappachantin* ("the person and his or her clothing"); *huaci canchantin* ("the house with its patio").

Thus, the suffix -*ntin* denotes relations of possession similar to what we saw in the earlier discussion of the semantic effects of the addition of -*yuq* to nouns and numbers. But in addition to indicating the possession of one thing by another (as with -*yuq*), the suffix -*ntin* can also specifically denote *kinship* relations (e.g., of descent, filiation) between two entities. This characteristic of -*ntin* helps us to make sense of several of the terms for the categories "even" and "odd" given in Table 2.5. For instance, in such related terms as *khallu* ("one alone") and *khalluntin* ("the one together with its mate/pair"), in which there is an indication of both kinship and part-to-whole relations, *the "mate" is possessed by the primary character*. That is, in the *khallu/khalluntin* formulation, the "two" (or "second") is possessed by the "one" (or "first") in the formation and naming of a pair.

In Quechua number ontology and terminology, the types of relationships signified by the suffix -*ntin* are extended throughout the (alternating) sequence of odd and even numbers; every even number is seen as completing the "unevenness" (i.e., the pairing) of the anterior odd number. In this way, the sequence of cardinal numbers is constructed throughout by the combined, and complementary, relations and values of kinship and affiliation—the latter of which is conceptualized primarily in terms of part-to-whole relations. In sum, the domain of the cardinal numbers is a world constructed explicitly on models of kinship and social organization. I will return in the conclusions (Chapter 7) to make use of the categories of odd and even as elaborated in the foregoing as a basis for stating a hypothesis for the logical principles and semantic categories underlying decimal organization in Quechua numeration. For the time being, we will turn in the next chapter to a discussion of how the values and relations discussed above are present as well in the syntactical structures and semantic values associated with the ordinal numerals.

Ordinal Numerals: The Reproduction and Succession of Numbers

The Vocabulary of Ordination

Ordinal numbers have the function of arranging (in semantic space) and labeling discrete objects or "places" in a set using an ordered sequence of terms usually connected with, or derived from, the cardinal numbers. This statement is generally true, with the common exception, which we see in many languages including English, of the "first" and "second" (i.e., not "oneth" and "twoth") terms of the sequence. The ordinals reflect natural or ascribed relations of precedence and succession that are found in, or projected onto, the set of things in question. When we look closely at some of the uses of ordinals in Quechua, we find that the ways in which they order and label the members of various sets look remarkably like, and often converge with, other principles for ordering and naming ordered sets, such as birth order and age grading. I will return to examine such ordinal-like, non-numerical ordering and labeling systems after giving an overview of the grammar and vocabulary for ordinal numerals in Quechua.

Generally speaking, Quechua ordinals combine cardinal number names with a term indicating the action of ordering, sequencing, or grading. In Cusco Quechua, this latter term is *ñaqen* (or *ñiqin*), which Padre Lira glosses as "order, hierarchy, gradation" (1982: 211). In Bolivian Quechua, *kaq*, the present participle of the verb *kay* ("to be"), is used as the ordinal marker. *Kaq* denotes the distinctive identity and position within an ordered group of the item in question—e.g., *iskay kaq* ("that

TABLE 3.1
Ordinal Numerals in Cusco and Sucre Quechua

Ordinal Numeral	Basic Term	Cusco Marker		Sucre Marker
first	*ñawpaq*	*ñaqen*	/	*kaq**
second	*iskay*	*ñaqen*	/	*kaq*
third	*kimsa*	*ñaqen*	/	*kaq*
fourth	*tawa*	*ñaqen*	/	*kaq*
fifth	*phishqa*	*ñaqen*	/	*kaq*
sixth	*suqta*	*ñaqen*	/	*kaq*
seventh	*qanchis*	*ñaqen*	/	*kaq*
eighth	*pusaq*	*ñaqen*	/	*kaq*
ninth	*isq'on*	*ñaqen*	/	*kaq*
tenth	*chunka*	*ñaqen*	/	*kaq*
etc.	etc.	etc.	/	etc.
last	*qhipa*	*ñaqen*	/	*kaq*

*In Bolivian Quechua, "first" may also be constructed as *uj kaq*.

which is two" [in the group/series]) = "second"; *kinsa kaq* ("that which is three" [in the group/series]) = "third."

There are two exceptions to the modes of forming ordinals in Quechua described above. These concern the "first" and the "last" members of a sequence. The standard form for indicating the "first" in Cusco Quechua is the construction *ñawpaq ñaqen*; the common forms of referring to the "first" in Sucre Quechua are *ñawpaq kaq* or *uj kaq*. *Ñawpaq* can be glossed "ancient, anterior; ancestor or ancestral." The "last" in an ordinal series is termed *qhipa ñaqen* (Cusco) or *qhipa kaq* (Sucre). *Qhipa* (*qhepa*) may be glossed as "posterior, later; straggler; coming, future." Table 3.1 gives the basic terms for ordinals for 1st through 10th and "last"; to the left of the slash mark is the ordinal marker used in Cusco (i.e., *ñaqen*); to the right is the marker used in Sucre (i.e., *kaq*).

Two of the fundamental principles organizing and motivating ordination are hierarchy and succession. That is, any position in an ordinal series, *save the "first,"* has, in the system of naming the ordinals, a well-defined position vis-á-vis its neighbors, the prior numeral and the one that follows. For example, the "fifth" is the successor to the fourth and the predecessor to the sixth. But, what of the relationship between the first two ordinals—the "first" and the "second"? How is the "first" established, or brought into being, and how does it give rise to the "second"? These are important, if not vital, questions in the study of the conceptual and semantic foundations of ordinal sequences in any number system, as is well attested by the enormous amount of energy and ingenuity devoted precisely to these questions by Western philosophers of mathematics (e.g., Dummett 1991: 315–317; Russell 1980: 241, 249–251). The crux of the problem is not so much how the "first" comes into being, for that is essentially the problem of Genesis, which must be resolved on the basis of criteria (such as logic, faith, or mythology) relevant to the particular case at hand. Rather, the central problem is how the "second" comes into being and what its relationship is to the "first." This is the central problem in the study of ordinal sequences because it is only when the "second" comes into existence that the *successor–predecessor* relationship, which is typical of an ordinal sequence as a whole, is set in motion, or brought into being.

It is important to note in regard to the above observations that González Holguín (1952 [1608]: 65) defines *naque,* which he combines with the cardinal numbers to produce the ordinal numerals, as "to wither." This notion is elaborated in the following entry from González Holguín: *"Ccochayan ccochayman, o naquen, o caunun, soncco o ccalpa"* ("to be greatly diminished in spirit and primary, or initial, strength"). This suggests that an ordinal sequence was conceived of as beginning in a state of strength, and perhaps purity, and then as undergoing a gradual deterioration, or diminution, of the initial state with each successive member. This image captures perfectly the notion that ordinal sequences are grounded in the principles of hierarchy and succession.

In addressing the analysis of ordinal sequences in particular and relations of hierarchy and succession in general from the perspective of a Quechua theory and ontology of numbers, which is the central objective of this chapter, I do not think we can succeed if we confine ourselves to the realm of explicitly ordinal numeral sequences, strictly defined (i.e., sequences in which the members/elements are only or primarily labeled "first, second, third, . . ."). Rather we will fare much better in our attempt to understand the principles that motivate and organize ordinal sequences if we turn our attention first to the investigation of several examples of non-numeral ordinal-like sequences. These are sequences organized by hierarchy and succession that are grounded in such qualitative and classificatory distinctions as older/younger, parent/child, upper/lower, which do not necessarily assign ordinal numerals to positions within the sequences, or at least which do not take ordinal designation as the primary ordering principle of the sequence. It is in such data, I will argue, that we will encounter most directly the principles and grammatical formulations that will expose the logic underlying true ordinal sequences from the point of view of Quechua cultural, ideological, and linguistic values and principles. Using this interpretive strategy, we will hopefully be able to arrive at a clear understanding of how ordinal sequences are conceptualized and why they are assigned certain symbolic and metaphorical characteristics.

Ordinal Series and the Non-Numeral Ordinal Sequences

In comparative and historical studies of counting and mathematical systems around the world, an important topic of investigation has concerned the origin of, and the relationship between, cardinal and ordinal numerals. Which came first? Does it *matter* which came first? How are the two sets of number names—cardinal and ordinal—related conceptually and lexically? In fact, it is probably not possible to determine which of the two came first, especially not at the lexical level, as they are so intimately and intricately interconnected. Indeed, as Hurford (1987: 169) notes, "this question cannot arise, as the notions of 'collection' [the basis of cardinals] and 'sequence' [the basis of ordinals] are both necessary (and neither is sufficient) for a grasp of the full significance of numbers" (similar ideas are expressed by Dantzig 1954: 9 and Russell 1980: 241, 249–251; but see Crump 1990: 9–11, in which he argues for the numerical ontogenetic sequence: ordinal numbers, natural numbers, cardinal numbers). Hurford further claims that the cardinal and ordinal meanings—i.e., "collection" and "sequence," respectively—are learned in the practice of the activity of counting (1987:

168–169, 173). However, this is not to say that the two types of number series are equally motivated. That is, in my opinion at least, ordinal sequences seem to have some priority at the conceptual and cultural levels, primarily through their affinity with and attachment to non-numeral ordinal sequences—sequences such as birth order, age grades, and others. While cardinal numbers and ordinal numerals are abstractions "drained" of any specific denotative content (other than quantity and position within a succession), non-numeral, ordinal-like sequences retain cardinality and ordinal succession *in conjunction with* semantic and symbolic content. It will be through an examination of a variety of these non-numeral ordinal sequences that we will be able to explore the conceptual and ontological foundations of Quechua ideas of numbers.

To anticipate the argument to be made in this chapter, we will find that in Quechua conceptions of the cardinal, ordinal, and non-numeral ordinal sequences, the primary motivating force—that is, the force that both brings sequential elements of an ordinal series into being and directs the classificatory and linguistic activity of naming the members in their proper hierarchical order—is *reproduction*. One of the clearest expressions of the incorporation of this principle into ordered sequences as conceived of in Quechua ideology is the designation of the first member of a series as *mama* ("mother"). Pursuing the use and meaning of this term, especially in the non-numeral ordinal sequences, will give us deeper insight into the nature of ordinal sequences and, in turn, of the meaning of numbers in Quechua thought and culture. We begin by examining the (for us) novel proposition that the reproduction of *animals* is one of several possible forces that gives rise to the numeral system.

The Reproduction of Animals and Numerals

The hypothetical situation motivating the discussion of this topic by my principal informant, Primitivo Nina, was the construction of a series of "corrals" (*kancha*) for holding sheep or llamas. His description began with the circumstance in which a family would build a single, large corral to hold all of its animals. Such a corral—the first to be built by a young family—is referred to as *mama kancha* ("mother corral"). Assuming good fortune on the part of the family in the reproduction of their livestock, a number of additional corrals would be built over time. When subsequent corrals are built, the first corral, *mama kancha*, will also begin to be designated as both *jatun kancha* ("large corral"), and *uj kaq kancha* ("first corral"). At full maturity (of both the heads of the household and the herd), the family will ideally have four corrals. *Mama kancha* will be used as the pen for adult female (*china*) animals; the "second corral," *iskay kaq kancha,* will house adult male (*machu*) animals; the "third corral," *kinsa kaq kancha,* will hold immature female (*china*) animals; and the immature male (*urqu*) animals will be placed in the "fourth corral," *tawa kaq kancha.* Thus, each one of the four corrals holds one member, or type, of a reproductive set; the corrals, and by extension their ordinal numeral designators, become glossed as reproductive units. Finally, in addition to the designation of the corrals in an ordinal seriation, the group of *four corrals* will be referred to as *uj kancha kinsa uñayuq,* "one [the "mother"] corral with three suckling babies."

The latter designation of the relations among the four corrals indicates the grounding of the conception of the generation and relations among the four corrals in terms of kinship and reproduction. But beyond this, we see here an explicit link between the reproduction of animals and the reproduction of numbers in the generation of an ordinal sequence. It is important to emphasize that there is a clearly conceived *causal* relationship between these two series. That is, the ordinal numerals do not cause the animals to reproduce; rather, the natural reproductive force of the animals—but more specifically that of the adult females (*china mamas*)—is the cause of, or the motivation behind, the *generation* of an ordinal sequence. By "generation," I mean the successive appearance or birth of a group of related members who collectively form an age-graded, ordered series. This motivation of ordinal sequences, and the privileged, generative role within them of the reproductive female, will be seen in each of the following examples.

Ayllu Ordination and Human Reproduction

The example that we take up now begins from the well-known circumstance in the Andes in which there are a number of interrelated *ayllus*[1] occupying a given territory over time. In such settings, it is commonly the case that the people belonging to the various *ayllus* will have traditions concerning the origin and evolution of the related groups. Such traditions are well attested in the Andes, both ethnohistorically and ethnographically.

TABLE 3.2

The *Ayllus* of Bustillos

Ayllu	Ordinal/Evolutionary Sequence of Appearance	Translation
Chayantaka:	*mama ayllu*	mother *ayllu*
	jatun ayllu	large, or great, *ayllu*
	ñawpaq ayllu	ancient/ancestral *ayllu*
	uj kaq ayllu	first *ayllu*
	ujninkaq Chayantaka ayllu	first united *ayllu* Chayantaka
Yanpara:	*Chayantaka qhipan ayllu*	*ayllu* following Chayantaka
	iskay kaq ayllu	second *ayllu*
	iskayninkaq Yanpara ayllu	second united *ayllu* Yanpara
Macha:	*Yanpara qhipan ayllu*	*ayllu* following Yanpara
	kinsa kaq ayllu	third *ayllu*
	kinsaninkaq Macha ayllu	third united *ayllu* Macha
Jukumani:	*Macha qhipan ayllu*	*ayllu* following Macha
	tawa kaq ayllu	fourth *ayllu*
	tawaninkaq Jukumani ayllu	fourth united *ayllu* Jukumani
Laymi:	*Jukumani qhipan ayllu*	*ayllu* following Jukumani
	phishqa kaq ayllu	fifth *ayllu*
	phishqaninkaq Laymi ayllu	fifth united *ayllu* Laymi

The example that we will use here for illustrative purposes is from the province of Bustillos, in the Norte de Potosí, where we find the following interrelated group of *ayllus:* Chayantaka, Yanpara, Macha, Jukumani, and Laymi (for descriptions of alternative configurations of *ayllus* in this area, see Izko 1992). One tradition of the origin and evolution of these *ayllus* that Primitivo Nina is aware of is shown in Table 3.2. The table illustrates the notion that Chayantaka *ayllu* first came into existence, and then, through the growth and continual sub-division of the ancestral group over time, a number of new *ayllus* came into existence.

Two things are important to take note of with regard to the sequence shown in Table 3.2. First, Chayantaka *ayllu*—the first member of the group of interrelated *ayllus*—is conceptually the same kind of entity that we saw earlier with the *mama kancha* as the origin of a group of corrals built by a family over time; that is, Chayantaka *ayllu* is *mama, jatun, ñawpaq, uj kaq* ("first") *ayllu*. *Mama ayllu* is the original, generative group of the series of *ayllus* that appeared in this territory over time. But, and this is the second point, whereas in the case of the corrals the generative force of the ordinal sequence was the reproduction of animals, in this case the generative force is human reproduction. I will come back to the topic of *ayllu* organization and ordinal sequences in the next section.

In summary, the image that we are developing here of *mama,* and of her role in the generation of numbers as offspring, is captured in González Holguín's gloss of a term derived from *mira,* "multiplicity." The term in question is *miraywa,* which he defines as "fecund woman; prolific female" (1952 [1608]). This image will be considerably amplified and clarified as we continue.

Fingers and Numbers

The problem that we examine in this section concerns the relationship between numbers and the fingers of the two hands. In Quechua, the fingers represent an important set of tools not only for counting but also for naming and organizing ordinal relations among groups of up to ten objects. This should come as no surprise to the reader, since the fingers have been put to similar uses in virtually every culture, even to the point, in some cases (as mentioned in Chapter 2), of serving as the foundation of number names themselves. But we should not allow the fact of the ubiquity of the relationship between fingers and numbers to lull us into seeing this as a trivial relationship, for we will find in these data explicit links among numbers, the classification and organization of the fingers, and ideas about human reproduction, age, gender, and kinship relations. These data, then, will allow us to expand further the paradigm we have been developing and exploring in which ordinal and non-numeral ordinal-like sequences are conceptualized in terms of reproductive processes and kinship relations.

We can begin by looking at several examples of the classification and naming of the fingers in Quechua. Table 3.3 presents information on systems of naming the fingers, five of which are drawn from Quechua sources. For comparative purposes, I have also included information from Bertonio's early seventeenth-century Aymara dictionary.

Table 3.3 shows clearly that the fingers are named and organized according to categories and principles defined on the basis of kinship, gender, and age relations. In all these naming systems, the *thumb* is the oldest/ancestral digit, while the little finger is the youngest/last. In addition, "one" (*uj*) and/or the "first" (*uj kaq*) of a series is commonly glossed as *mama;* as we see also in Table 3.3, the thumb is often glossed as *mama.* Thus, the initial suggestion is that thumb = *mama* = "one." But where do we go from here? That is, how (if at all) can we assign numbers to the fingers? There are a variety of data and approaches that will help accomplish the matching of the sequences of numbers and fingers. The model that we will derive is one in which the numbers 1 through 5 will be matched, one-to-one (in the same order), with the sequence thumb–little finger.

To begin, Table 3.3 shows that the thumb is always the oldest, ancestral digit, while the little finger is the youngest, or last. I have heard the thumb given priority over the other fingers in indirect, and somewhat ironic, designations of the thumb as *tawaq ujnin* ("of the four [i.e., the fingers], the one intimately connected to them [= the thumb]"), and as *tawaq kuraqnin* ("of the four [i.e., the fingers], the elder intimately connected [= the thumb]"). Table 3.3 also shows that the temporal sequence of the age grading of the fingers is oriented from the perspective of the thumb. The time scales extend from thumb = ancestor (*machu*), parent, or parent's sibling (*mama/tayca*), or older sibling (*hila*), to little finger = youngest or last-born (*sullk'a/uña*).

A complementary principle of organization to those discussed above is the identification of the third digit as the "middle" or "center" (*chawpi/taypi*) finger. Because all the traditions of naming fingers shown in Table 3.3 classify the fingers in temporal terms—that is, as an age-graded sequence—we may conclude that *chawpi* and *taypi* have the meaning not only of the "middle" of the span of the fingers, but also of

TABLE 3.3

**Names for the Fingers in Quechua
and Aymara, by Language and Source***

Finger Order and Name	Translation or Explanation
Quechua:	
I. Santo Tomás (1951 [1560]):	
1 - *ñaupa rucana*	ancient, or ancestor, finger
2 - *catec rucana*	following, or accompanying, finger
3 - *chaupi rucana*	middle finger
4 - *catec rucana*	following, or accompanying, finger
5 - *sullca rucana*	youngest finger
II. González Holguín (1952 [1608]):	
1 - *mama rukana*	mother finger
2 - *tocsiq rukana*	pointer finger
3 - *chaupi rukana*	middle finger
4 - *siui rukana*	ring finger
5 - *sulca rukana*	youngest [last-born] finger
III. Cusihuamán (1976):	
1 - *maman-riru*	mother finger
2 - *t'oqsiq-riru*	pointer finger
3 - *chawpi-riru*	middle finger
4 - *anillo-ch'olqona*	ring-joint
5 - *uña-riru*	suckling baby finger

TABLE 3.3

(*continued*)

Finger Order and Name	Translation or Explanation
IV. Urton (Pacariqtambo, Peru, 1983):	
1 - *machu riru*	old, or ancestor, finger
2 - *riru*	finger
3 - *chawpi riru*	middle finger
4 - *chawpi riru*	middle finger
5 - *uña riru*	suckling baby finger
V. Primitivo Nina (Sucre, Bolivia, 1994):	
1 - *mama riru*	mother finger
2 - *juch'uy riru*	small[er] finger
3 - *chawpi riru*	middle finger
4 - *sullk'a riru*	younger finger
5 - *sullk'aq sullk'an riru*	younger sibling of the younger [i.e., youngest, or last-born] finger
Aymara:	
VI. Bertonio (1984 [1612])	
1 - *hila l.[-ucana];*	older brother finger
tayca lucana	mother's sister finger
2 - *hilakharu lucana*	older brother's descendant finger
3 - *taypi lucana*	middle finger
4 - *siuittaña lucana*	ring finger
5 - *sullca lucana*	younger [last-born] finger

Key: 1 = thumb; 2 = index finger; 3 = middle finger; 4 = ring finger; 5 = little finger.

the middle of the age-grading *and* of the numerical sequence of the members of the "descent group" represented by the fingers.

Let us return to the point mentioned earlier concerning the classification of the thumb as an "ancient," "ancestral" (*machu/ñawpaq*) digit and note that the cardinal number "one" and the ordinal numeral "first" may both be replaced by the adjective *ñawpaq* ("ancient, anterior"; see Table 3.2). *Ñawpaq* plays an important role in establishing the relationships of age and succession in the generation and organization of numerical sequences in general. For instance, *phishqa* ("five") may be referred to as *tawaq ñawpaqin* ("four is earlier" [i.e., 4 is the number before this number = 5]), *suqta* ("six") may be referred to as *phishqa ñawpaqin* ("five is earlier" [i.e., 5 is the number before this number = 6]), and so on. Here, *ñawpaq* represents something of an instrument for moving *prospectively* through the number sequence. That is, *ñawpaq* motivates a natural sequence of counting by identifying, or naming, the number *preceding*, or anterior to, successively higher numbers in the sequence— "pushing" the higher numbers along, as it were, ahead of it.

The above discussion of *ñawpaq* calls to attention the system of naming the fingers given by Santo Tomás (see Table 3.3). In this system, the thumb, as the oldest (*ñaupa*) finger, and the middle (*chaupi*) finger each has a "following," or "accompanying" (*catec*) digit. I would suggest that we can gloss the term given by Santo Tomás for the second finger, *catec rucana* (*katiq rukana* = "following/accompanying finger"), as "the pairing/paired finger." Thus, the beginning of the number/finger sequence is the oldest digit (= 1), which is followed by its "pair" (= 2). This stage in the sequence is suggested by González Holguín's gloss of *ñaupacta katiquen* as "*el segundo*" ("the second"). Next, and *continuing the sequence,* the next digit (= 3) is followed by its "pair" (= 4). The end of the sequence is the youngest digit (= 5). Santo Tomás's data suggest that we should consider again the relationship between one/odd and two/even (see Chapter 2). We can best accomplish this by shifting our focus for a moment from the fingers to the two hands.

In Quechua, the hands (*maki* = "hand") are conceived of as two separate, symmetrical parts of a unified whole. A single hand, which represents an existential state referred to qualitatively by the term *khallu* ("one apart, alone, separate"), is a prototype of the condition known as *ch'ulla* ("uneven, odd"; i.e., without a/its pair). *Ch'ulla* is a thing that has a natural pair which, for some reason, is separated from it; when the two are brought together, their unity is referred to as *khalluntin*, "the two separate parts of a pair, intimately bound together" (see the discussion of odd and even numbers, and "pairs," in Chapter 2). When the two hands are brought together to form a complete "set," or pair, this is termed *yanantin* ("the two opposite but complementary things intimately bound together"), or *iskaynintin* ("the two/pair together"; see Platt 1986b). That the fingers of the two hands form a natural, complementary pairing is expressed in one of the conventions used to denote "ten"; that is, *phishqa phishqa* ("five [and] five"). The terms *yanantin* and *iskaynintin* represent what we could call imperative forces that "urge" the linkage of things considered to have a natural, complementary relationship to each other.

Following upon the various observations made above, I would argue that we can identify in these data the fundamental principle and logic of the successor function in the Quechua ontology of numbers. That is, the motivation for *two* is the "loneliness" (*ch'ulla*) of *one*. "One" is an incomplete, alienated entity; it needs a "partner" (*ch'ullantin*). This principle and motivational force obtain, I will argue, regardless of whether the unit that composes the "one" is indivisible (e.g., a single digit) or divisible (e.g., a hand with its five digits). This latter point, however, raises a larger question: What is the relationship between the group (e.g., as with one hand) of 1–5 and its paired, or accompanying group of 6–10 (e.g., the other hand)? The full answer to this question will form the basis for my theory of the (Quechua-) logic of decimal numeration, to be presented in the conclusions (Chapter 7). However, we can address certain issues raised by this question here.

The central problems that are raised in the above discussion are the following. How are the two sets of five joined together to form a single, ranked group of ten? And secondly, how are corresponding positions in the two sets (1 and 6, 2 and 7, 3 and 8, etc.) considered to be related to each other? Here we may turn to evidence from classificatory models of decimal groupings elsewhere in Andean societies. For instance, in my earlier study (1990) of the organization of the ten *ayllus* within the community of Pacariqtambo, I found that the ten *ayllus* are organized into two sets of five; one set is called *Hanansayaq* ("of the upper part"), the other is called *Hurinsayaq* ("of the lower part"). Each set of five is organized by a ranking of members from first to fifth (or last). When there arises the necessity of placing both sets in a single series of ten—e.g.,

TABLE 3.4

Ordinal Sequences and the *Ayllus* of Pacariqtambo, by Group

Rank	Hanan. Ordinal No.	Hurin. Ordinal No.	Hanan. Ordinal No.	Hurin. Ordinal No.
1	1	6	1	2
2	2	7	3	4
3	3	8	5	6
4	4	9	7	8
5	5	10	9	10
	(a)		(b)	

when calling the roll of the *ayllus* in an assembly—this is accomplished in either of two ways. In both systems (to be outlined below), numbering begins from the "first" member of *Hanansayaq;* this is the group known as Nayhua *ayllu,* the *ayllu* classified as *collana* ("first") *ayllu* in the village. Nayhua *ayllu* is said to be the "oldest" *ayllu;* it was the first group to appear at the beginning of time (see Urton 1990: 79; see Zuidema 1964: 211–235 for analyses of Inka five- and ten-part organizations in Cusco). The unity of the *ayllus* in Pacariqtambo is emphasized by referring to them collectively as *ayllu wauq'intin* ("the united brother *ayllus*"), a phrase that employs the suffix *-ntin,* discussed in Chapter 2.

One way of placing the ten *ayllus* in a sequence, which focuses on the unity *within each set* (i.e., moiety), begins with *collana ayllu,* continues in sequence through all five members of that group and then switches to the other set of five (see Table 3.4[a]). The other way of sequencing and assigning ordinal positions to the *ayllus* focuses on the order and hierarchical relations *between the two sets;* this ordinal sequence goes from *collana* ("first") *ayllu* of the first set, to the "first" *ayllu* of the other set (= "second"), back to the second *ayllu* of the first group (= "third"), and so on (see Table 3.4[b]).

Now, I have never seen anyone number the fingers of the two hands as shown in Table 3.4[b] (i.e., right thumb = "one/first," left thumb = "two/second"; however, see Rivière [1983] for an example of this pattern in the seating of political officials). Counting off numbers on the fingers always proceeds as shown in Table 3.4[a], with no particular priority, that I have noted, for beginning on one hand over the other. However, there is today, as has been true in the past, a general ritual and formal priority of the right hand over the left (see Urton 1984, 1992; Rivière 1983). For example, in 1567 Matienzo noted the following organization of seating among the headmen, or *kurakas,* of the moiety groupings of Inka *ayllus:*

> *In each* repartimiento *or province there are two divisions: one is called* hanansaya, *and the other* hurinsaya. . . . *[T]he curaca of the hanansaya division is the principal lord of all the province; the other curaca of hurinsaya obeys him when he speaks. He of the hanansaya has the best position of the seats and in all the other places they repeat this order. Those of the hanansaya division seat themselves at the right-hand side, and those from the hurinsaya at the left-hand side. . . . This leader from hanansaya is the principal of all and he has domination over those of hurinsaya. (Matienzo [1567, Pt. 1, Chapter 6] 1967: 20).*

Thus, we see here grounds to argue that in certain formal settings, as when the dual division of decimal groups is at issue, 1–5 = right hand, and 6–10 = left hand. Such assigned values could, of course, be extended for whatever purpose and whenever appropriate to the overall organization of relations among the digits, in the sequence 1–10.

In summary, I want to make two general observations concerning the relationship between numbers and the hands and fingers. First, whichever hand one begins with, the thumb of that hand is usually labeled "one/first," and the little finger of the opposite hand ends the count at "ten/last." And second, even when the two groups of five fingers are organized into a sequence of 1–10, the hierarchical position of any digit/number can be established by placing, or reconfiguring, it within the hierarchical organization of the five fingers on whichever hand it happens to fall. In this (re-)configuration, the sequence runs from one = thumb through five = little finger. The larger point to take from this is that the organization and classification of a set of *five* appears to be the nuclear model for the organization of ordinal sequences in general; the paradigm for this model is the age/number sequence: oldest/1–youngest/5. Gender enters explicitly only at the beginning of the sequence in the form: *mama* ("mother") = *uj* ("one"), or *uj kaq* ("first"). This paradigm is evident not only in the ethnographic material we have analyzed above, but also in the ethnohistorical documentation (e.g., see the discussion in Chapter 6 of the considerable attention given to "groups of five" in the Huarochirí document; Salomon and Urioste 1991).

Before moving on to the next topic, I would note that the naming of the fingers according to models based on social and kinship relations, including ideas about procreation, is not unique to the Quechua and Aymara. Among the Iqwaye of Papua New Guinea, for instance, Mimica (1992: 59–64) reports that the fingers of each hand are organized as a group of siblings and named using birth-order suffixes. However, we do not have to search in such exotic locales as Papua New Guinea for comparable ideas about finger naming and organization, for my Colgate colleague, Anthony Aveni, informs me that as a boy growing up in New Haven, he used the following names in referring to his fingers: thumb = me; first finger = mother; middle finger = father; ring finger = mother's next oldest sister; and little finger = baby brother (A. Aveni, personal communication, 1995). Although I have not done a great amount of general comparative research on this topic, I suspect that the unity and diversity of the fingers—based on their fixed order and different sizes— make them a powerful (not to mention handy!) model of a family grouping with its diverse kinship and age relations.

Jurk'a: The Paradigm of the Pitchfork

The example of a non-numeral ordinal sequence that we will take up now is particularly appropriate for consideration at this point because it pertains to a model of divisions numerically and symbolically equivalent to the fingers of the hands. In this case, however, both the finger-like divisions and the spaces in between them are numbered. As we will see, the numbering is staggered in a way similar to that seen above in the combination of a cardinal number with *ñawpaq,* a construction that has the effect of generating, or "bringing into being," the next higher number beyond the cardinal number named. The example that we will examine now concerns, of all things (after such a buildup!), pitchforks.

As anyone who has spent time doing agricultural work in the Andes knows, the pitchfork (*jurk'a*) is an essential tool in a variety of agricultural tasks. While some people in communities have been able to purchase metal pitchforks, the more common form of this device is a tool made from a forking tree branch that has been stripped of its bark. If the tines are not naturally of the appropriate shape, they will be reshaped by exposing them to the flames of a fire and then applying pressure, usually by weighing them down with heavy rocks to produce an efficient working head. While the minimum number of tines in a pitchfork is, of course, two, the number that is considered to be both ideal and "traditional" is *five* tines—like the fingers of the hands.

Before discussing the naming of the tines of pitchforks, we should note that a comparison between fingers and tines, or between the "hand" (*maki*), and the "pitchfork" (*jurk'a*), is logical and highly motivated in mechanical as well as economic terms. That is, it is the hand that grips the shaft of the pitchfork in the performance of agricultural tasks, and it is the latter that gives to the former a greater productive capacity. As we will see, the metonymic link between *maki* and *jurk'a* is reformulated in metaphorical terms that, again, will provide us with additional insights into Quechua ideas about numbers, sets, and collections.

We should note to begin with that the tines of a pitchfork are referred to as *palqa* ("branch; division"), while the spaces between the branches are called *palqayuq* ("of the branch"). Thus, as we saw with incomplete numbers that are attached to and possessed by a complete decimal unit by means of a grammatical construction denoting possession (e.g., *chunka tawayuq*, "10 with its 4"), the opening formed by branching tines is possessed by or, we could say, is the product of, the two adjacent tines. Figure 3.1 shows the system of naming the branches and openings of pitchforks made up of from two to five tines.

The people with whom I have discussed the different shapes and qualities of pitchforks consistently pointed out that the best, most useful type of pitchfork is the one with five branches (and four openings). Curiously, it is also said that, although pitchforks of this type were once fairly common, they are now very rare. One gets a clear sense from such statements that the "ideal," five-tined pitchforks are not only from an earlier time, but also that, since there used to be a lot of five-tined pitchforks, the world was a better place in the past than it is today. Although I never actually heard the five-tined variety of pitchfork referred to in this way, such a tool has the status of *ñawpaq jurk'a* ("ancestral pitchfork"). However, such pitchforks *are* specifically referred to both as

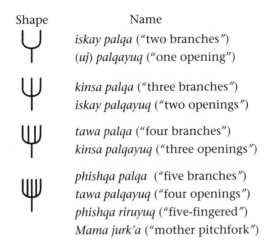

Shape	Name

iskay palqa ("two branches")
(uj) palqayuq ("one opening")

kinsa palqa ("three branches")
iskay palqayuq ("two openings")

tawa palqa ("four branches")
kinsa palqayuq ("three openings")

phishqa palqa ("five branches")
tawa palqayuq ("four openings")
phishqa riruyuq ("five-fingered")
Mama jurk'a ("mother pitchfork")

FIGURE 3.1.   The classification and naming of pitchforks.

phishqa riruyuq ("five-fingered")—a designation likening them explicitly
to the hand with its thumb and four fingers—as well as *mama jurk'a*,
"mother pitchfork." What is implied in the comparison between the
five-fingered pitchfork and the hand is, first, that the five-tined variety
of this tool is the complete, fully mature set composed of a mother and
her offspring. And second, it is clear in turn that the other members of
the set of four types of pitchforks illustrated in Figure 3.1 are "immature" versions of the five-tined variety; that is, they are in various stages
of growth and maturation.

Curiously, then, we seem to have *reversed* the age metaphor in its
connection to both the cardinal numbers and the fingers developed in
earlier examples (e.g., see Tables 3.2 and 3.3). That is, we saw earlier in
the sequence of naming the fingers that the thumb—i.e., the "mother"
(*mama*), "ancient" (*ñawpaq*) digit—is the *lowest* whole number, "one"
(*uj*), whereas in the "paradigm of the pitchforks" the ancestral, mother
form of this tool is the one containing the *highest* number in the sequence, the five-tined variety. This apparent paradox is due to the fact,
of course, that the succession of types of pitchforks is not a *sequence*;
that is, three-tined pitchforks do not grow to become four-tined ones,
and so on. Rather, the succession of pitchforks shown in Figure 3.1 is a
set, the complete, highest, and ideal cardinality of which is five. The
three earlier forms—those composed of two, three, and four tines—are

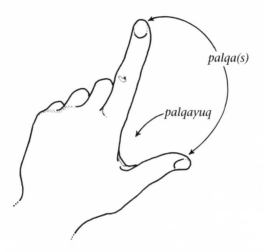

FIGURE 3.2.   Maki "prototype" of *iskay palqa/uj palqayuq.*

"immature" versions of the complete, mature "mother" form. In other words, *mama jurk'a* contains within itself all the previous forms. Thus, for instance, in the metaphorical comparison between fingers and tines, I would argue (although I was not told this explicitly) that the digital prototype of the two-tined pitchfork is not just any two adjacent fingers that form an "opening" (*palqayuq*); rather, the prototype should be the pair that contains the ancestral digit, the *thumb* (= *mama*), together with her first, oldest offspring, the index finger (see Figure 3.2).

I would also note that in the organization of numbers in the set of pitchforks in Figure 3.1, in which the cardinality of *palqayuq* ("openings") is always one less than the cardinality of the "branches" (*palqa*), we see a strategy of number production that is similar to the process of counting discussed in the previous section by the use of the term *ñawpaq* to generate, or "push ahead of it," each successively higher number (see Chapter 2). These observations, and the two examples we have now seen of a particular strategy for the generation of numbers (i.e., *one* opening requires *two* branches; *two* openings require *three* branches) take us back to two of the questions raised at the beginning of this chapter. That is, how does the "first" number of a sequence give rise to the "second"? And what is the relationship between the "first" and the "second" in a series? The answer to this question, which we have been developing to this point, is that the "first" is the "mother" (*mama*) and the "second" is her first offspring.

Birth Order and the Origin of Ordination

Now, we have already established through several examples a consistent *identity* for the "first" in an ordinal sequence—this is the appellative *mama*, the "title," we might say, of the state or condition of *ñawpaq* ("ancient, ancestral"). The more specific question to address is: How is the link between *mama* (the "first") and her first offspring (the "second") conceived of and projected in metaphorical terms? The most direct answer to this question comes by way of a model articulated in relation to an all-important economic resource in the Andes—corn.

As everyone knows, corn grows as a cane "stalk" (*wiru*) topped by a "tassel" (*parawi*). The ears of corn sprout from "joints" (*muju, phaki,* or *sinkha*) along the cane that are located just above a "leaf" (*laqhe*). It will be noted that, in these identifications of the various parts of a corn plant, the only part that was not named were the ears of corn. The reason for this is that the ears of corn receive different names, depending on their location on the plant and their order of appearance. These two characteristics of ears of corn—location and sequence of maturation— are linked to each other. That is, as we see in Figure 3.3, the first ear of corn to sprout from a stalk, which is the highest (or top-most) and largest ear on the plant, is called *chuqllu*.

Chuqllu usually matures early in the harvest season—around March, or so—and is harvested and eaten at that time with great excitement. The *chuqllu* ear is also called *mama,* as well as *madre* (in Spanish). Thus, the largest, first, highest and "oldest" ear of corn is *mama*. In Bolivian Quechua, the second ear of corn, which grows lower down on the stalk, is called *apaña*. The third ear is *iskay apaña* ("second *apaña*"); and the fourth is *kinsa apaña* ("third *apaña*"). Following the maturation of three lower ears of corn, as shown in Figure 3.3, one may now refer to the first ear of corn—that is, the *chuqllu*—as *kinsa apañantin,* "[the one] together with three *apañas.*" What is obviously of interest to us here is the term *apaña*. What does this term mean? Earlier (Chapter 2), I glossed this

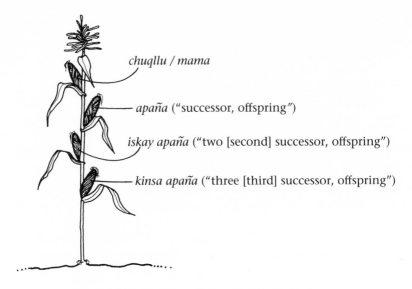

chuqllu / mama

— *apaña* ("successor, offspring")

iskay apaña ("two [second] successor, offspring")

— *kinsa apaña* ("three [third] successor, offspring")

FIGURE 3.3.   The "birth order" and naming of ears of corn.

term in the form *apañayuq* (*-yuq* = possessive suffix) as "pair," and "twins." I have given in Table 3.5 several additional glosses of this term drawn from Quechua and Aymara dictionaries.

As I have suggested in Figure 3.3, the best glosses for the term *apaña* are "successor," "kin by blood," "offspring," and (adjacent) "siblings." *Apaña* is an important term for our study, particularly as we are concerned with the relationship between the first and second members of an ordinal sequence. *Apaña,* which has as one of its primary meanings the notion of "twins" (i.e., *two* of a kind), is the first descendant of *chuqllu mama.* Thus, the pair *chuqllu mama/apaña*—i.e., one (or the first) and two (or twins)—combines the principal characteristics of an ordinal sequence: hierarchy and succession. "Succession" also implies "contiguity," and this trait is also clearly present in the corn-plant model of the ordinal sequence. As what we may consider to be the principal marker of an ordinal sequence (i.e., the successor function), *apaña* is repeated with each successive member of the series descended from *mama.* In addition, beginning with the *third* member of the sequence, *apaña* is preceded by the appropriate cardinal number. In the case of the *third* member, the "appropriate" cardinal number is *iskay* ("two"). Therefore, the cardinal numbers do not designate in this case the ordinal position of

TABLE 3.5

Forms of *Apa-:* The "Successor" Relation

Forms of *Apa-*	Translation or Explanation
Quechua:	
apa	Brother(s) or sister(s) born (pl.) successively.
apantin, or *apapura*	Two siblings born successively. (González Holguín 1952 [1608])
apaña	Kin by blood.
apa	The arm, or the space between the arms. May be said of the adjacent siblings by birth order, both ascendant and descendant.
apantía	The twin that is born last, or after the first. (Lira 1982)
apa	Contiguity of birth between an older and a younger sibling. (Lara 1991)
Aymara:	
apañani (also: *apañata* and *apañasiri*)	Brother, or younger sister who is born immediately after [the first birth]; although not in the same birth event. (Bertonio 1984 [1612])

members as counted from the point of origin of the sequence (i.e., *mama*/*chuqllu*/"first"). Rather, they indicate the number of each successor as counted from the ear of corn that is *first* designated "*apaña*"; this is the second ear of corn on the stalk, the first-born offspring of *mama.*

This naming of the ears of corn by "birth order" elaborates further the paradigm that we have been developing in this chapter. That is: ordination is constructed as a set of relationships having as its prototype a "natural" set of four or five members beginning in a principle associated with *mama,* the mature, reproductive female, and ending in an immature, essentially nongendered member of a consanguineal group, the child. In addition, this is the most compelling example we have to answer the question: What is the nature of the relationship between the first and second members of an ordinal series? The answer is: The second is to the first as the first-born child is to its mother. All subsequent members of the series fall into place by birth order and age. Thus, as we have seen in earlier examples involving animals and humans (i.e., *ayllus*), the force that gives rise to an ordinal sequence is *reproduction*.

The system of naming ears of corn described above is based on information that I collected from informants in Marawa, Bolivia. It is interesting to note here another system of naming that was collected in K'anas, in southern Peru (Province of Chumbivilcas, Department of Cusco), and reported (in an abbreviated form) by Valencia Espinoza (1979). In his listing and brief description of different types of corn recognized in K'anas, Valencia (1979: 77) describes *Taqi Sara* ("granary corn") as follows: "Those principal, large ears of corn, surrounded by other smaller ones or ones adhering (*adheridas*) to the central ear of corn, which is the *Sara Mama*, mother corn or goddess (*diosa*) of corn, since she [*Sara Mama*] is considered as a woman surrounded by her children" (my translation).

I will have more to say about *Sara Mama* in a moment. The point to note is that, while stating that the largest ear of corn may be in the center of a corn plant (thus contradicting ideas about the location of *Sara Mama* that I heard in Marawa), the image here of multiple ears of corn on a corn stalk is still one of a mother with her children.

I do not want to leave the impression that reproduction is the only process implicated in Quechua ideas about the origin of, and the forces driving, ordinal sequences. For instance, the life process of aging, or maturation, also is shown in certain circumstances to have these qualities. One particularly compelling example of this is seen in a study (Cereceda 1990) of the symbolism associated with color changes in plumage that occur over the life cycle of the Andean falcon (*Phalcobaenos megalopterus*), known in Quechua as *allqamari*. With respect to color, the life cycle of the *allqamari* is divided into two phases: as an adolescent, the bird has monochromatic, coffee-colored plumage; however, on reaching maturity, the plumage changes to black and white. In her analysis of the symbolism of *allqamaris* as expressed in myths, as well as in statements by informants about the characteristics of these birds and the qualities of the color contrast *coffee/black and white,* Cereceda emphasizes the symbolic importance of the transition from *one* color to *two* (her analysis takes account of the expression of this relationship between colors and numbers in textiles, as well). Thus, we see here another *natural* model on which to base a logical argument explaining the "successor function" that operates within an ordinal sequence, which finds its first expression in the relationship between *one* and *two*.

Sara Mama, "Corn Mother"

In bringing this discussion of ears of corn to a close, I would like to offer a reprise on symbolic constructions relating corn to the reproductivity of *mama* and ideas about the predecessor-successor relationship. For these comments, we turn to the object called *Sara Mama* ("corn mother"); this is a double *chuqllu* ("first ear of corn"), one larger (the *mama*) ear of corn linked to the other by a thin, umbilicus-like attachment. It was during the corn harvest of 1993, in Marawa, Bolivia, that I encountered an example of *Sara Mama*. The one that I saw was similar to that illustrated in Figure 3.4.

The *Sara Mama* that was harvested that day in Marawa caused a good deal of excitement. This was considered to be a good augury for the harvest, because *Sara Mama* is the very image of fertility and reproductive power.[2] *Sara Mama* provides an intriguing perspective on the relations and principles organizing ordinal sequences and the nature of the force(s) that set such sequences in motion. That is, "corn mother" presents a direct model for the relationship between the "first" and "second" members of a consanguineal group. As seen in this condensed model, the "second" is the child, which is linked by the umbilicus to its mother.

I should note that I was not given a separate name for the smaller of the pair of ears of corn included in the unit called *Sara Mama*. In this regard, it is interesting to take note of a type of corn that Valencia Espinoza calls *Apayoq Sara* ("blood kin/successor-possessor corn"). Valencia (1979: 79) describes *Apayoq Sara* as follows: "Those that have more than one ear of corn; it can be of two or three ears of corn each

FIGURE 3.4.   *Sara Mama.*

with its grains" (my translation). It is unclear from Valencia's description if "those" (*son las*) refers to a combined (two- or three-unit) ear of corn, or to a corn plant that has two or three separate ears of corn along the stalk. The latter interpretation would not seem to identify a circumstance that is remarkable enough to assign the corn a specific name. Therefore, I interpret his description to apply to the former circumstance, which is similar to the arrangement shown in Figure 3.4. If this is the case, then I would suggest that we can combine Valencia's *Sara Mama* (see above), which he describes, in one variant, as the largest ear of corn with one or more smaller ears of corn "adhering" to it, with what he calls *Apayoq Sara*. If this is the case, then we have a situation very much like that illustrated in Figure 3.4; the larger ear of corn would be *mama*, while the smaller, attached ear of corn would be her *apa-* ("blood kin; successor; offspring").

In *Sara Mama,* the umbilicus is like an abbreviated version of the stalk, which links successive ears of corn on a corn stalk. What is significant about the representation of this principle in *Sara Mama* is that it appears here as a highly fetishized (given the attention and treatment I saw accorded to it) *token* of a model of ordination. The fully elaborated version of the model of which *Sara Mama* is a token is the succession of ears of corn sprouting along the stalk of a fully mature corn plant.

We now turn to the last example of non-numeral ordinal-like sequences to be discussed here; this involves the most spectacular natural model displaying relations of hierarchy and succession—the rainbow.

Kinship and Ordinal Relations in the Colors of the Rainbow

Perhaps the most striking model of a continuum of linked categories in the natural world is the colors of the rainbow. In Quechua, rainbows are called *k'uychi* ("making the arc"; see my discussion of ideas and beliefs about rainbows in the Cusco area in Urton 1988: 87–90). Since the colors of a primary rainbow are always ordered in the same manner,[3] rainbows are of singular importance in establishing and displaying the proper order of relations (e.g., of contiguity, hierarchy, and succession) among colors. Because of their (generally) fixed positions in the color spectrum, one might think that the colors of the rainbow would be good candidates for organizing and naming by the ordinal numerals. That this is not the case, at least not in Quechua, is explained by the fact that the colors of the rainbow are considered to form an inseparable continuum, or "gradation," of colors, called *sayt'u* ("taper"). Since numbering, or counting is thought to result in breaking things up into discrete units (see Chapter 4), assigning number names to the colors of the rainbow would violate the natural continuum of colors in a rainbow; thus, one is prohibited from counting the colors of the rainbow.

So, if the colors of the rainbow should not be numbered, how then are they to be classified? There are several different traditions for accomplishing this in Quechua-speaking communities in south-central Bolivia. The various traditions combine two sets of nomenclature; one involves color names (in Quechua, Spanish, or a mixture of the two), while the other is made up of terms and phrases indicating the relative position of color hues as they appear, one next to the other, in the rainbow. The different traditions of naming the colors differ not only in the terms that are used in the two sets of nomenclature, but also in the number of colors that are recognized and named; in general, the various traditions identify six, five, or four color hues. The most complex of the traditions, as well as the one my principal informant, Primitivo Nina, was most familiar with, since it is found in his home community of Betanzos (located between Sucre and Potosí), is the six-colored rainbow series. This is the tradition shown in Table 3.6.

It will be obvious from a review of the sets of color terms used in the town of Betanzos, as recounted by Primitivo Nina, that some of the same kinship terms and relationships that we encountered in previous discussions of the classification of the members of non-numeral, ordinal-like sequences are employed in naming the colors of the rainbow (e.g., *mama*, first child, younger sibling, last child). It is important to note that whereas I was told by people in Candelaria that the first color to appear in a rainbow is the color at the bottom, with the higher colors then gradually and successively coming into view, the proper order that one should follow in naming the colors always begins at the top and goes down to the bottom—ending with *ultimito* [*wawan*]/*qhipakaq*. To name the colors in the "reverse order" (i.e., from the bottom to the top), as they actually appear in succession in the sky is referred to as *kutiray* ("to turn around [up-side down] the order of things"); such an inverted order of naming is said to "confuse" (*pantakuq*) the natural order of the colors. What seems to be at issue here is the principle that a series of things organized vertically should always be named from the top down

TABLE 3.6

Names and Identifications of Rainbow Colors in Betanzos

Color	Gloss	I.D.	Position	Remarks
yana murado	"dark purple"	*mama*	*patankaq*	"top thing"
guinda/panti	"maroon"	*wawan*	*urankaq*	"lower thing"
q'illu	"yellow"	*larun* [*ladun*] ("sus partes")	*qhipankaq*	"next thing" (the later and younger companion[s] of *guinda*)
q'umir	"green"	*larun* [*ladun*]	*qhipankaq*	(same as above)
rosada	"rose"	*larun* [*ladun*]	*qhipankaq*	(same as above; said to be the most dangerous color)
qhaqya q'illu	"pale yellow"	*ultimito* ("last")	*qhipakaq*	"last thing" (losing purity of color; thus, it is independent of the others)

to the bottom. This was, of course, the order that we saw in the naming of the ears of corn growing along the stalk of a corn plant. I will discuss in more detail why this is considered to be the proper order of naming and enumerating such arrangements in the discussion of *yupay,* "counting" (Chapter 4).

What is of utmost interest and importance to us here concerning the classification and naming of the colors of the rainbow is that the sequence begins at the top with *mama,* proceeds downward to her first offspring, *wawan* ("baby"), then through a series of "sides" (*larun* = Sp., *lado*), which Nina glossed as *sus partes* ("the rainbow's/mother's parts/sections"), and ends with the "last-born" child, *ultimito* [*wawan*]. Thus, *mama* once again has the status of progenitrix of a natural, non-numeral ordinal-like sequence.

But, what can we say, finally, about the nature of the "reproductive force" at work in this example? That is, in all the previous examples, we have seen that ordinal-like sequences are generated by the reproductive forces of plants, animals, or humans as set in motion by *mama,* the mature reproductive female. Noting to begin with that I do not have explicit testimony from informants on this matter, the most satisfactory explanation I can provide in this case begins from the symbolic characteristics associated with *yana* ("dark; black"). As we see in Table 3.6, *mama* is identified with *yana muradu* ("dark purple") in the classification of the colors of the rainbow in the town of Betanzos. A similar and quite consistent association between *mama* and *yana,* or the darkest hue of a particular color, is also found in the classification of the rainbow in the weavings of the Tarabuco area (see Dávalos, Cereceda, and Martínez 1992: 24–27). The obvious question for us to address is: What manner of force of reproduction is associated with *yana* ("black; dark") in Quechua ideology?

One important body of material to be taken into account in relation to the symbolism of *yana* concerns a type of constellation in Quechua astronomy, which I have analyzed at length elsewhere (Urton 1988: 169–191). These constellations, called *yana phuyu* ("dark cloud"), are deep black clouds of interstellar dust that cut through the bright clouds of the Milky Way, primarily in the south celestial hemisphere. The *yana phuyu* are said to be composed of a very fecund, feminine form of "earth," called *pachatira.*[4] This substance is absorbed into the Milky Way during its passage under the earth. The "dark cloud" constellations are identified as particular animals (e.g., snake, toad, partridge, llama, fox), which are considered to be responsible for the reproduction of these same animals on the earth (Urton 1988:169 ff; see also Polo de Ondegardo 1916 [1571, Chapter 1] for similar beliefs among the Inkas).

As I have earlier demonstrated a direct link in Quechua ideology and symbolism between the Milky Way, with its "dark cloud" constellations, and rainbows (see Urton 1988: 174, 191), I would argue now that the essential blackness of the *yana phuyu* provides us with one answer to the question raised above concerning the nature of the reproductive force associated with *mama* when she is identified with blackness, or the darkest color(s) of the rainbow. That is, insofar as dark colors, or black, are symbolically associated with the image, figure, or persona of *mama,* darkness is the origin of colors. The fecund, reproductive force of *pachatira,* as seen in the patches of dark clouds in the Milky Way, is the reproductive force driving the generation of colors in the rainbow from *mama,* the darkest color, to her youngest child, the lightest color. We see similar ideas concerning the fecundity and the originary quality of blackness (or black things) expressed elsewhere in Andean symbolism. For instance, Cereceda (1990: 77) notes that in the Bolivian community of Chuani, a black form of wild quinoa (*Chenopodium quinoa*, a high-protein cereal grain), called *aara*, is considered to have been the principal food of the ancestral peoples of the area, who are called *ch'ullpas*. *Aara* is itself said to be the ancestor of all present-day domesticated varieties of quinoa, which come in a profusion of bright colors (see also López-Baralt 1987 on Andean myths of the "black rainbow").

Therefore, *mama* is now recognized to be the origin both of colors *and* numbers.[5] Now, when we turn to a discussion of weaving in the next chapter, we will see there that the art of weaving is realized in the practices of counting threads and of combining colors in skillful and aesthetically pleasing ways. We should not be surprised, then, when we find that the title that is commonly used to refer to the highly skilled female weavers of the Bolivian Andes is "*Mama*."

Summary

In this discussion of ordinal numerals and the ontology of ordinal sequences, we have seen that ordinal numerals are employed in the task of ordering relations among a variable number—but very commonly that number is four, or five—of entities according to the principles of hierarchy and succession. While the surface features of ordinal sequences may be identical from one culture to the next, therefore offering the possibility of translating the particular terms used in each language to a single set of terms in any given target language (e.g., "first, second, third, . . . "), such a translation cannot be taken to represent the total value, or significance of ordinals viewed cross-culturally. Perhaps in some cultures, ordinals are drained of any connotative, or metaphorical, values (although I suspect this is only an epiphenomenon of formal, philosophical language, not of everyday language and thought). Certainly we are able to conclude from the foregoing discussion that this is not true in the constructions of such sequences in the Quechua ontology of number(s). For we have found consistently that ordinal sequences are conceptualized in terms of a "descent group" composed of, "first," a mother who gives rise to numerous offspring ("second, third, . . .").

I would suggest that ordinal sequences have the character which they do in Quechua ideology for two basic reasons. First, as elements of ordinal numerals, cardinal numbers are not considered to have any independent existence, much less force, as abstract entities; that is, cardinal numbers cannot *alone* order anything. Rather (and this is the second point) in Quechua ideology it is *social relations*—especially those formed biologically, emotionally, and politically within a reproductive group—that constitute the principal sources of order (that is, of hierarchy, succession, and so on). Thus, it is only by coupling the number series with the organizing forces of social relations that ordinal sequences emerge as meaningful, rational expressions of the relations and forces organizing and uniting the members of a group.

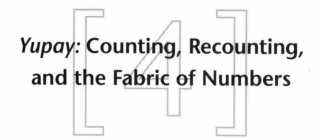

Yupay: Counting, Recounting, and the Fabric of Numbers

Introduction

During the course of this discussion of counting, we will consider such questions as: What kind of activity do the Quechua take counting to be? That is, what kinds of propositions and conceptions about (for example) order, space, magnitude, time, and succession does the *act* of counting consist of? What is implied concerning the nature and meaning of number(s) in the relationship that is posited when a cardinal number name is assigned to an object in the act of counting? In addition, since counting is a—if not *the*—central activity in weaving, we will turn at the end of this chapter to a discussion of numerical knowledge and counting practices in warping and weaving textiles. This discussion of counting will also serve as an introduction to the study, in Chapter 5, of other forms of operations on and with numbers, such as addition, subtraction, multiplication, and division.

In order to address the topics raised above, we will begin by examining the basic terminology for "counting" and considering the range of meanings conveyed by these terms.

The Vocabulary and Grammar of Counting and Recounting

The principal term used in Quechua to refer to counting is *yupa*. This word may be glossed as "count" and "account," although it also has the sense of the "value, merit, or price" of something. *Yupa* is the core term on which is built a very large assortment of nominal and verbal constructions denoting the activity of enumeration and the results thereof. This being said, we nonetheless should note from the outset that the primary meaning of *yupa* is adjectival; that is, in this form, without modification by any one of the numerous suffixes that can be added to the word, the term denotes "much, many, and quantity." In certain constructions, *yupa* takes on the generalized meaning of "multiplicity," or the immense, uncountable quantity of things that exist in the world. This sense of *yupa* is further emphasized by the redoubled form of the word—*yupa yupa*—to indicate the superlative.

Yupa is also used in the nominal form *yupana*. The suffix *-na*, added to a verb (or, as in this case, a nominalized verb stem), converts the verb root into a common object, or an abstract noun. *Yupana* is the term used for numbers—the abstract objects that are both the products and the instruments of, and for, (ac-)counting. Numbers are also referred to as *yupaykuna* (*-kuna* is a pluralizer).

When we move to the use of *yupay* as a verb (*-y* is the infinitive ending), we encounter a number of additional meanings and associations for this term. Most directly, *yupay* denotes the actions of counting, accounting, and enumerating. It is important to note here the point made by Hurford (1987: 114–115) to the effect that numbers higher than, approximately, the number 3 are learned through the counting sequence; the numbers 1, 2, 3 are learned from the practice of making small collections. In the Quechua of the colonial era, a lexical distinction was drawn between counting *people,* which was called *yupturani,* and counting all other types of things, which was known as *yupani* (González Holguín 1952 [1608]).[1] As far as I am aware, such a distinction does not exist in Quechua today. The principal point that I want to stress here with regard to the range of meanings associated with the verb *yupay* is the link that is consistently made between counting and *accounting.* In Quechua, the latter term carries with it some of the same *non*-numerical associations that are found in this English word. That is, in English, the act of "accounting" can refer to such numerical and statistical activities as recording quantitative records and balancing books, but in addition, the term is used to denote the process of, for instance, relating a series of events, in narrative fashion, that explains some circumstance or state of affairs, as well as the process of giving a justification of the causes and the rationale for one's actions. The Quechua verb *yupay* has this same dual—numerical and explanatory—set of functions.

The importance of the above observations, which I will only outline here but will take up in more detail in a later work, concerns the relationship between counting with numbers and "recounting," as in storytelling. The link between the two (both in Quechua and English) is the comparison between *counting* as a process of enumerating items one-by-one and *recounting* as the process in narration of moving one-by-one, in a linear fashion, through the events or episodes that make up a story. This dual meaning of *yupay* should be of central importance in our studies of the numerical and narrative capacities of the Inka *khipus.*[2]

Another gloss on the term *yupay,* which shares certain properties with its use in denoting the "counting off" of episodes in a narrative, is its relation to the act of honoring and paying respect to someone. This is a long-standing sense of the term; for example, González Holguín (1952 [1608]) noted the familiar use of *yupay* to indicate the "appreciation, estimation and honor that a person receives in recognition of his merits, or rank." In a closely related usage, *yupay* denotes the acts of grieving and of paying respect to the dead. Such actions are conceived of in Quechua as a process of running through a mental or verbal inventory of all the items that one can recall about a grievous situation or, for instance, about the life of a recently deceased person who is the object of the act of mourning. This use of *yupay* is usually signaled by the addition of the enfix *-ku.* For instance, the verb *yupakuy,* in addition to being used to denote the action of making an inventory of the things that belong to one (by touching them one by one), also means to grieve, or mourn, repeatedly. In the Norte de Potosí, there is the special, technical use of *yupay* in the form *yupaykakamuy* to denote a highly ritualized act of mourning for the recently deceased. This act occurs when a group of mourners goes to the cemetery. The person who performs *yupaykakamuy* takes a position to the side of the group of mourners, but within hearing distance of them, and there mourns the loss of the dead person. This mourning takes the form of a loud wailing and of rapidly repeating, between sobs, the things that one remembers—"recounts"—about the dead person.

In sum, *yupay* refers to various forms of counting, recounting, and enumerating. The feature shared by all of these acts is the identification and "naming-off"—by means of numbers, or items composing an account, or a set of memories of the deceased—of collections of objects in an ordered sequence.

The lexical and semantic connection between the numerical activity of counting and the ritual act of recounting the deeds of the dead, expressed in Quechua through forms of the verb *yupay,* is found more widely in the Andes and elsewhere in South America. For instance, Isbell mentions the ceremony called *pichqa* ("five") that occurs in the Ayacucho region of south-central Peru. In this rite, which combines elements of divination and purification, the deceased's clothing is washed and the funeral participants' hair is cut and burned five days after the burial of the dead (Isbell 1985: 6–7). There are also reports that in some communities a kind of dice game, called *pishqha/pichqa* ("5") is played in connection with funerals and the burial of the dead. Karsten (1930) discusses a number of such rites, including various forms of dice games (for example, *pichqha, chunka, taba,* and *huayru*), played by peoples of Peru and Ecuador at the time of funerals. The purpose behind the playing of such games at that time, Karsten notes, included the division of the deceased's property, as well as divination and prognostication. In one such game, which Karsten observed being played in Ecuador, the dice were actually thrown over the corpse, the idea being that, as the dice passed over the body, the soul would enter the dice cast by a player favored by the deceased and would bring that player good fortune (Karsten 1930: 9–11). Salomon (1995) has analyzed colonial sources dealing with rituals of death and mourning in late-pre-Hispanic and early colonial times. It is clear from the data discussed by Salomon that a five-day period of intense mourning, ritual purification, and the playing of dice games by the deceased's relatives is of considerable antiquity in the Andes.

More distantly, Altschuler (1965: 89–90) reports that among the Cayapa, the only time games are played is at the time of funerals. The one game described by Altschuler, which is called "plantain money," involves the use of *five* pieces of plantain cut into slices, which are said to be money. In the playing of this game—the details of which we need not go into here—the number five appears again in terms of ordering the number of turns, or rounds, by which the game proceeds.

The point to stress about the relationship between numbers and/or counting and the dead is the power of numbers to (re-)establish order when a threat to stability, balance, etc., is perceived to exist in a community. In most, if not all, cultures, death is conceived of as offering such a threat because of the feelings of loss, insecurity, disorder, and confusion unleashed by the death of a loved one. As Salomon (1995: 325) notes, "death disrupts the durable interests vested in a system of power (especially rights in land and water or political office)." Thus, because of their exactitude, regularity, and precise order, numbers—in the form of divinatory counting, games, gaming pieces, etc.—are very often a focus of funereal activities.

But beyond the appeal to numbers in general on these occasions, it is interesting to note the special attention paid to the number *five,* or to sets of five things (such as days, plantains). Although five is not the only number accorded special, ritual significance in Quechua ideology, it is— and was—clearly of considerable importance. The explanation for this, I would suggest, has already been alluded to in Chapter 3. There, we saw a preoccupation with ordering relations among groups of (more-or-less) five objects, or entities; two common models, or "prototypes" of this grouping, as I suggested, include the hand with its five digits and a mother with her offspring. Therefore, we should not be surprised to find that, in situations when order and stability are threatened, as at the time of the death of a loved one, there is a direct appeal to "fives" as a part of the rituals and discourse of reordering relations among the survivors.

We will return for a further discussion of the issues raised above in Chapter 5 in connection with the philosophical principle underlying arithmetic as an art of "rectification." This is the principle whereby such operations as addition and subtraction are conceived of as being motivated by the requirement to maintain, and/or regain, a state of balance, harmony, and equilibrium.

Finally, I should mention another term, *khuchu,* that is used (although less commonly than *yupay*) for the act of counting. *Khuchu,* which means "divide," or "partition," emphasizes the quality of counting as an act of separating a group of things/objects into discrete units. As we saw earlier (Chapter 3), the act of "separation" can be a problematic and potentially dangerous undertaking, which results in a prohibition on counting certain types of objects. I will elaborate on this latter point in the next section.

What May and May Not Be Counted

While most things in the world are susceptible to being counted, certain things are not. However, what is considered to be uncountable is *culturally* determined. In our own culture, for instance, we are fairly insistent that all physical matter is classifiable and countable down to its most elemental parts. Nonetheless, we also maintain—at least metaphorically—that there are certain things you either should not, or cannot, count (on). You should never, for instance, "count your chickens before the eggs are hatched." And each of us knows certain people whom you simply can't "count on" (to tell the truth, to give support, etc.). While the "uncountable" is relatively limited in our own culture, it occupies a much larger domain of knowledge and experience in Quechua life and thought.

There are basically two types of uncountable objects in the Quechua formulation of such things. The first is made up of those objects that cannot be counted because they are too numerous, such as the blades of grass in a field or the stones on a hillside. In most respects, we would probably agree with Quechua people on this first category of the uncountable, since, while such things as the number of stones on a hillside theoretically *could* be counted—the numbering systems are sufficient, in both English and Quechua—who would want to actually count them! Who has the time, or the patience? However, while such things are, practically speaking, uncountable in our culture, in Quechua they are considered to be uncountable both practically and philosophically speaking. The way of phrasing the uncountability of such things as the blades of grass in a field is quite emphatic in Quechua; that is, one says of such a challenge, *mana atikuq,* "it is not doable"; "it cannot be done." We may perhaps think of this as a Quechua proposition on the philosophical *and* corporeal limitations on counting "infinitely"(cf., Rotman 1993).

The other category of the uncountable in Quechua ideology is somewhat more unusual, and culture-specific. It involves not what *cannot* be counted, but rather what *should not* be counted. The principal types of things in this category are harvested produce and herd animals. For instance, a person who would count his harvested potatoes is called *papa yupa,* "potato counter." This is an insulting epithet, one that is used more broadly, outside its agricultural context, to mean "penny-pincher," or, as is also said in English, "bean counter." It is considered to be bad luck to become so obsessed with your production. The point is that counting one's harvested produce courts disaster. The same thing goes for domesticated animals in general (such as pigs and chickens) and for herd animals in particular (such as sheep, llamas, alpacas, and goats).

In fact, we should not make a strict separation between what cannot and should not be counted, for often the two complement or reinforce one another. For instance, among people on the island of Taquile, in Lake Titicaca, ideas about the stars include the belief that:

> Chaska [*Venus*] and cabrilla [*"goat," the Pleiades*] are explicitly related to fecundity, but so it seems, are all stars. This fecundity is not restricted to agriculture. Taquileans believe that you should not count stars, because you will have as many children as stars. My informants never counted them, and one in particular said he had always counted "one, two, one, two," and therefore has two children. This can be seen as prediction for a family "harvest." (Prochaska 1988).[3]

I often heard sentiments similar to those expressed above in relation to mice; that is, you should never count the mice in your storeroom, because you will have as many children as the number of mice you count.

The reader may be wondering at this point how certain practices relating to the numbering of sequences discussed in Chapter 3 can be squared with the prohibition on counting agricultural produce. The obvious example is with the naming of the ears of corn on a corn plant—a system of nomenclature that, in certain instances, incorporates cardinal number names, as *iskay* ("2") *apaña* and *kinsa* ("3") *apaña*. The explanation for this seeming contradiction is that the numbers used in naming, for example, ears of corn do not constitute an act of *counting*, or summing ("one, two, three, . . ."); rather, they are used to identify positions in an ordered sequence ("second successor, third successor, . . ."). Thus, the point, and the force, of the use of numbers in the corn plant example is not to arrive at a *sum*, which is the goal of counting; rather, the purpose is to identify or specify the relations of hierarchy and succession uniting a group of things into an ordered set without regard to the total number of members making up the set.

The injunction against counting herd animals noted above also needs some clarification. Since herd animals are out in the field most days, and they therefore are exposed to numerous dangers, such as falling off a cliff or being taken by a predator, one needs some way to assure oneself that all the animals have returned to the corral in the evening. This is done through a system of names, not numbers. That is, each individual animal in a herd has its own name, usually derived from some peculiarity of the animal ("crooked ear" or "spotted face," for example). In "counting"—or better, *inventorying*—the animals, the presence of each animal is noted, name by name. If the presence of an animal corresponding to a name in the inventory is not noted, then it is known that that particular animal is missing. However, it should also be said that it may occasionally be the case that one actually needs to count, or enumerate, one's herd animals. If such a need arises, it is considered appropriate only for the woman of the household to do the counting. A man who would count his herd animals, I was told, is a *maricón* ("pansy; homosexual"). Although I was not given an explanation for why a woman but not a man may count the herd animals, I would suggest, based on the material presented in Chapter 3, that women are allowed this privilege because every woman is (potentially) *mama*—the origin (and owner?) of numbers.

Now, we must ask: What *is* the problem with counting one's produce or herd animals? When I pressed this question on my main informant and friend, Primitivo Nina, he responded that the principal problem is that counting has the effect of *separating* things. If what one proposes to count are the members of a reproductive group—whether plant, animal, or human—then the act of enumerating the parts of the group one by one is a threat to, and undermines, the reproductive force of the group. The potential for reproduction is, in all cases, considered to be based on the unity and the interdependence of the members of the group. This makes us aware, then, of an important principle in Quechua ideas about the nature of numbers and the possible consequences of assigning numbers—and thereby of either creating or emphasizing individualism—to certain objects in the world. Insofar as reproductive groups are concerned, enumeration or counting represents a force of alienation. The act of counting the members of a group, as though they were individuals, constitutes a threat to the reproductive capacity and unity of the group *if* the things in question are considered to be inseparable; on the other hand, it is fine to count trucks or (as we will see below) threads making up the warp of a fabric.

The above comments obviously raise a number of important and perplexing questions concerning the practice of census-taking. How has the process of counting the members of a community been viewed historically by Andean peoples? We may suppose that since the time of the Spanish conquest, neither the colonial state nor modern nation-state bureaucrats would have been deterred from census-taking by attitudes, like those outlined above, about the potentially harmful consequences of counting "reproductive units." However, we must then ask how such attitudes—assuming that they did exist (which we cannot affirm with certainty)—were accommodated in the *khipu*-based census-taking procedures of pre-Hispanic Andean societies. We should recall here that, according to González Holguín, counting people was lexically distinct from counting all other types of things.

While I am not prepared now to address the problem identified above in any detail, I would state, as alternative hypotheses for future analysis, that *either* the *khipu* records may have never been intended to represent sums of the members of reproductive units; rather, the "values" recorded were intended to be interpreted as establishing ordinal relations (of hierarchy or succession) among "reproductive units" identified as political groups, such as *ayllus*. *Or,* that the prohibitions on counting reproductive units noted earlier in this section were based on local values and practices, and that these were violated by the greater interests of the state—both Inkaic and Spanish—in order to keep accurate census records. It is also possible, of course, that the prohibition on counting reproductive units that I encountered in my research was not, in fact, operative in pre-Hispanic times; that is, this scruple may be a product of historical processes and attitudes that arose during or since the colonial era. I will return to discuss these questions and hypotheses at a later date, in the context of a more detailed study of the values and symbolism of numbers and counting in the Inka *khipus*.

The Space and Time of Counting

An important characteristic of certain expressions that are used to denote the act of counting is their implication that such an activity is conceived of as moving within, or through, both space and time. For instance, if we were to ask someone who had just finished counting a group of objects to give an account of what had been done, we would word our question as follows: *Maymanta maykama yuparqanki?* (literally, "From where [and] to where did you count?"). *May* ("where") is the principal interrogative used in Quechua to ask questions regarding the location or site of some object, event, or activity in space. In addition to other uses, *may* is employed with the suffix *-manta* ("from; about") in questions concerning the origin or place *from* where/which a movement proceeds, and with *-kama* ("to") to indicate the point or site *to* where/which the movement ends. *Maymanta maykama* ("from where to where") implies movement within a spatial continuum having distinct beginning and end points. Another common grammatical construction denoting the beginning and end points of counting is the combination of *qallarispa* ("beginning, setting out") or *ñawpaqta* ("earlier, anterior") with *chayay* ("to arrive," as at one's place of destination). The construction *qallarispa . . . chayay,* which is commonly used to talk about goings and comings or departures and arrivals, likens the act of counting to a journey.

The question that we should address is: How is the image of the space through which the "journey" of counting proceeds conceptualized? We begin by noting the incorporation of directionality into such images. In this context, directionality refers to the spatial orientation of hierarchy and succession in the organization of relations among numbers. Although largely unstudied to date, the existence of such parameters must be a fundamental element in the conceptualization of numbers and counting routines in all languages. For English-speakers, for instance, I would hazard the guess that we most commonly imagine the spatial arrangement of counting the sequence of numbers 1, 2, 3, . . . *n* as extending from left to right, or (less saliently) from top to bottom. That the former of these two schemes mimics the organization of written numbers (in the form of both numerals and number names) suggests that, in literate societies, mental images of the organization of numbers may be closely linked to the directional and spatial schemes of writing. If such a relationship does in fact exist in literate societies, it would then be interesting and instructive to examine cross-culturally how, and to what degree, differences in the directionality and spatial organization employed in various writing systems are, in turn, reflected in syntactical and semantic constructions defining the mental conception of the "placement" of one number next to, behind, above, or below the other.

For Quechua-speakers, there are a number of fairly standard, well-attested terms and phrases indicating how numbers are organized in the space-time of the imagination. In some cases, these schemes may be projected onto some ready-to-hand physical arrangement whereby a one-to-one correspondence of the spoken number series can be illustrated, such as in "counting off" numbers on the fingers—moving from thumb (= 1) to little finger (= 5). In other cases, the verbal descriptions stand alone, dependent on the grammars of space/time shared between speaker and listener for evoking the desired structuring of the space of the image of counting.

To be more specific, when counting a sequence of numbers in Quechua, one begins spatially at a position referred to as *umapi* ("in/at the head"). Temporally, the beginning of a counting sequence may be termed as either *kunanqa* ("now") or *ñawpaqtaqa* ("anterior, or first"). The "next" number, referred to as *qhipa*, is located to the back of, or behind, the first, with subsequent numbers emerging (or being placed) progressively farther back until the end of the sequence is reached. The end point, or "last" number, is termed *qhipan* ("last"), or *qhipatataq* ("finally"). The term *qhipa* ("after, later, behind; front") also has the meanings of "future," or "future time," and "successor." The "last" number is situated behind, or in back of, the penultimate number. The dimensions of the space-time of counting imagined here are not ones in which the higher numbers are located (as though occupying two-dimensional space) either to the right or left, or above or below, their predecessors. Rather, the image is of a sequence proceeding from the lower numbers in the near-upper (or "head") part of the frame, with subsequent, higher numbers moving downward and away into three-dimensional space, as it were (see Figure 4.1).

In summary, Quechua counting projects the ordered, hierarchical sequence of number names into a space-time continuum, the spatial dimension of which is built on a body metaphor moving from the first number, at the "head," away and downward to the last number, at the lower back, or bottom, of the imagined space. The temporal dimension of a number sequence goes from the beginning, in the present, to the end, which is located "toward the back (i.e., in front of the speaker) in the future." This combined space-time framework for counting does not take into account the specific arrays into or onto which counting sequences using cardinal and ordinal numerals are projected. For instance,

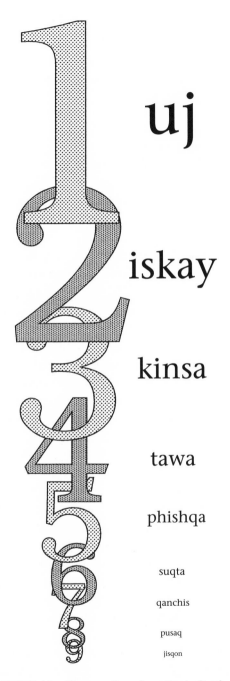

uj

iskay

kinsa

tawa

phishqa

suqta

qanchis

pusaq

jisqon

FIGURE 4.1. The space-time of counting in Quechua.

we saw in Chapter 3 an arrangement for counting with ordinals that shares some properties with the imagined mental framework described above. That is, in the naming of the ears of corn appearing successively on a corn stalk, the sequence proceeds from *chuqllu* (the first ear of corn to appear), which is located at the top or "head" (*umapi*) of the corn plant, to the last "successor off-spring" (*apaña*) ear of corn, which is located at the foot of the corn stalk. We also saw in Chapter 3 how the colors of the rainbow are always named, or identified, from top to bottom, although they (are thought to) actually make their appearance in the sky from bottom to top (see Classen 1993, for additional examples of such body and plant metaphors in Inka cosmology).

Counting: The Foundation of Arithmetic and Mathematical Operations

In Chapter 5, we will turn to the study of arithmetic operations—such as addition, subtraction, multiplication, and division—as they are talked about and performed in Quechua. What is important to recognize concerning these manipulations of numbers is the primacy to them of the ability to count. That is, not only in Quechua but (undoubtedly) in all cultures, counting constitutes the practical and conceptual grounding for manipulating and making propositions about the nature, organization, and structure of relations among numbers that are central to the activities of addition, subtraction, multiplication and division. The "primacy" of counting to these activities can be explained on two levels; the first concerns the principles of hierarchy and succession that are shared between counting and mathematical operations; the second deals with the implications for the manipulation of numbers of the grammatical constructions employed in producing compound number phrases in counting. I will discuss these two topics in the order mentioned here.

By linguistic, cultural, and historical precedent, the numbers of any particular language are formally organized in a hierarchical progression—as, for example, *tawa, phishqa, suqta,* . . . (4, 5, 6, . . .). The absolute fixity of the order of the elements in such a series is fundamental to the definition of a particular set of adjectives as numbers. The notion of a fixed order, specifically as applied to numbers, is expressed in the term *ujnintin* ("together with one/another"; see the discussion of *-ntin,*

Chapter 2). Primitivo Nina glossed the term *ujnintin* as (in Spanish) *la se-quencia de los números* ("the sequence of the numbers"). I would stress, however, that *ujnintin* indicates only the proper sequence, or order of numbers; it is neutral with respect to whether the "adjacent number" (another possible gloss of *ujnintin*) is greater or less than the number named. For example, the number phrase, *pachaq chunka pishqhayuqpa ujnintin,* may be glossed "one [number] in sequence with (or adjacent to) 115"; the number in question may be either 114 or 116.

Quechua children begin to learn the rules and regimes of counting from an early age, especially in such activities as games, riddling (see Isbell and Roncalla Fernandez 1977), and weaving (see below). Through the experience and continual reaffirmation of the fixed order of the number sequence that comes with the practice of counting, children begin to incorporate this sequence as a part of their world view. That is, the sequence of words and values regularly produced in counting constitutes a central element of "the way things are" in the child's world. Once the number sequence has been mastered, it is then possible to move on to learning more complex operations using numbers, such as addition and subtraction. However, what is important to recognize is that by virtue of simply learning to count, the child has already received training in certain basic principles of these higher-level operations (this is one of the central problems addressed, and conclusions arrived at, in Piaget's study, *On the Child's Conception of Number* [1969: 161–220]).

For example, the arithmetic operations of "addition" (*yapay*) and "subtraction" (*jurquy, pisichay*) are contained, in nuclear form, in the procedures of counting either progressively *higher* (one, two, three, . . . = addition) or *lower* (three, two, one = subtraction) in the number sequence. Thus, the reproduction of the order and relations among numbers realized in counting are at the base of routinized experiences that provide one with practice in, and insight into, the principles and relations on which arithmetic operations are built.

The second reason that the perfection of counting serves as a foundation for the conception of, and discourse about, mathematical operations (especially addition and multiplication) concerns the grammatical structures and classificatory entailments of the formation of compound number names used in counting. In Chapter 2, we analyzed some of the syntactical features of the formation of compound numbers. What is important to note is that the syntax of higher number names and phrases in Quechua incorporates the *results* of manipulations of numbers that are characteristic of the basic *additive* arithmetic operations; for Quechua, these were identified in Chapter 2 as *yapay* ("to add") and *miray* ("to multiply"). This proposition is in agreement with Piaget's conclusion that, "in the case of multiplicative operations, as in that of additive operations, qualitative composition of classes is not achieved on the operational place before that of numbers, but at the same time" (1969: 220). In Quechua, a phrase such as *chunka tawayuq* ("10 4" = 14) is an additive statement, composed as it is of the combination of "ten" (*chunka*) and "four" (*tawa*) through the techniques of juxtaposition and the use of the possessive suffix *-yuq* (see Chapter 2).

The principle of multiplication is, like addition, directly employed in the formation of compound number words as produced in the counting sequence. For instance, the number *tawa chunka* ("4 10" = 40) appears to be, like its English equivalent "forty" (i.e., "4 10"), expressive of the process of multiplication. However, *tawa chunka* could also be interpreted as a kind of notational instruction for repeated addition (rather than multiplication), a process that would also give rise to the number name "forty." I will leave aside for the moment the question of the complex relationship between multiplication and repeated addition and return to this problem in Chapter 5. The principal point that I want to make here is that expressions such as *tawa chunka* are generally "additive" in nature and that learning the place and value of such constructions in the counting sequence has implications for acquiring some basic arithmetic knowledge and skills. (Posner [1982] arrived at a similar conclusion from her studies of school children in West Africa.)

While subtraction and division are not overtly a part of the operations for forming compound number phrases in Quechua, they are nonetheless implicit in them. That is, "counting forward" is the additive side of the coin of the act of counting, the subtractive side of which is "counting backward." The two equally involve principles of, and skills in, number manipulation that are crucial for learning arithmetic operations. Similarly, while not used overtly to form number words or phrases in Quechua, division is present implicitly in the potential "decomposition" of multiplicative statements that are contained in such number names as *tawa chunka* ("forty"). That is, imbedded in the number name *tawa chunka* (literally: "four ten") is the proposition that "forty" is composed of—and can thus be decomposed, or divided, into—four groups of ten, or ten groups of four.

Learning and practicing the art of counting (especially using compound numbers) inculcates in the speaker various principles of number manipulation that (will) become formalized and abstracted in the language of the arithmetic operations of addition, subtraction, multiplication, and division. Therefore, counting—a skill which children learn in a variety of everyday practices in growing up as productive members of their households—provides the foundation for learning the formal rules and procedures of mathematical operations on numbers. A similar point has been made elsewhere with respect to other non-Western societies (Mimica 1992; Hallpike 1979) as well as in the West (see, for example, Lave 1991; Piaget 1969).

The principal difference that I would identify as distinguishing the development of these abilities in Quechua society and at least the Western version of these activities that I am most familiar with (North American English), is that in the former the vocabulary and grammar of counting and ordering in ordinal sequences are accompanied by metaphorical propositions linking numbers to social relations and kinship positions and statuses; for instance, that *uj* ("one") and *ñawpa kaq* ("first") are *mama; iskay* ("two") and *iskay kaq* ("second") are the first offspring; etc. Because of such comparisons and connections that are made to everyday, lived categories of social and kinship relations, the Quechua child must—almost inevitably—experience numbers and arithmetic as a more rational and sensible enterprise than does a North American child, who is taught that numbers are abstract entities devoid of social values or moral connotations (see Lave 1991, on the disjunction between formal and informal mathematics in American culture). However, the Quechua-speaking child will also encounter numbers as abstractions in the arithmetic classes taught in school, which are, with few exceptions, conducted in Spanish.[4] In this new setting, as well as in the money-based market systems operating throughout the Andes, the conception of numbers as categories of kin is a naive and ultimately dysfunctional conceit.

We turn now to the activity in Quechua-speaking communities in which the art of counting is most highly developed and valued—weaving.

Counting and the Art of Weaving

In any community where there is a significant division of labor by sex, age, or whatever criterion, which describes most societies that have existed in human history, the different tasks that are performed by various groups or types of people will both require and reinforce specific skills and bodies of knowledge. For instance, a task that regularly involves counting and the execution of arithmetic operations can be expected to produce individuals who are more skillful than the population at large at counting, adding, subtracting, and other arithmetic operations. This situation describes perfectly the relationship between the art of weaving and the presence in Andean communities of a group of people who are highly skilled in counting and mathematical practice.

In the remainder of this chapter, I will discuss weaving, and its associated task of warping threads, by way of investigating what is, arguably, the most important domain of knowledge and practice employing the arts of counting and arithmetic in Andean communities. It should be stated that when talking about the art of weaving in the Andean context, we are not discussing just another, or an ordinary, example of a form of production that is known in communities worldwide. Rather, throughout much of human history in the Andes, weaving has been of the greatest economic, symbolic, and even political importance (see Murra 1962). The fabrics made by Andean weavers beginning several thousand years before the time of Christ and continuing down to the present day represent some of the finest and most complex examples of the art of weaving produced anywhere. The modern weavers of the Andes are heirs to this tradition in both aesthetic and technical terms.

I should state here explicitly the bases of my own understanding of weaving. Some of this comes from a kind of generalized sense of how weaving is performed that derives from having lived for some four years, prior to my principal fieldwork for this project in 1993–1994, in various communities in southern Peru (see Urton 1988, 1990; Meyerson 1993). Many of the day-to-day activities of women, and occasionally of men, involve one or another of several weaving-related tasks. From observing and helping with these various tasks, one comes slowly to a general understanding—at least in a theoretical and statistical sense—of the operations that are required in the art of weaving. In addition, while carrying out fieldwork on numbers and mathematics in Bolivia in 1993–

FIGURE 4.2.   Irene Flores Condori.
From Dávalos, Cereceda, and Martínez (1992), fol. p. 28.

1994, I actually apprenticed myself out to weavers in the village of Candelaria (near Tarabuco) for a period of about three months (for further discussion of weavers and weaving in Candelaria, see Meisch 1986).

While I resided in Candelaria, my principal teacher was a twelve-year-old girl, Irene Flores Condori (see Figure 4.2). I also studied with Irene's fifteen-year-old sister Benedicta. Irene and Benedicta are the daughters of María Condori, who is one of the directors of the *taller* (weaving "workshop") in Candelaria and a weaver of wide renown. I also studied with two of the adult master weavers—who are called *Mamas*—in Candelaria. One of these women was Santusa Quispe, the wife in the household that served as my host family while I was living in the community (see Figure 4.3). My other teacher was Valentina Flores Vargas, the sister-in-law of Santusa. While I insisted on paying an hourly sum for the lessons that I received from my teachers in Candelaria, these four women were all willing and generous teachers who had a seemingly genuine interest in instructing me in weaving—this despite my obvious clumsiness and the fact that it is quite unheard of, not to mention a

FIGURE 4.3. Santusa Quispe and Damián Flores.
From Dávalos, Cereceda, and Martínez (1992), fol. p. 28.

most egregious violation of gender stereotypes in the division of labor in Candelaria, for a man to weave.

In relation to the latter point, I do want to mention that my efforts to learn to weave in this village created a certain amount of amusement, confusion, and (generally good-natured) consternation. The master weavers of Candelaria are all women, and the view there is that weaving is an activity appropriate only for females. Therefore, the sight of a middle-aged *gringo* sitting in the shade of a fruit tree taking instructions in weaving from teenage girls was often too funny for people to silently ignore. On one occasion, a stern old woman who was the mother of one of my principal informants asked me point blank if, by weaving, I was trying to be like a woman. I answered by telling her that in some villages that I know of, it is the men rather than the women who do the weaving; my friend then jumped to my defense, saying that in Potolo (west of Sucre), for instance, the men do some of the weaving. The old woman gave us both a wry look and asked, if that was the case, then is it the women in those villages who have the penises! From these and other experiences—such as people asking me if perchance I had ever heard of the term *mari-machu* ("confusion/confusing-old man"), a derisive term applied to a man who takes on the behavior and activities appropriate to a woman—it was clear that my behavior was being tolerated to the degree that it was only because, as an outsider, I was not subject to the same rules and expectations as local men.

As it turned out, working with young girls proved to be a very good approach to studying weaving. Older women—the master weavers—have routinized and incorporated the rhythms of weaving so deeply into their bodily movements that it is difficult for them to articulate clearly the step-by-step movements, especially the regimes of counting, that are required to weave a particular design. While young girls learn the fundamentals of weaving from years of observing their mothers weave, and then practicing the movements they have observed (in addition to a certain amount of verbal instruction on their teacher's part), my time was more limited. Thus, I needed a teacher who could still easily produce detailed, verbal instructions for how one should proceed, move by move, to weave a particular design. My twelve-year-old teacher proved to be perfectly suited to this task. From Irene and her older sister Benedicta, I learned to weave some five or six different types of standard geometrical designs, known as *ch'askas* ("stars"), on narrow bands, called *watus* ("cord; line"). From working with older teachers—the *Mamas* Santusa and Valentina—I learned several more *ch'aska* motifs, as well as a couple of examples of broader bands (called *layas*, "type, class") that combine the geometrical *ch'aska* motifs along the borders with at least one figural design in the interior space (of this type, I learned to weave *yuthus* ["partridges"] and two styles of ducks). Thus, while I am a purely novice weaver, I did learn enough to stand in awe of the accomplishments of the few "outsiders" who have learned this craft well (among these are Ed and Chris Franquemont, Elayne Zorn, Lynn Meisch, and Mary Frame).

The name for the master weavers in the Tarabuco region—*Mama*—is of obvious interest in relation to topics discussed earlier. As we saw in Chapter 3, the term "*mama*" has an important and unique status in ideas concerning numbers, colors, and the relations of hierarchy and succession in organizing numeral and non-numeral ordinal sequences. "*Mama*" is the status position of the origin of numbers and colors; furthermore, *mama* has within her the power of reproduction and multiplication that gives rise successively to new members of a species. This, by analogy, is the role played by the *Mamas*, the master weavers of the Tarabuco region. Not only do these women produce fine weavings for their own and their family's use, as well as for sale at market, but they do so utilizing highly developed skills in counting and manipulating sets of threads. In the discussion of weaving and counting later in this chapter, we will see how these women continually reproduce a whole class of stylized domesticated animals (*uywas*) in the designs of their weavings. In addition, the sale of these weavings has considerable importance for the reproduction of the women's household economies.[5]

In the following sections, I will discuss those aspects of weaving that most directly bear on numerical knowledge, counting, and arithmetic practice. That is, I will not discuss here the tasks of shearing wool, or of spinning, plying, or dyeing the threads. Rather, I will take up the topics of warping and weaving. These two tasks demand knowledge of, and skill in, many of the forms of numerical knowledge and counting discussed earlier. In order to talk about weaving, we must first discuss the procedures for warping threads and the role of numbers, counting, and mathematical calculations in this process.

Before discussing the warping of various design elements of an Andean-style weaving, I should note that the complex geometric and

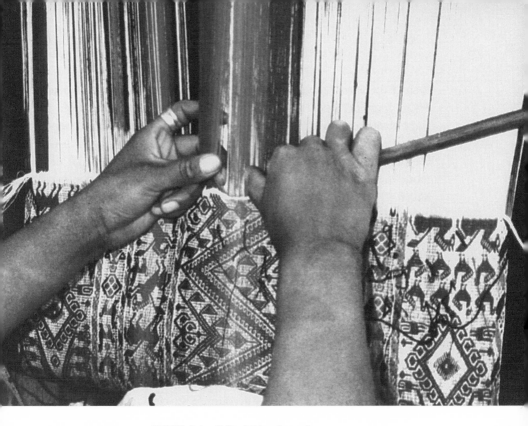

FIGURE 4.4. *Pallay* (pick-up) weaving.
From Dávalos, Cereceda, and Martínez (1992), fol. p. 42.

animal motifs woven into these fabrics are produced by the technique known as *pallay* ("to pick up"). The warp of a fabric is strung with paired threads, one white and one colored. Weaving is performed by working the heddle to alternately raise and lower the white and the colored sets of threads. When the heddle is raised, the weaver selects, or "picks up," a predetermined patterned group of colored and white threads; the weft is then passed between the threads that were picked up and those that were not. After packing the weft snugly between what is now (after "picking") a new set of upper and lower threads, the heddle is once again pulled up to establish the next upper and lower groups of working threads, and the appropriate pattern of the "picking up" of threads is performed (see Figure 4.4).

Since most textiles bear a number of different design elements arranged next to each other across the width of the warp threads of a fabric, the weaver must know what set of threads must be selected for each of the several designs of a fabric with each pass of the weft thread. While some of these "picking sequences" repeat after as few as six or eight passes of the weft, on more complex designs it takes some twenty to thirty (or more) passes of the weft to begin to repeat a design. All of the information on the proper picking sequence for each design of a fabric is held in the head of the weaver. However, a master weaver—a *Mama*—generally does not consciously repeat to herself, or become aware of, this information as she weaves. Weaving is usually performed extremely quickly by a master weaver.[6] Her movements are performed automatically, without counting to herself, according to hand and body routines of movement that become habitual through long training.

Warping and Counting

"Warping" (*allwi*) refers to the process of laying out, on a frame, the parallel longitudinal threads of a fabric; the weaving process involves the insertion of transverse elements, known as the "weft" (*mini*), through the warp threads (for a definitive account of warping and weaving structures and processes, see Emery 1994). Textiles are usually warped by two women who often work together on this task as warping partners. There are certain women who are known for their ability to warp. These women will often be sought out when a *Mama* wishes to warp a fabric whose design layout she may not be familiar with, or which is especially complex in its organization of threads. The most complex fabric woven by women in the Tarabuco area is the *axsu*—the woman's over-skirt. In the following discussion, it should be assumed, unless otherwise stated, that my comments concern the warping of an *axsu*.

It is impossible to generalize about how the challenges of warping are met, given the large number of solutions that are actually arrived at as evidenced in the finished products, the woven *axsus*. Nonetheless, there are certain what might be called guiding principles of design that organize elements in most of the *axsus* produced today in Candelaria. These are based on varied arrangements of three basic design elements: *pampa, layas,* and *ch'askas* (see Figure 4.5). These three design elements may be characterized as follows:

a) *pampa* ("open field"): This is a large plain weave section, often making up as much as one-half of the total space of the

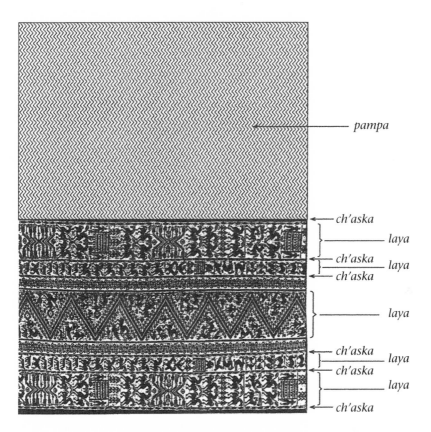

FIGURE 4.5. The design layout of an *axsu*.

finished *axsu*. The *pampa* is warped as a single continuous run of monochromatic, dark (usually black) threads. The pampa is usually warped and woven separate from its companion colorful section, the latter of which is composed of *pallay* ("pick up") designs; the two parts of the *axsu* are stitched together later.

b) *laya* ("group; kind, species"): These are warp-patterned woven panels that carry the main woven designs of geometric shapes, animals, humans, etc. Each *axsu* carries a number of *layas* of different widths, usually varying from narrow bands an inch or so wide to wider ones measuring some six to eight inches in width. As noted above, in *axsus* of the Tarabuco region, the total area occupied by the *layas* is separate from, and usually roughly equal in size to, the space occupied by the *pampa*. I will illustrate the naming and organization of the *layas* of different widths and function in a moment. As stated above, the *laya* panels are warped in paired threads—i.e., one colored (usually woolen) thread together with one white cotton thread. The actual hues of the colored threads will usually vary within each *laya,* and across the numerous *layas* of an *axsu.*

c) *ch'aska* ("star; shaggy hair"): This design element is composed of narrow bands, usually measuring one-fourth to three-fourths inch (ca. 1 to 1½ cm) in width, that are woven exclusively in geometric designs. *Ch'askas* serve as dividers between the *laya* panels. Although the *Mamas* refer to the sets of threads for warping *ch'askas* as *pares* ("pairs"), in fact, these "pairs" are actually composed of *three* threads, one white cotton thread plus two colored woolen threads.

The best way to characterize how these three elements—*pampa, laya,* and *ch'aska*—are incorporated into the design of an *axsu* is to give a couple of examples of fabrics that I actually saw being warped, and whose warp counts I am therefore certain of. Two examples of the warp counts of *axsus* are presented in Figure 4.6 a and b.

The actual warping of an *axsu* is a (usually) day-long process carried on between two *Mamas.* The women sit on the floor at either end of the warping frame (see Figure 4.7). The lead warper—the most experienced of the two women in warping the fabric in question—has near her a pile of several balls of yarn, which she combines in various ways as the warping proceeds. The stringing of the "paired" (sets of two *or* three) threads, always proceeds from left to right. Warping is fundamentally an act of *counting,* either explicitly or "intuitively." As for the latter—intuitive counting—this pertains especially to warping the *ch'askas* and the narrow, monochromatic edge stripes, called *simun.* These narrow bands require some three to six sets of threads each; therefore, the *Mamas* are able to warp these sections by just being aware of the proper "number" (kinesthetically, rather than arithmetically, speaking) of passes of the warp thread back and forth between them.

However, when the *Mamas* begin warping the wider *laya* panels—those having at least ten pairs of threads—these are meticulously counted. This is usually not done, however, by way of counting off each run of the warp threads as they are laid down. Rather, the lead warper

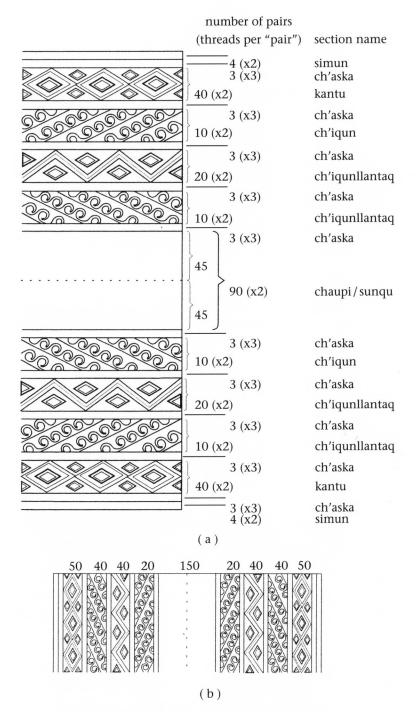

number of pairs	
(threads per "pair")	section name

4 (x2) — simun
3 (x3) — ch'aska
40 (x2) — kantu

3 (x3) — ch'aska
10 (x2) — ch'iqun

3 (x3) — ch'aska
20 (x2) — ch'iqunllantaq

3 (x3) — ch'aska
10 (x2) — ch'iqunllantaq

3 (x3) — ch'aska

45

90 (x2) — chaupi/sunqu

45

3 (x3) — ch'aska
10 (x2) — ch'iqun

3 (x3) — ch'aska
20 (x2) — ch'iqunllantaq

3 (x3) — ch'aska
10 (x2) — ch'iqunllantaq

3 (x3) — ch'aska
40 (x2) — kantu

3 (x3) — ch'aska
4 (x2) — simun

(a)

50   40   40   20   150   20   40   40   50

(b)

FIGURE 4.6.   Warp counts on two *axsus* from Candelaria.

knows approximately how wide any particular design panel should be. The women will warp a panel by sight—chatting all the while—up to the point at which the lead warper thinks they are nearing the desired number of threads. The women will then stop and count the paired runs of threads; from that point on, they will keep a close count of the actual number, or pairs of threads, laid down. As far as I have experienced, the *Mamas* always count warp threads in pairs using Quechua numbers (*uj* = "one" [pair of threads], *iskay* = "two" [pairs of threads], and so on).

I want to make three observations concerning the warp counts shown in Figure 4.6. First, as far as I have observed on both warped fabrics and on a larger sample of fully woven *axsus,* the design panels of *axsus* are laid out symmetrically on either side of the middle of the "center" (*chaupi*), or "heart" (*sunqu*) *laya.* Thus, in warping the two halves of the colorful section of an *axsu,* the number of thread pairs in the *laya* panels on the right side repeat exactly the counts established earlier in the warping of their mirror-image panels on the left side. Second, in all examples with which I am familiar, the number of pairs of warp threads in all *layas* of an *axsu* represent full decimal unit values (10, 20, 30, etc.). Therefore, we can say that the decimal values constitute a strong organizing principle in the layout of design panels in these weavings. A weak version of this principle is that—except insofar as the *ch'askas* (divider bands) are concerned—even numbers predominate in the warping of fabrics.

The third point to note with respect to the warp counts illustrated in Figure 4.6 a and b is that there is usually, but not always, a close correspondence between the number of pairs of threads in the central, *chaupi/ sunqu* design panel and the total number of pairs in the two sets of design panels on either side of the center. That is, in Figure 4.6b, there is a total of 150 pairs of threads in the central panel; this is mirrored in the combined number of thread pairs (50 + 40 + 40 + 20 = 150) in the wide *laya* panels on either side of the center. It will be noted, however, that such an equivalence is not present in the fabric illustrated in Figure 4.6a; there, the center panel contains 90 pairs of threads, whereas the totals on each side are 80 pairs (10 + 20 + 10 + 40 = 80).

FIGURE 4.7. (*opposite*)   A completed warp for an *axsu* (Candelaria).
ASUR (Antropólogos del Surandino).

Several things are notable about these observations. First, there is a strong impression of symmetry in the spaces occupied by the three main sections of the *axsus*, the central panel and the combinations of the narrower *laya* panels on each side. Second, these examples make it clear that the *Mamas* are working with fairly large numbers, combining and recombining various groupings of decimal values in sophisticated and generally symmetrical arrangements. And finally, warping is very much concerned with the art of counting, but it is not *just* about counting; clearly there is a complex interplay of attention to, and knowledge about, both numerical information *and* spatial arrangements and organization involved. A *Mama* is a master weaver not just because she is proficient at counting threads, but also because she combines that technical skill with aesthetic considerations based on producing pleasing and compelling arrangements of threads through the manipulation of color and space. The fact that the spatial arrangements are products of different thread counts provides the link between precise knowledge and aesthetics that is the hallmark of a master weaver.

The calculations made by the *Mamas* in warping textiles involve addition, subtraction, and division. I have not heard a woman make a multiplicative statement (such as, "this panel contains 5 groups of 10 pairs of threads, which totals 50 pairs") in totaling the number of thread pairs in a section. The additive process seems to remain at the level of addition, with multiplication being handled as repeated addition. Division is seen when the *Mamas* count, as well as "decompose," analyze, or break down a large number of pairs of threads into decimal groupings.

As I suggested at the beginning of this discussion, warping is a process intimately connected with the art of counting. As we will see below, this is a—if not *the*—fundamental activity in weaving as well.

Weaving and Counting

Whether performed on back-strap looms, as in much of Peru, or on horizontal or up-right looms, as in much of southern Peru and south-central Bolivia, Andean weaving is a complex art whose mastery requires years of patient study and practice. At about four to five years of age, young girls begin "playing" at weaving as they watch their mothers weave day in and day out. By six to eight years of age, the girls begin to receive more direct instruction in weaving, perhaps from a friend, an older sister, or their mother or grandmother. At this stage, the girls will learn to warp and weave a variety of geometric designs on narrow (ca. one-fourth- to one-half-inch) bands, called *watus*. *Watus* are constructed of a few three-string "pairs" of threads, two colored and one white thread in each pair. The *watus* that a girl learns to weave at this age are, in fact, the set of narrow geometric bands that will later form the dividers— called *ch'askas*—between the *layas* of *axsus*. As the girl matures, she begins adding larger working units such as *laya*-like bands of varying widths that are bordered on either side by *ch'askas,* as well as increasingly more complex design motifs, to her repertory. By puberty, the girl will be ready to undertake the weaving of her first *axsu* (for an excellent description of the life-stages in the maturation of master weavers in Chinchero, Peru, see Franquemont, Franquemont, and Isbell 1992).

Most of the operations involved in weaving geometrical, animal, and other patterns are learned by young girls as numerical formulas, or "recipes," passed on from older, more experienced weavers to younger ones. By practicing these recipes, they gradually are able to reproduce them not as a matter of conscious manipulation, but of habit—of the smooth flow of body movements and the feel of the proper rhythms. A close analogy to this process drawn from activities the reader might be familiar with is typing. Typing quickly demands that the typist perform the operations without thinking about them; nevertheless, when the typist makes an error his or her body will be fully aware of the mistake. It is at this level that most weaving occurs (see Connerton 1989 and Bourdieu 1979 on the social, symbolic, and historical significance of such bodily routines and habits). Such an ability, however, depends upon years of practice in counting and calculating the proper moves. In order to understand better the nature of the processes through which such skill is developed, and the implications of such skill for questions concerning counting and mathematics, we must look more closely at the numerical patterns and counting schemes incorporated in the weaving "recipes" alluded to above.

The recipes, or detailed instructions, that I will describe here are for weaving geometric *ch'aska* motifs on narrow bands, or *watus*. These represent the foundation of knowledge of weaving on the basis of which

TABLE 4.1.

Picking Sequences for *Chakrupatacha Palmita*

1) 6 white / drop one white and one red / 4 red / 6 white

2) 4 white / 8 red / drop one white and one red / 4 white

3) 2 white / drop one red and one white / 12 red / 2 white

4) 6 red / 4 white / drop one red and one white / 6 red

5) 4 red / drop one white and one red / 8 white / 4 red

6) 2 red / 12 white / drop one red and one white / 2 red

7) Repeat from #1

more complicated motifs are learned. What is important about these recipes are the counting regimes that they contain and the practice one gains in performing these operations in forming and recombining sets of threads of different quantities.

Table 4.1 contains the *pallay* or "picking" instructions for producing one of the simplest of the *ch'aska* designs in the Candelaria repertory, called *chakrupatacha palmita* (see Figure 4.8). This design has the form of a series of Vs, in the color(s) selected, on a white background. Each complete working series of *chakrupatacha palmita* requires the six picking sequences described in Table 4.1.

To clarify the meaning of the notations given in Table 4.1, the translation of line 1, in operational terms, is as follows:

a) beginning from the right side of the band, moving to the left, pick up the first 6 white threads; this implies not selecting (i.e., "dropping," or pushing down) the colored thread associated with each of these 6 white threads;

b) drop or push down the next (i.e., the seventh) white thread, as well as the subsequent red thread;

c) pick up the next 4 red threads; and

d) pick up the following 6 white threads. Now, insert weft between the threads that were picked up and those that were pushed down. Pull the heddle and move on to the picking sequence in line 2.

FIGURE 4.8. The *ch'aska* design *chakrupatacha palmita* (woven by the author).

TABLE 4.2

**Number Grid from Picking Sequences
for *Chakrupatacha Palmita***

6	-	1/1	-	4	-	6
4	-	8	-	1/1	-	4
2	-	1/1	-	12	-	2
6	-	4	-	1/1	-	6
4	-	1/1	-	8	-	4
2	-	12	-	1/1	-	2

When we look more closely at the arrangement of numbers (setting aside for the moment the color differences) in the six picking sequences, we see that they are organized in two sets of three sequences each; the first set (lines 1–3) differs from the second (lines 4–6) by rotation/vertical reflection symmetry (see Ascher 1991: 160). This can be seen more easily if we create a grid showing, in order, the number of threads specifically indicated for picking up, pushing down to the resting position, etc., through each picking sequence; such an arrangement is illustrated in Table 4.2. From Table 4.2, we see that if the upper three rows are rotated right-for-left, as a group, 180° on the vertical axis, the order of the numbers of threads selected in each picking sequence of the upper set of three duplicates that in the lower set of three.

Therefore, in the short term—the course of each picking sequence—the production of different *ch'aska* designs entrains in the young weaver various patterns in the selection of numbers or sets of threads. In the long term—over the course of performing and repeating several full sets of picking sequences—the production of these designs instills and reinforces an awareness of, and a sensibility to, "reciprocal" relations between larger sets of numbers through the various forms of rotational and reflection symmetry that are used in producing the different designs.

The design used for the above exposition is among the simplest motifs in the entire weaving repertoire of Candelaria. Its production is so

easy and straightforward that young girls master it by the time they begin school, and even younger children (boys and girls) often try to warp
and weave this (and other similar) motifs while sitting around the house.
However, this leads us precisely to the point I want to make in giving
this example. For the *chakrupatacha palmita* motif represents the kind of
encounter with numbers and spatial arrangements that Andean children experience from a very young age. Such experiences provide them with an
understanding of counting, the relationship between even and odd
numbers in set formation, and the properties and relations of different
geometric shapes that serve as the practical grounding for more complex notions about, and manipulations of, cardinal numbers, ordinal sequences (such as the order of thread selection in a picking sequence),
and arithmetic calculations. As young weavers practice these simple
designs, skill in counting as well as in the performance of arithmetic
operations and the (re)organization of space become sublimated and
serve as the foundation for solving the challenges in counting, set formation (as in selecting groups of colored threads), mathematics, and
spatial manipulation presented by more complex design motifs. Such
performances and activities are excellent examples of the activities of
collecting and *correlating,* which Kitcher sees as the bases of the acquisition of knowledge and experience central to the formation of abstract
ideas in mathematics:

> *One central ideal of my proposal is to replace the notions of abstract*
> *mathematical objects, notions like that of a collec*tion, *with the notion*
> *of a kind of mathematical activity, collec*ting. . . . *In its most rudimen-*
> *tary form, collecting is tied to physical manipulation of objects. One way*
> *of collecting all the red objects on a table is to segregate them from the*
> *rest of the objects, and to assign them a special place. . . . We learn how*
> *to collect by engaging in this type of activity. . . . However, our collecting*
> *does not stop there. Later we can collect the objects in thought without*
> *moving them about. We become accustomed to collecting objects by*
> *running through a list of their names, or by producing predicates which*
> *apply to them. . . . Thus our collecting becomes highly abstract. . . .*
>
>   *Collecting is not the only elementary form of mathematical activ-*
> *ity. In addition we must recognize the role of correlating. Here again we*
> *begin from crude physical paradigms. Initially, correlation is achieved*
> *by matching some objects with others, placing them alongside one an-*

other, below one another, or whatever. As we become familiar with the
activity we no longer need the physical props. We become able to relate
objects in thought. (Kitcher 1983: 110–111).

The above discussion provides us with an excellent outline of the theoretical orientation that I have tried to develop here in relation to the art and language of weaving. The relationships between practice, thinking, and signing stressed by Kitcher are what I would argue are at the base of developments in the language of numbers, arithmetical operations, and mathematical concepts which we have been investigating up to this point in relation to numbers, and which we will investigate in relation to arithmetic operations in Chapter 5. I would also note here that it is precisely in terms of Piaget's emphasis on collec*tion* over collec*ting*, for instance, that Mimica criticizes Piaget's studies on children's conceptions of number (Mimica 1992: 114–121).

The last topic to discuss with regard to the subject of counting and weaving has to do with the act of enumerating threads in the production of the more complex designs alluded to above, especially the nongeometric, figural designs. If we confine ourselves to the design inventory in the weaving tradition of the Tarabuco–Candelaria region, there are a large number of figural designs in the repertory. These include a variety of nondomesticated animals (such as condor, fox, vizcacha, *"león"* [puma], monkey, and duck), domesticated animals (horse, dog, cat, chicken), architectural forms (house forms and the *pukara,* or carnival altar), and humans. The animal forms in this repertory are referred to collectively as *uywas,* a term otherwise used to refer specifically to domesticated animals.

When a *Mama* lays out, or warps, a weaving that includes any combination of this group of figures, she will provide a predetermined number of thread pairs for the production of each figure; these counts must be coordinated with, and worked into, the thread counts for the *laya* bands as a whole. Thread counts (in pairs) for several of the more common *uywa* designs in the weaving repertory of Candelaria are given in Table 4.3.

As she weaves any one of these figures, the *Mama* will know exactly how many threads are available in the warp for the production of that figure. These thread counts represent another body of numerical knowl-

TABLE 4.3

Thread Counts for Some Figural Motifs

Motif	No. of Pairs of Threads
Horse	45–50
Condor	30
Vizcacha	25
Cat	"
Duck	"
Dog	"
Monkey	"
Chicken	"

edge (in addition to those contained in the picking sequences of a large repertory of *ch'aska* designs) which each *Mama* has at her disposal to direct and organize her work. As she moves across the wide expanse of an *axsu* during the course of a single picking sequence, the weaver must know where she is numerically, spatially, and "rhythmically" (that is, in terms of body movements established in the skillful performance of weaving techniques) in the picking sequence *of each one* of the variety of geometric (*ch'aska*) and figural (*uywa*) forms that are located along that row. Since a *Mama* rarely, in fact, has a free, uninterrupted moment to weave—she is constantly being diverted by such interruptions as a baby that wants to nurse, children having an argument, or a fire that needs stoking—she will return after the interruption, *count* off thread pairs to determine where she left off in the weaving of a particular design, and then resume her smooth, instinctual weaving movements.

Interestingly, several *Mamas* claimed to me that they are constantly counting while weaving. However, when one sees how rapidly an experienced woman picks threads and weaves across a row (see note 6), it is clear that the word "count" (*yupay*) is being used in two senses. One is in terms of the conscious, thread-for-thread act of counting to reassure oneself of where one is during a moment of uncertainty; the other is in terms of the smooth flow of bodily movements that is associated with the rhythms and "habit of numbers" deriving from years of practicing the craft of weaving.

Conclusions

The ability to count and the range of numbers utilized in a system of counting have consistently been used as yardsticks for evaluating the level of complexity of numerical and other forms of precise knowledge in different societies (see, for example, Hallpike 1979). However, such data have often been presented in texts dealing with the history of mathematics more as ethnographic curios than as the subjects of serious analysis (see, for example, Dantzig 1954). This style of approach is unfortunate because it closes off from critical appraisal the questions of how and why simpler, less complex systems of numbering and counting could exist in contemporary settings; that is, since it mistakes description for explanation, it does not insist on the need to examine the meaning and significance of such conditions. Such views are especially pernicious when they attempt to use decontextualized, unanalyzed data to enunciate evolutionary arguments. This has led in some cases to drawing comparisons between the knowledge of numbers and counting on the part of "primitive" adults, on the one hand, and children in complex industrialized societies, on the other (see Piaget 1969, 1972; Hallpike 1979). In many cases, however, such evaluations and comparisons proceed on the basis of only a superficial understanding of the ethnographic particulars of the "primitive" side of the equation (on this point, see Mimica 1992: 114–121). An example will be helpful in clarifying the problems presented by the kind of approach to simpler numbering systems I am concerned with here.

Holmberg, in his ethnography of the Siriono, a people of the tropical forest of eastern Bolivia, states that "the Siriono are *unable* to count beyond three" (Holmberg 1985: 121; my emphasis). Interestingly, Holmberg (ibid.) goes on to note that despite their "*inability*" to count beyond three, the Siriono are able to perceive, by some "gestalt" form of perception, if one ear of corn has been removed from a bunch containing a hundred ears. However, my concern here is with the way Holmberg chose to characterize the cause of the absence of counting beyond three.

That is, he does not say simply, for instance, that the Siriono *do not* count beyond three, nor that they *feel no need* to count beyond this limit; rather, he states that the Siriono are *unable* to count beyond three. Holmberg's observations might seem to provide invaluable data for a project of attempting to delineate the levels of evolutionary complexity represented by different types of societies—a project undertaken explicitly, for instance, by Hallpike (1979). Holmberg himself never asked, nor does he appear to have considered, the most obvious question that presents itself from his observation; that is: How do we explain how it can be that adults in this (or any other) society are unable to count beyond three?

Now, we might be content to let the implications of Holmberg's implicit interpretation of why the Siriono don't count beyond three—that they are "unable" to do so—go unquestioned were we not to read the rest of his ethnography carefully. What we find later in his study, for instance, is that the Siriono of the time had exceptionally complex systems of teknonyms and nicknames. Teknonymy is a system of changing one's name at the time of the birth of a child or the death of a family member. As Holmberg describes the naming systems:

> *Every time a Siriono is the father or the mother of a child, his [/her] name is changed to that of the child with an additional suffix indicating father or mother. This, coupled with the fact that nicknames are also frequently changed, makes it possible for an Indian to have as many as fifteen or twenty names during the course of a lifetime. One's father, for instance, will not have the same name after one's own birth that he had after the birth of one's elder brother. (Holmberg 1985: 129)*

Holmberg struggled for months, through at least two field sessions, to understand the Siriono systems of teknonyms and nicknames. He finally arrived at a rough-and-ready understanding of the system that let him get on with his work and begin to ask reasonably intelligent questions about Siriono kinship.

Now, we have here a very odd situation. People who do not possess the ability to count beyond three *do* have the ability to operate daily with shifting, ever-changing systems of names that require them to make exceptionally complex, abstract genealogical calculations (re)defining (reclassifying) the identities of their neighbors with each birth and death that occurs in the village. How can we square these two characterizations of the intellectual and mental capacities of the Siriono? They cannot, of course, be rectified *unless* we are willing to view and critically evaluate one body of data (Siriono counting) in relation to the other (Siriono naming). If we do pursue such an evaluation, we will surely be forced, specifically, to reject such interpretations as Holmberg's of the reasons for the relative simplicity of a system of numbers and counting, and generally, to develop not just different but more ethnographically and linguistically informed criteria for evaluating numerical knowledge and systems of counting in such a society.

As a counterpoint to Holmberg's approach to and comments on Siriono counting, let us look briefly at what Martín Gusinde had to say in 1931 concerning the counting system of the Selk'nam Indians of Tierra del Fuego. Prior to noting that the Selk'nam had numbers only from one to five—anything beyond which was designated as "much"—Gusinde (1931: 1107) says: "proceeding from their extremely limited property in material cultural goods, one expects from the outset only a limited development of *counting* and the number system." Here, we have what seems to me to be a rational and thoughtful description and explanation of a simple numbering system, one that accounts for simplicity (or the comparative lack of complexity) as a function of need, rather than as a reflection of deficient mental capabilities on the part of the people in question. This view is reinforced later when Gusinde notes:

> *Almost never, however, does one [i.e., the Selk'nam] strive for scrupulous mathematical exactness in figures,* since no one feels the need for it. *It therefore seems as if these Indians always act in the loftiest fashion in statements of numbers and amounts, whereas in reality the* linguistic expressions *for unequivocal exactitude are lacking. (Gusinde 1931: 1107; my emphases)*

To credit simplicity in a particular domain of culture to the absence of a need for complexity helps us to avoid absurd arguments suggesting that the vocabulary and conceptions current in any particular area of the culture of adults in a fully *Homo sapiens* community reflects a lower stage of the evolution of intelligence. The latter interpretation can easily (and unfortunately) be drawn from statements in Piaget and Hallpike's characterizations concerning the "pre-operatory" level of apprehension of numbers on the part of "primitive" peoples (Piaget 1972; see also Hallpike 1979). Hallpike does provide disclaimers on this point. For instance:

> *One is therefore not implying that adults in primitive society are intellectually merely the equivalent of children in our society, but that in primitive societies cognitive skills predominantly of the pre-operatory type will be developed to a very high degree of skill and that these will be complemented by the accumulation of experience and wisdom throughout the lifetime of the individual. (1979: 39–40)*

Such disclaimers notwithstanding, the overall thrust of Hallpike's presentation is to place "primitive" thinking roughly on a par with that of children in "modern" societies. This is easier for him to accomplish, given the absurd criteria that he establishes for evaluating "primitive" thinking in a more favorable way.

> *. . . if we, as ethnographers, had found that members of primitive societies were, for example, quite capable of generalizing to us in abstract terms about the way in which their societies worked and the purposes of their institutions, of distinguishing between logical and narrative order in their myths, of discussing with us logical flaws in argument and analysing the structure of their syntax, even though they were not accustomed to talking in this way among themselves, we should rightly conclude that primitive thought was nothing more than a response to local circumstances and had nothing to do with the cognitive capacities of individuals. But we do not find that primitives can in fact communicate in these ways. . . . (1979: 57)*

The only comment I would make in response to Hallpike's final point is that neither do we find that 95 percent of adult Americans could accomplish the tasks he establishes for "primitives" in order to demonstrate to him that they are mature and "logical!"

Thus, the position that I adopt on the significance of different levels of complexity in a particular area of culture, knowledge, and practice as found in different cultures—as we might have need to explain significant differences, such as, for instance, why American kinship terms and relations are so impoverished *vis-a-vis* Australian Aranda, Kariera, or

Walpiri terms (see Ascher 1991: 70–81)—is that the differences ought to be viewed as products of the varying levels of interest that the people of each society have in the subject matter at hand and/or of the different types and levels of tasks to which they expose the bodies of knowledge and practice in question. This position is consistent with that articulated by Cole et al. (cited in Crump 1990: 22) in their study of learning among the Kpelle of Liberia: "cultural differences in cognition reside more in the situations to which particular cognitive processes are applied than in the existence of a process in one cultural group and its absence in another."

At this point, the reader might well be asking: What does this digression on the Siriono and Selk'nam have to do with the Quechua? Surely after the above discussion of weaving we can be confident that the Quechua people do have a complex numbering system and a sophisticated ability to count. I can establish the relevance of the above discussion with the following brief anecdote.

One day I and a few young men, who were employed by the development project ASUR to work on the promotion of textile production in and around the town of Candelaria, were watching the *Mamas* as they received cash payments for their weavings. I became aware that as most of the women received their handsful of money, they would go immediately to one or the other of a couple of women in the group and hand her their money. The woman who received the money would count it and then hand it back to the first woman. When I asked the men from ASUR what was going on, I was informed that most of the *Mamas* "can't count." This explanation was as shocking to me then as it may be now to the reader. How can we account for the fact that most *Mamas*—women who spend the better part of every day counting threads in warping and weaving textiles—are unable to count the money they earn from their labor?

In this case, I think it is fair to say quite concretely (unlike the generalized statement given by Holmberg for the Siriono) that the *Mamas* of Candelaria are, indeed, *unable to count money.* The qualifier "money" is, of course, crucial. For we know that the *Mamas*—"the origin of numbers"—can indeed count threads in extremely complex and sophisticated ways. That they *cannot* count money is thus not a result of the lack of a knowledge of numbers, nor is it due to an inability to use numbers abstractly to compare sets of objects of different magnitudes. Rather, their inability to count money is perhaps partially a consequence of their unfamiliarity with the basic units of the currency, but more likely (I have a strong suspicion) it is due to a fear of taking sole responsibility for counting their profits. For it is in the market and in their exposure to the money economy where *campesinos* are most often at a disadvantage and can most easily be cheated.

What we can conclude from the above observations is that counting is a culturally specific activity, grounded in the rules, routines, needs and values peculiar to each society. It is only in terms of an evaluation of "counting" as a generalized kind of *activity* (see Kitcher's comments on collec*ting vs.* collec*tion;* above), based on daily practices and procedures, that we can meaningfully compare numbering and counting systems from one culture to another.

Quechua Arithmetic
as an Art of Rectification

Introduction

In discussing arithmetic and mathematical operations and philosophy in Quechua language and culture, we need to begin by reviewing four topics that will help lay the groundwork for ideas and practices relating to addition, subtraction, multiplication, and division presented later in this chapter. These topics include: (a) the evidence for the high level of mathematical knowledge and practice among pre-Hispanic Andean societies; (b) the arithmetic implications and uses of terms which, on the surface at least, appear to be mathematically oriented; (c) the notions of "key concepts" and "core terms" that I want to introduce into this discussion; and (d) the cohering, philosophical principle of Quechua arithmetic as a set of processes aimed at "rectification."

Arithmetic Operations and Mathematical Concepts in Pre-Hispanic Societies

Evidence that Andean peoples, such as the Quechuas, Aymaras, "Yungas" (Chimus), and the ancestors of these and other groups, engaged in sophisticated manipulations of numbers, sets, geometrical shapes and surfaces, etc., before the arrival of the Spaniards is seen clearly in the archaeological record. For example, there is ample testimony in pre-Columbian textiles that Andean weavers were among the most skillful people in history in the arithmetic arts of counting, of creating and manipulating sets of threads in highly complex patterns (Cereceda 1987, 1990; Conklin n.d.; Desrosiers 1992) and even of reproducing—in the flat, two-dimensional surfaces of fabrics—the illusion of perspective (Sawyer 1967). In the engineering arts, the Inkas (like other Andean peoples before them) developed highly complex traditions of geometrical knowledge and mathematical calculations for dealing with the challenges of load, mass, the fracturing patterns of stones, etc., in cutting and seamlessly fitting together massive, irregularly shaped polygonal blocks of exceptionally hard stone into some of the most impressive architectural forms known in the New World (see Protzen 1993). In metallurgy, the products of which were, of course, of utmost interest to the gold-hungry *conquistadores,* Andeans had developed, beginning several centuries before the time of Christ, means for extracting precious metals from their ore-bearing deposits, of processing silver using mercury, and of mixing metals to produce a variety of types of alloys. All of these activities demanded considerable skill in manipulating and "mixing" (*chakruy*) substances in precise ratios and proportions (see Lechtman 1980; Shimada, Epstein, and Craig 1983). The astronomical and calendrical systems that were developed by Andean peoples demonstrate a high level of achievement in observing, recording, and intercalating periodicities of a variety of astronomical cycles to produce accurate annual solar calendars. Such bodies of knowledge and precise calculations were used in the construction of calendars for the coordination and regulation of agriculture, herding, and other economic activities, as well as of ceremonial and ritual observances (Earls 1972; Urton 1988; Sullivan 1985; Zuidema 1982, 1990).

Finally, as discussed more thoroughly elsewhere (Chapters 1 and 6), evidence for sophisticated traditions of numeration and mathematical knowledge and practice ranging from the "basic" procedures of addition, subtraction, multiplication, and division, to more complex quantitative manipulations, such as the calculation of fractions, ratios, etc., are at least indirectly documented for the Quechua, Aymara, and other peoples of the pre-Hispanic Andes in the knot records of the *khipus* (see, for example, Ascher and Ascher 1969, 1975, 1981; Mackey 1990; Radicati de Primeglio 1979; and Zuidema 1989). Although the Aschers have argued convincingly that the *khipus* do not appear to have been used in the manner of, for example, abacuses actually to make arithmetic calculations, nonetheless, the numbers that are recorded on certain of the *khipus* clearly express the *results* of such calculations. One of the best sources of information for reconstructing the methods whereby such calculations may have been carried out are the colonial documents that contain Spanish translations and transcriptions of native readings of *khipus* (Urton n.d.).

From achievements in these and other areas, it is clear that Andean peoples had developed highly complex systems of numeration and arithmetic and mathematical calculations in pre-Hispanic times. The importance of these observations for our purposes here is that to the degree that Quechua was the language of communication used by pre-Hispanic populations in different times and places in the Andes, we may suppose that its grammar, syntax, and lexicon evolved to accommodate the requirements of communication with respect to the various substances—fiber, stone, metals, celestial bodies, and numbers—manipulated in the arts and crafts mentioned above, as well as to the quantification and arithmetic manipulation of relations among properties of those objects and substances as they were brought into contact with one another in cultural productions, such as textiles, calendars, *khipu* accounts, and so on. I argue that many of these same grammatical structures and lexical items are still a part of the Quechua language spoken today. It is the latter that we will explore in this chapter.

The main point that I want to make in the introduction to this chapter is that, unlike much of South America, where we lack explicit historical or ethnographic evidence for highly developed practices and procedures for the manipulation of numbers according to such basic arithmetic operations as addition, subtraction, etc., we *do* possess such evidence in the case of the Andes. Therefore, when we examine (as I intend to do in this chapter) linguistic and other evidence for Quechua arithmetic and mathematical concepts, we will be doing so in the context of a culture that has a long and well-documented history of the existence of such ideas and activities. These comments raise a broader and more perplexing issue for our study of the language of arithmetic and mathematics.

The Arithmetic Implications of "Mathematical" Terms

I would venture to say that in any given language on which one might wish to focus, one could encounter terms and grammatical constructions that would serve as appropriate glosses for what we would recognize (in

English) as constituting an "arithmetic" vocabulary. For instance, every language undoubtedly has words that could be used to translate fairly accurately the English words "add," "subtract," "multiply," and "divide." The universality of such terms doubtlessly results from the fact that these terms refer to operations and forms of action that are fundamental strategies of human life, regardless of the cultural setting (see Brown 1991 and Dixon 1977 on lexical and semantic universals). For example, semantic equivalents of the terms mentioned above would be needed by people in any society to talk about circumstances in which (respectively): (a) one quantity is put together with another; (b) one member of a group is removed from that group; (c) an operation is performed repeatedly; and (d) a quantity of things is apportioned out in some fashion (equally, unequally, etc.).

Now, in English, we would have no difficulty in assigning the terms "addition," "subtraction," "multiplication," and "division," respectively, to the series of circumstances mentioned above. I suspect, in fact, that *every* language has a term or grammatical construction that would fairly accurately correspond in meaning to each of these circumstances, operations, or states of being. But the point that I am driving at, and what is critical for our discussion here, is that in English, at least, the terms used to describe everyday occurrences of these circumstances are *also* used, in more technical senses, to refer to the manipulation by these various operations of more abstract entities, such as *numbers* and *sets*. These terms (among others), then, define a part of the language of arithmetic in the English language and culture(s). The question for us here is: To what degree can such "arithmetic-like" terms and grammatical constructions in another culture be taken to constitute evidence for actual, technical *arithmetic* and *mathematical* knowledge and practices on the part of the people of the society who speak that language? For instance, to what extent are we justified in inferring a technical, *arithmetic* significance for the term "addition" when people use their term for that operation in merely talking about the everyday activity of "putting one thing/quantity together with another?"

The positions that I would take with respect to the questions raised above are the following. First, it is clear that when "arithmetic terms" are used explicitly in the manipulation of numbers (as in craft production, storytelling, etc.), we of course can pursue a direct analysis of the arithmetic implications of these terms and grammatical constructions in that language and culture. Second, when the arithmetic application of such terms is not made explicitly but can be consistently inferred from the evidence for complex procedures in the manipulation of quantities and sets of objects in craft production—as in warping and weaving threads in the production of textiles, or of complex formulas for mixing substances in metallurgy—such information can be interpreted as indirect evidence for the existence of bodies of knowledge and practice relating to what is classified, in Western science, as "arithmetic operations." Third, when arithmetical terms referring to the actual manipulation of numbers are found in the historical documents pertaining to a society (as in the Spanish accounts that chronicle highly complex accounting procedures performed by bureaucrats of the Inka state), but when that society has subsequently experienced a long history of colonization and an active process of "underdevelopment" (thereby creating the conditions for the loss of those earlier forms of arithmetic knowledge and practice), then I think we are justified in pursuing a mathematical interpretation of the lexicon of arithmetic-like terms and grammatical constructions in the language linking the contemporary peoples with their precolonial forebearers. This is a legitimate undertaking since we know—according to the terms of the historical conditions outlined above—that arithmetic ideas and practices formed a part of the forces shaping the linguistic and cultural traditions of the ancestral speakers of that language. And fourth, in the case of a society for which we have no explicit historical or ethnographic evidence for the practice of the mathematical "sciences" (either in the direct application of mathematical operations to numbers, or in indirect evidence for such practices in complex craft production, etc.), then we cannot pursue with any confidence a mathematical interpretation of the arithmetic-like terms and grammatical constructions that, as I have pointed out above, will undoubtedly exist in the language spoken in that society.

On the grounds of the abundant evidence for the existence of the first three circumstances outlined above among past and present-day Quechua-speaking populations, I argue that we have every reason to pursue with confidence an interpretation of the arithmetic significance of lexical, syntactic, and semantic elements of mathematical-like terms in the Quechua language spoken today in the Andes. To be more precise about the actual vocabulary of arithmetic terms that may have been used in the Quechua spoken in the area of southern Peru and Bolivia in pre-Hispanic times, we can take note of what types of arithmetic operations are implied on the basis of the evidence of the numbers that the Inka bureaucrats appear to have recorded on the *khipus*. From their studies of the numbers recorded on the Inka *khipus,* Ascher and Ascher (1981: 151–152) have concluded that "the body of arithmetic ideas used by the Incas must have included, at a minimum, addition, division into equal parts, division into simple unequal fractional parts, division into proportional parts, multiplication of integers by integers, and multiplication of integers by fractions."

Therefore, in our study of the lexicon and grammar of arithmetic operations in Quechua, we should find that the language is adequate for talking precisely, and in detail, about the above operations—*at a minimum.*

Key Concepts and Core Terms in Quechua Mathematics

The vocabulary of what I propose to call "key concepts" in Quechua arithmetic and mathematics is large, and the meanings or glosses of these terms in English are varied. By "key concept," I am referring to a classification of concepts that represents basic forms of human action in the world—concepts such as "make," "talk," "walk," "carry," etc. Among such arguably universal concepts, I would include the four basic arithmetic operations that we are concerned with here: addition, subtraction, multiplication, and division. Furthermore, I argue that a general feature of such operations and concepts is that there will be a number of different words in the language under investigation (the so-called target language) that will share the semantic domain occupied by the key concept. The characteristic of key concepts notwithstanding, I also argue that among the various terms there will be one, or perhaps (at most) a couple, that will define and evoke most directly and powerfully the semantic domain of the key concept; such a term I will refer to here as the "core term." To summarize, a core term is a word in the target language that occupies the "center" of the semantic domain of the key concept under investigation. The central challenges raised by these notions are, first, the identification of core terms in the language and culture under analysis, and second, the identification of a particular term in the language of analysis (in this case English) that can be used to translate accurately the "core terms" of the key concept in the target language.

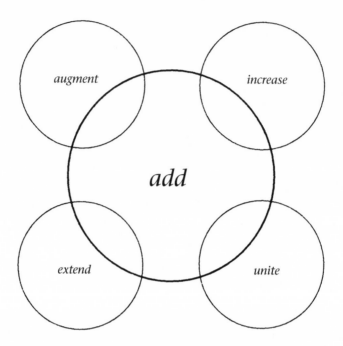

FIGURE 5.1.   The core term "add" and related terms.

The best way to clarify the points I am trying to make above is by appeal to a specific example; this I will do by considering the first arithmetic operation to be analyzed below: "to add; addition." The word "add" is the core term for the semantic domain of a key concept in English that also includes: "augment," "increase," "extend," "unite," "join together," and a few other terms. A part of the meaning of each one of this series of words intersects with the meaning of the English word "add" (see Figure 5.1).

Of the five words in the diagram in Figure 5.1, the semantic field which they all share—that is, the area of the four subsidiary circles included within the central circle—is defined by the core term "add." Add is the core term because it may be used as a gloss for the other four terms, whereas none of the four peripheral terms is an appropriate gloss for all the others.

The question now is: What term in Quechua (if any) can occupy the central place of a group of interlocking circles, like those in Figure 5.1, the central member of which has a meaning approximating that of the

English word for the arithmetic operation "to add"? As we will see below, this term in Quechua is *yapay*. The principal gloss of *yapay* (the infinitive form) in colonial Quechua–Spanish dictionaries is the Spanish word *añadir*, "to add." Putting aside for the moment various objects that are accorded special linguistic treatment (especially things considered to be natural "pairs," such as the hands), any act of putting two or more things together is, or can be, referred to as *yapay*. *Yapay* also refers to the activity of adding two or more numbers together to obtain a sum.

This discussion helps establish a methodology for presenting and analyzing the language and cultural practices associated with arithmetic operations in Quechua. That is, for each operation—addition, subtraction, multiplication, and division—we will need both to identify the core term of that operation and concept in Quechua and to investigate other terms that are peripheral to, but still evocative of, the key concept (this strategy is similar to Mannheim's [1991: 188–200] analysis of "associative sets" of terms in Quechua). Before doing so, however, we should explore in greater detail and depth the ideology and values motivating arithmetic and mathematical practice in Quechua language and thought. This involves a peculiar attribution and significance attached to the term discussed above—*yapa(y)*.

Arithmetic as Rectification

As a basis for examining both the philosophical conceptions and practices relating to arithmetic operations in Quechua language and culture, we have to take account of the purpose and motivation for which such operations are considered to be appropriate actions. The question here is whether or not there exist any prototypical conditions or values that motivate the execution or performance of any one of the arithmetic operations in Quechua ideology. That there is one such overarching value, and that this is one feature that clearly distinguishes Quechua arithmetic practice and mathematical conceptions from those in the West, has already been alluded to in the introduction to this study.

The purpose, or what I would call the teleology of Quechua arithmetic practice, is realized in a principle that I will refer to here as "rectification." Simply stated, rectification is grounded in the idealistic, philosophical, and cosmological notion that all things in the world—from material objects to habits, attitudes, and emotions—ought to be in a state of balance, or equilibrium. Depending on the object(s) in question, "balance" can have, among other forms, a distributive, constitutive, or moral significance. For instance, if duties, goods, or resources are distributed in an inappropriate way, as defined according to Quechua *cultural* values, then an act of (re)distributive adjustment should be carried out in order to address the imbalance. Adjustment can take a number of different forms, depending on the particular circumstances that brought about the state of imbalance in the first place; for instance, one circumstance may call for redividing the items in question, taking something from one site (subtraction) and applying it to another (addition). At the moral level, the principal cause of the emergence of a state of imbalance and disequilibrium is attributed to a variety of activities known collectively (that is, as a "class" [*laya*]) as *qhincha*. Such activities include adultery, lying, theft, and other forms of bad behavior, *all* of which represent acts that disturb the balance of social relations. Persons engaging in *qhincha* must mend their ways, that is, (re)establish rectitude, by changing their behavior and, if possible, by making restitution for the harm done to society, the family, etc.

Now, I stated above that rectification takes a variety of forms. In the contexts that we are interested in, the major forms of rectification include addition, subtraction, multiplication, and division. While each of these concepts and practices has a variety of labels in different mathematical contexts (see below), collectively they are grouped together as corrective actions aimed—each in a slightly different way from the others—at achieving rectification in a circumstance of imbalance, disequilibrium, and disharmony. The inclusive label for these four forms of corrective action is *yapa*.

As discussed above, in a limited technical sense *yapa* has the meaning "addition"; the verb form *yapay* means "to add." *Yapa* will be recognized by anyone who has ever lived and worked in the Andes as one of the most common terms used in market transactions. That is, when one purchases some item of food—from fruits and vegetables to meat and coca leaves—from a vendor, it is customary for the vendor to give a small "additional" quantity of the product to the buyer. This additional quantity is referred to as the *yapa*—or, more commonly, "*yapita*" ("a little extra"). In such transactions, the *yapa* expresses appreciation to the buyer for making the purchase and "asks"—through the obligation created by the spirit of prestation, which partially underlies the giving of a *yapa*—the buyer to return to the vendor in the future. As Marcel Mauss

(1967 [1925]: 6–12) noted long ago, gifts (of which the *yapita* is one Andean example) help to establish and maintain social relations and interactions having, as they do, a force calling for reciprocity in the form of a response, generally in the form of a counter gift. The theme of the *yapita,* then, is the theme of the gift in general; it is the agent of action in the cycle of disequilibrium (created by the initial gift) and the regaining of equilibrium accomplished in the return gift. As we will see below, this is as well the central theme of *yapa* as it is concerned with arithmetic procedures used as strategies for regaining equilibrium, or achieving rectification.

Beyond the common uses of *yapa* discussed above, the term also has the technical sense of one of a variety of means of affecting corrective actions addressing disharmony, *qhincha,* disequilibrium, etc. On this level, the arithmetic operations of addition, subtraction, multiplication, and division all constitute different forms of *yapa.* Thus, to return momentarily to the question of the relationship between *yapa* and the gift and the return gift, in Quechua arithmetic philosophy, *yapa* has more the status of the return gift, which reestablishes equilibrium by complying with the requirement to reciprocate, rather than the original, disequilibrium-provoking gift. We must stop to ask specifically what is the logic whereby, for instance, subtraction and division are classified as alternative forms of *yapa,* a term whose primary meaning is "addition"? The answer is that, since, according to the foundational logic of the arithmetic system, subtraction and division will only be performed in order to rectify an imbalance, therefore, the performance of either one of these operations will have the effect of moving an existing situation of imbalance *toward* a state of balance. That is, subtraction, for instance, is a form of "augmentation/addition," or *yapa,* when the effect of the act of subtraction is to cause things to become *more* balanced and harmonic. The general label for, and the prototypical form of, the "sameness of effect" of the four arithmetic operations is *yapa.*

This characterization of the term and concept *yapa,* which constitutes what we could call the first principle of Quechua arithmetic and mathematics, is the appropriate logical and cultural point of departure for a study of Quechua mathematical operations because it provides the rationale for the conceptualization of arithmetic and mathematics both as a type of human activity and as a cultural production. It should be clear from this outline how radically Quechua mathematics differs from at least certain traditions of pure mathematics (especially formalism) in the West. In the latter, mathematics neither has nor needs justification for its practice beyond the full and free exploration of the properties of number(s). On the other hand, since in no case are mathematical theories in the West founded on the basis of a well-articulated set of sociocultural principles, nor do they have a specific motivation, set of values, fixed goals, or utility comparable to the goal of "rectification" that motivates Quechua mathematical practice, Western mathematics has had a far more difficult time articulating its purpose and meaning—hence, the vast, and decidedly arcane, literature in the West relating to the exploration of the logical and philosophical foundations of mathematics. For instance, as the great mathematician G. H. Hardy (1967 [1940]: 119–120) noted, in his waning years: "The 'real' mathematics of the 'real' mathematicians, the mathematics of Fermat and Euler and Gauss and Abel and Riemann, is almost wholly 'useless' (and this is as true of 'applied' as of 'pure' mathematics). It is not possible to justify the life of any genuine professional mathematician on the grounds of the 'utility' of his work."

I should stress that the view expressed in this quotation from Hardy is not to be taken to represent a consensus view on the part of all Western mathematicians. For even as vehement a defender of Platonism as Frege argued that the proper business of mathematics was the analysis of what makes its applications possible, and that it was this that renders mathematics a science (Dummett 1991: 300–301).

To return to the topic of rectification in Quechua arithmetic philosophy, what is required for the practical operation of an "arithmetic of rectitude" is a set of terms for comparing and evaluating the relative size, power (or force), quality, and other such features of one object or set of things with respect to another, as well as terms mandating the (re)establishment and maintenance of harmony, equilibrium, and balance. Before giving examples of these two types of terms, I want to note that the general act of "comparing" things is referred to as *tinkuchiy* ("to cause things to be brought together"). Terms used then for evaluating the results of comparisons include (but are not limited to): "much, or too much/many" (*ashka; ancha*); "greater, or more than" (*astawan*); *aswan ashka* indicates that one is "more than two times" the other (as 33 is to 16); *aswan ancha kuraq* indicates that one unit is "three times larger"

TABLE 5.1

Examples of the Language of Equilibrium and Rectification

Quechua	English
ayniy	(v.) to cooperate, reciprocate (esp. in labor exchanges)
aysamuy	(v.) to provide a counterbalance
chimpuy chimpu	(adj.) equality of measure(ment)
kalin kalin	(adj.) in balance, equilibrium (esp. as in the equal distribution of weight)
kikinchachiy	(v.) to make things alike (e.g., to even them out)
kuskachay	(v.) to even out in weight; to divide/distribute the weight evenly; to level out, or even up, the liquid in two or more glasses
purachiy	(v.) to cause to be alike; to even out (esp. in weight)
ujchanakuy	(v.) to divide things up in an equal manner; to convert something into two equal groups

than another (as 48 is to 16); "little, or less" (*pisi*); "much less" (*aswan pisi*); and "to be insufficient, or to lack [something]" (*pisiy*). Terms indicating acts and/or processes of "evening out, or establishing a balance of things" include those defined in Table 5.1.

Having laid out above the terms and principles that will help guide our description and analysis of Quechua arithmetic and mathematics, we now turn to the analysis of the language and culture of the principal arithmetic operations. Given that we cannot be exhaustive in our presentation, the strategy that I will adopt in the following discussions of specific arithmetic operations will be, first, to present the basic terminology representing the core term(s) of each of the key concepts, and second, to then provide examples of the application of these terms and the various forms of action that they denote in as many different settings as I am aware of. It is hoped that such a strategy, combining language and practice, will provide the reader with a clear and comprehensive understanding of the role and meaning of the various arithmetic operations in Quechua language and culture. Again, I would emphasize that the purpose for discussing this information is to suggest, on the basis of our sound knowledge of the existence of fairly complex arithmetic and mathematical practices in the pre-Hispanic Andes, that somewhere within the various broad semantic fields of arithmetic terms and concepts outlined below there are doubtlessly situated many of the fundamental ideas, principles, and practices underlying Quechua arithmetic and mathematics as they have been conceptualized and put into operation in Andean communities over time.

I will introduce each of the following four subsections by providing English definitions of the verbal and nominal forms of the arithmetic operations in question. The source of these definitions is *Webster's New Collegiate Dictionary* (1956). These definitions are *not* intended to (de)limit the nature or range of Quechua linguistic and ethnographic data to be taken account of in the discussion that follows; rather, my purpose in giving these definitions is to establish, through a set of core terms in English, a shared (between myself and the reader) vocabulary and point of departure from which to investigate Quechua glosses and activities pertaining to the particular arithmetic operation under consideration in each subsection.

Finally, I would note that, for sentence-level constructions employing various terms for the different mathematical operations that are discussed in the following sections, I have made use of examples provided in the excellent (Bolivian) Quechua dictionary of Herrero and Sánchez de Lozada (1983).

To Add; Addition

Add, v.t. . . . 1. *To join or unite so as to increase the number, augment the quantity, or enlarge the magnitude.* 2. *To combine into one sum or quantity.* 3. *To append.*

Addition, n. . . . 4. Math. *The process of combining two or more numbers so as to obtain a number called their sum . . . Syn. Accretion, increment, accession.*

Sum, n. . . . 5. *The number or quantity resulting from the addition of two or more numbers or quantities . . . ; an aggregate; a total.*

As I have already noted, the Quechua term that most centrally defines the action "to add" is *yapay*. For example: *Manaraj romananchej khuskan pesadata oqharisanchu; uj loq'o junt'ata jinatawan papata **yapay**.* ("The needle of the balance is still not showing 50 kilos; **add** a sombrero full of potatoes more.") We also saw earlier in this chapter that just as the English word "add" shares semantic space with other terms (see esp. Figure 5.1), so, too, is this true for *yapay*. These words can be grouped logically and semantically under four different but related headings. In order to arrive at a comprehensive understanding of *yapay* and, thus, to appreciate the full and varied significance of "addition" in Quechua, we need to take account of the overlap in meaning among *yapay* and the four other word groups organizing the information listed in Table 5.2.

Several comments are in order regarding the information in Table 5.2. First, I do not pretend that the terms included under each heading are exhaustive. Unless otherwise noted, the terms listed are ones that I have either heard used explicitly in the field or in interviews, or which were given by my principal informant, Primitivo Nina, as illustrations of the meaning and significance of a particular additive form, strategy, or concept. Second, in those cases in which a particular number is mentioned in the formation of a term or phrase (for example, *chunka* = "ten"), the specific number should be taken as illustrative; that is, in most cases, and speaking in general terms, any other number could substitute for the one that is given. However, this general statement needs some qualification. In practice, constructions such as *chunkachay* ("to bring the number up to ten") and *chunkamuy* ("to add on more until ten is reached") will tend to employ *even* numbers (since odd numbers are considered, by their nature, to be "incomplete"; see Chapter 2) if not full decimal unit values (as 10, 20, 100, . . .). The third point to stress, or actually to reemphasize, is that the terms included in Table 5.2 share a part of their meaning with the core term *yapay* ("to add"). For example, the meaning of the verb *t'inkiy* ("to bind, put together") is seen in the following usage to share semantic value with "to add": *Wallpastaqa chakipurata watarqospa iskaymanta iskay **t'inkiy*** ("Join/bind the chickens together two by two, tying them together by their feet"). The term *yapay* articulates, directs, and focuses the various meanings of this collection of terms as representative not only of the arithmetic operation

TABLE 5.2

Word Groups Related to *Yapay* ("to add")

Word Groups	Quechua	Translation or Commentary
1. *"augment"*:		
	palltay	(v.) to place a small, supplemental quantity on top of the principal (and larger) quantity; specifically used to refer to placing a smaller load (*carga*) on top of the main load
	patampi	(adj.) one on top of the other/another
	umallikuy	(v.) to perform one action "on top of" another (*-lli* = "to place on top of"; see *wiqsalliy*)
	uywakuy	(v.) to adopt; to take on additionally
	wiqsalliy	(v.) to make pregnant; i.e., to place one/another child "on top of" the (mother's) stomach
	yupaykakamuy	(v.) to add one's self to an existing group (depending on one's own volition)
2. *"unite"*:		
	tantay	(v.) to reunite (bring back together)
	t'inkiy	(v.) to chain, link, or bind together (as in uniting, or joining together, a suffix with a verb root)
	t'ullkuy	(v.) to double (as in plying threads together)
	ujchakuy	(v.) to group together; to unite; to increase the group (-ing)
3. *"expand"*:		
	ashkayachiy	(v.) to increase, augment (but to do so through a third party)*
	jatunyachiy	(v.) to stretch (out); to cause to grow; to increase, promote*
	wiñay	(v.) to grow, increase (in an activist, interventionist sense, as in Clinton's phrase, "to grow the economy")

TABLE 5.2

(*continued*)

Word Groups	Quechua	Translation or Commentary
4. *"part-to-whole"*:		
	ch'ullantin	(n.) pair; i.e., the two natural parts (of a pair) joined together
	chunkachay	(v.) to bring the number up to 10 (i.e., add whatever is necessary to arrive at 10)
	chunkamuy	(v.) to add on more until 10 is reached (i.e., if you want 10 and are only given 8, this is how you ask to have the quantity increased to the level requested)
	khalluntin	(n.) pair; i.e., two things bound/sewn together
	pañantin	(n.) two things of the same line, type, or "species" together (*paña* = "right")
	yuntantin	(n.) team; i.e., the two natural members of a work pair together

*-*chi* = causative suffix; added to a transitive verb, indicates action of ordering, motivating, or doing something *through an intervening third party,* apart from the speaker (Morató n.d.).

yapay but also of the *additive mode* of *yapa*—the "calculus of rectification" (see discussion of arithmetic as rectification, above).

In addition to the general terminology for "to add; addition" listed in Table 5.2, there are several ways of directly phrasing addition statements using numbers. Among these are the following:

a) *phishqa phishqa:* "5 5" [= 10]; as an expression of the operation of addition, I am aware of the use of this form only in the *doubling* of a single number word. The juxtaposition of two different number words, such as *kinsa tawa* ("three four"), is taken to be a statement of multiplication (i.e., *kinsa tawa* = 12).

b) *phishqamanta phishqawan . . . chunka:* "of/from 5 with 5 [is] 10."

c) *phishqayunta ch'ullayuq:* "a pair of fives together with an unpaired/odd one"—i.e., (5 + 5) + 1 [= 11]; this construction specifically characterizes the number sequence as an alternation of even (i.e., *yunta* = "pair"; even) and odd numbers (i.e., *ch'ullayuq* = "uneven"; that is, the one having a natural pair, but now separated from its partner).

d) *tawaq kuraqnin:* "four and its senior" [= 5]; *kuraqnin* has the sense of "the next higher one/number," or "plus one."

e) *taway tawa:* "4 'plus' 4" [= 8]; in such constructions, *-y* has the sense of "and," or "plus." Addition statements of this type are formed only when adding a number to itself (e.g., 4 + 4); however, this form is used only for numbers greater than 3 (it is not used for "1 + 1" or "2 + 2").

To Subtract; Subtraction

Subtract, v.t. *and* i. *To withdraw or take away, as a part from a whole or one number from another; deduct.*

Subtraction, n. . . . 2. Math. *Act or process of subtracting one number or quantity from another.*

Remainder, n. . . . 1. *Residue; residuum; remnant.* . . . 5. Math. *That which is left over after subtraction or any deduction; the undivided part, less than the divisor, left after division (cf.* quotient*).*

The core term in Quechua for the arithmetic operation of subtraction is *jurquy.* This term may be glossed in English as "take out," "extract," "remove," and "pull out/up." González Holguín gives the interesting usage *hurccuni humayman,* "tomar de memoria" ("to take from memory," or literally, "to extract from the head"). The act of telling a story from memory is thus considered to be based on an operation having a semantic relationship to the mathematical operation of removing, or "subtracting," a part from the whole. *Pisiyachiy* ("to make smaller/less") is also commonly used for the action of "subtraction." The following example of the use of *pisiyachiy* also emphasizes the notion of a state of "excess," which must be rectified: *Ancha ashkhata qosanki Estersita khuskanpaj khuskannintajina* **pisiyachiy** *chay qosqaykimanta* ("You're giving a huge quantity, Estercita, **reduce it** [the quantity] by about one-quarter [i.e., one-half of one-half]"). Terms for the various groupings, or subcategories, of "subtraction" are given in Table 5.3.

TABLE 5.3
Word Groups Related to *Jurquy* ("to subtract")

Word Groups	Translation or Explanation
1. *"Reduce/remove" (size/quantity):*	
q'intichiy	(v.) to reduce a little bit (i.e., minutely)
pisiyachiy	(v.) to diminish, lessen, decrease something; to discredit; to shorten, reduce
juch'uyay	(v.) to get small (but by a natural process, as the waning of the moon)
chhalaq	(adv.) lessen; reduction or lowering of the price in order to sell something
ujnintin	(adj.) diminished (literally: "brought together down to one"); omission of the last sound/syllable of a word
2. *"Reduce/lighten" (weight):*	
urquy	(v.) to reduce the weights on a balance (as by re-moving the weights)
qhituy	(v.) to reduce weight on a balance (as by rubbing, or scraping, the surface off the weights)
sulluchiy	(v.) to slip, slide; to cause to abort; to arrange a cargo poorly, so that a part falls off (esp. the *palta* [see "addition" terms])
3. *"Disunite/disaggregate":*	
t'aukaray	(v.) to level, dismantle, take apart, knock down
4. *"Remainder; part-of-whole":*	
ayphuyanayay	(v.) to parcel; to have/make a very small part
chhikanin	(n.) the little bit needed (in order to [be] complete)
kuraq	(n.) the rest, remainder, excess, surplus
puchun	(n.) left over, extra, remainder; part of the whole (fraction?)
q'asa	(n.) what is lacking (in order for something to be complete); chip (off); deduction; omission
t'una	(n.) fragment, change (as in the change remaining after a monetary transaction)

Compared to "addition," there are fewer phrases, or discursive strategies, that I am aware of for making subtractive statements using numbers. The ones that I am familiar with are the following:

iskayachiy: "to make 2 [through a third party]"; e.g., $x - y = 2$
tawaq qhipan: "of 4 the anterior [one]" (i.e., $4 - 1 = 3$)
tawaq sullk'an: "of 4 the younger [one]" (i.e., $4 - 1 = 3$)

As has been noted in many contexts, subtraction and addition are inverse operations (see, for example, Piaget's analysis [1969: 175–181] of the progressive, developmental discovery of this fact). That is, every statement or act of addition may be reversed so as to become a statement or act of subtraction, a fact that we are aware of and make use of in our everyday practice of checking addition by subtraction, and vice versa. Beyond this, what is interesting about subtraction is the status of what I have referred to in Table 5.3 as the "remainder," or the "part-of-whole." This value—the "remainder" that results from the process of matching one to one a part of a larger quantity with the whole of a smaller one (for example, $413 - 26 = 387$)—may become the reference value for fractional and proportional (or ratio) statements.

Now, the remainder in subtraction statements such as that given above has an "unfinished" quality to it. For example, the statement $413 - 26 = 387$ begs the questions: (a) How many times can 26 be subtracted from 413? (Answer: 15) And (b) what, if anything, remains after the last full unit of 26 has been matched with successively smaller sums produced by repeatedly subtracting 26 from 413? (Answer: 23) These two questions potentially move us from the domain of subtraction to division and fractions. Therefore, while deceptively simple on the surface, the language of subtraction raises for the native Quechua speaker a number of problems that require for their resolution various ways of talking about the four basic arithmetic operations in relation to each other. This—the inverse nature and the interrelations between sets of arithmetic terms and operations—represents one of the principal ways in which the motivations directing the language of "rectification" in Quechua arithmetic discourse (as in the use of any one of the terms in Table 5.1) will be phrased.

To Multiply; Multiplication

> Multiply, v.t. . . . 1. *To increase in number; to add quantity to.* 2. Math. *To take by addition a certain number of times.* . . . - v.i. *To become greater in number.*
> Multiplication, n. . . . 2. Math. *The process of repeating or adding any given number or quantity a certain number of times.* . . . *The inverse of division.*
> Multiple . . . - n. . . . 2. Math. *The product of a quantity by an integer; as 4 is a* multiple *of 2.*

In discussing multiplication, we are confronted with a somewhat different situation from what we found with addition and subtraction. For each of the latter operations, we were able to identify a core term of the key concept in question and then to group the various secondary terms under the core term. With multiplication, we have a situation in which there are actually two core terms, each related to a particular and unique aspect of the concept and operation of "multiplication." The English equivalents of the two core terms are *"turn"* and *"multiplicity."* The core term in Quechua for "turn" (or "times") is *kuti* (n., "turn(s), duplicate, repeat"); for "multiplicity," the core term is *miray* (v., "to multiply, augment, increase").

Two features of the process of multiplication, which are also seen in the English definitions, are worthy of special note. These are the link between multiplication and addition, on the one hand, and that between multiplication and division, on the other. The former is seen in the fact that multiplication is often difficult to distinguish from repeated addition. A first indication that these two operations may be distinct in Quechua is suggested by the two different syntactical and semantic strategies for forming compound number words and phrases (see Chapter 2). One action is termed *yapay* ("to add"), the other is *miray* ("to multiply"). In the *miray* principle, for example, *tawa chunka* ("four ten") is the construction used to denote the number "forty." While this kind of construction looks like a multiplicative statement, we cannot state definitively that such a phrase is conceptualized as multiplication rather than constituting instructions for the act of "repeated addition." I will address this ambivalence directly in discussing the ontology of "multi-

plication," below. It is interesting to note that such conceptual ambivalence is also present in the earliest mathematics book printed in the
West, the *Treviso Arithmetic,* which was printed in Treviso, Italy, in 1478.
In this work, multiplication is identified by the term *moltiplicare,* which
refers to the process of "repeated addition" (Swetz 1989: 197).

The connection between multiplication and division is found in English, as well as in the Italian of the *Treviso Arithmetic.* In the latter, we
read that: "To understand this [multiplication] it is necessary to know
that to multiply one number by itself or by another is to find from two
given numbers a third which contains one of these numbers as many
times as there are units in the other" (Swetz 1989: 197). This passage
makes it clear that multiplication and division are inverse processes
(i.e., $2 \times 4 = 8 /=/ 8 \div 4 = 2$). We will see in the Quechua data similar
links among multiplication, addition, and division (the link between
multiplication and division will be discussed more thoroughly in the
section on division, below).

In Table 5.4, I have organized the terms and suffixes relating to the
Quechua vocabulary and grammar for multiplication under the two
broad headings identified earlier—that is, *kuti* ("turn") and *miray* ("to
multiply, or augment").

The following are the grammatical constructions that I am aware
of that are used in making statements of multiplication employing
numbers:

iskay kinsa: "2 3" [= 6]
iskay tawaq kuraqnin: "the elder of 2 4" [i.e., $2 \times 4 + 1 = 9$]
kinsanchay: "to repeat three turns/times"
kinsakuti: "three turns/times"
kinsa kinsamanta chunka iskayniyuq mirachiy: "to cause to multiply
    twelve three times repeatedly" [i.e., $12 \times 3 = 36$]

The Ontology of "Multiplication"   The comments made thus far with
respect to multiplication concern terms and statements in Quechua for
particular aspects of the concepts involved in, or certain operations that
are potentially (although not necessarily exclusively) representative of,
multiplicative acts on numbers. What is lacking is an explanation of the
theoretical and conceptual foundations, or the ontology, of multiplication in Quechua. Such an understanding is important because (as

TABLE 5.4

Word Groups Related to *Kuti* ("turn") and *Miray* ("to multiply")

Word Groups	Translation/Commentary
1. *"turn"*	
kuti	(n.) turn, time(s); duplicate
kutipay	(v.) to imitate, repeat; to do something successively
kutin kutin	(adv.) repeat a thousand times (i.e., an "infinity" of times)
[number +]-*chay*	(v.) to repeat the specified number of "turns/times"; e.g., *tawanchay* ("to repeat four times")
-*rara*	(adv.) "how/so many times; repeatedly"
2. *"multiply/multiplicity"*	
askhayachiy	(v.) to cause to augment, multiply, or reproduce through the intervention of a third party
askhayay	(v.) to augment; multiply
miray	(v.) to multiply; multiplication; to augment a predetermined group of living beings (but not of things)
mirachiy	(v.) to cause to multiply (through the intervention of a third party)
-*riririy*	(enfix; v.) to multiply; to perform the action of the verb repeatedly
wiñashan	(v. 3rd per. sing.) it is multiplying, augmenting, accumulating, growing
-*ya*	(enfix) denoting a thing that engenders more things (of the same type); e.g., *qhapaqyay* ("to accumulate wealth")

pointed out above) multiplication seems to be so intertwined with at least two of the other basic mathematical operations, addition and division. How does multiplication differ from these other operations? *Does it actually differ from them,* or are these three operations perhaps bound together at various levels in ways that do not leave room for the ontological independence of any one of these concepts and operations? Given the ambiguity of the status of multiplication and the potential for confusion that exists with respect to these questions, I will clarify to the extent that I am able to do so how "multiplication" does, in fact, appear to have an independent ontological foundation in Quechua.

But first, we should take note of Hurford's comments following his demonstration that, in English (in which a similar confusion between multiplication and repeated addition is apparent, at least superficially), multiplicative constructions are in no sense—grammatically or logically—built on or derived from additive constructions.

> [T]he evolutionary relationship between addition and multiplication is not as conveyed by the usual picture of multiplication as serial addition. Multiplication emerges from pluralization, and addition from conjunction. In principle, although both multiplication and addition arise, I claim, from the same psycho-ontological scheme of aggregates and collections, a language could possibly develop multiplicative constructions before additive constructions. (Hurford 1987: 211; my emphases)

I will take Hurford's observations as the basis for arguing that the same holds true for Quechua as well and that, therefore, the challenge is to confirm the independence of pluralization (multiplication) from conjunction (addition).

In order to grasp the basic principle of "multiplication" in Quechua thought, we need to focus attention on two terms: *miray* and *askhayay*. *Mira*—which is identified in Table 5.4 in its infinitive form (*miray*) as one of two core terms for multiplication—has the basic meaning "from one, many appear." Now, females are considered to possess most profoundly the capacity for multiplication. More concretely, the capacity for multiplication, or pluralization, expressed in the term *miray* refers to the reproductive force situated in the female genitalia. The vagina is the prototypical object in the world of humans and animals that gives rise to more things, or examples, of the same type. In this regard, the vagina, which is commonly (and vulgarly) referred to in Quechua as *chupila* (literally: "a soup of meat and potatoes"), is the locus of the reproductive and creative powers of *"mama"*—the origin of numbers and ordinal sequences. *Miray*, then, refers to the capacity for augmentation, multiplication, and pluralization that is characteristic of a type of humans and animals—adult reproductive females. It is interesting to note at this point that González Holguín (1952 [1608]) glosses the terms *mirayhua* ("multiplier; reproducer") and *huahua ccoto* (literally: "baby pile") as "a woman or animal that multiplies [reproduces] a lot." I give below an example of the use of the verb *miray* to express the combined notion of the reproduction and "multiplication" of humans:

Walejilata Mamanikuna **miranku**, *ashkhaña kanku; kinsalla wayna kasajtiy chayamurqanku Putojsi qolqe qhoyamanta.* ("The Mamanis have **greatly increased/multiplied** in number; when I was young, only three of them came from the mine in Potosí.")

Like *miray,* the term *askhayay* ("augmentation") refers to the process of, and the capacity for, multiplication and pluralization identified in the expression, "from one, many appear." *Askhayay,* however, is more commonly used for the (re-)production of plant products from a seed. For instance, the "multiplication" that is realized in the act of planting a single seed potato and of receiving, at the time of the harvest, a multiplicity of potatoes is termed *askhayay.* I would suggest that the difference in terminology between human and plant "multiplication" is between the (generally) *one-by-one* reproduction of humans as opposed to the *exponential* reproduction of plants. Between these extremes of biological reproduction, there is the (often) *multiple* reproduction of animals.

To remain for a moment in the domain of plants, it is significant to note that, while Andean farmers recognize that many new potatoes can be produced by a single seed potato, nonetheless, potatoes are always (in my experience) planted in *pairs,* or occasionally in triplets, of seed potatoes. This is done in order to ensure that the farmer will receive from the patch of soil where each set of seed potatoes is planted a profusion, or a multiplicity, of new potatoes. The point here is that, although it is clear that Andean farmers are aware that a single seed potato has the potential to multiply and reproduce itself, such an outcome is considered to be more certain when two or three (i.e., "multiple") potatoes are planted together. That is, multiplicity of production is dependent upon a relationship between at least two representatives of the type in question (in this case, "seed potato"). This is, of course, true as well in both the human and animal domains. That is, although the reproduction and multiplication of a type or species in the human and animal domains comes about as a result of the birth of babies from the female body, nonetheless, this process requires the union of two sexually differentiated mem-

TABLE 5.5

Terms for Human and Animal Reproductive Partners

Set	Female	Male
Animal	*china*	*urqu*
Human	*warmi*	*qhari*

bers of the species. The terms used for the male and female of each of these reproductive sets, animal and human, are identified in Table 5.5.

I argue that Table 5.5 displays a model of the prototypical relations that underlie the key concept of multiplication, or pluralization, in Quechua ontology. I would stress that the two elements are not reproductive if they are only conjoined, or *added* together (see Hurford's point concerning the distinction between conjunction and pluralization in the quotation above). Such a process is, in fact, recognized as a potentiality in Quechua ideology; however, the result of conjunction is explicitly considered to be *non*-reproductive. That is, the addition or conjunction of the two terms and types produces an entity called *qhari-warmi* ("man-woman"); this is one of the terms (in addition to *mari-machu*, see Chapter 4) used to refer to a homosexual. Therefore, simply adding *qhari* to *warmi*, or *china* to *urqu*, does not cause multiplicity; rather "multiplicity" is the process of bringing the two different types (or sexes) together in a way—commonly (and vulgarly) referred to, in the case of humans and eatable animals, as *sachuy* ("to fuck")—that results in the multiplication or pluralization of the species (for non-eatable animals, the term used for this act is *tinkukuy*).

Thus, the quality of *mira* ("from one, many appear") is the process of setting in motion the multiplicative powers of the female through the *reproductive* interaction between the male and female. This general principle is expressed in the following example:

> *Uj china llamawan uj orqo llamallawan tiapuwarqayku, chaylla-manta iskay chunkamanña* **mirachiyku**. ("We had only one female and one male llama, and with this [pair] alone we have now succeeded in **increasing/multiplying** them up to a total of twenty.")

I should note that in this sentence, the causative suffix -*chi* is added to *miray* in order to indicate the action of causing, or bringing about, some action. In this case, the speaker's actions—of caring for the herd, etc.—caused, or were responsible for, the reproduction and multiplication of the llamas.

The material discussed above should help to clarify for us why we found so consistently in Chapter 3 that the reproduction of numbers and the production of ordinal sequences in the form of an age-graded set of siblings had as their origin the figure of *Mama,* the reproductive female. Beyond this point, however, the question that is raised by the above comments is: Are the relations and forces contained in the human/animal multiplicative model outlined in the above paragraph applied directly to the reproduction—but more specifically the *multiplication*—of numbers? That is, are *numbers* seen as having certain properties such that the multiplication of any two numbers may be likened to the *china/urqu//warmi/qhari* model? From what I understand, such a comparison cannot be made, at least not directly. The reason for this is that numbers are neither human nor animal; rather, numbers are *things*. Since both *miray* and *askhayay* refer specifically to the "multiplication/ multiplicity" inherent in living beings (plants, animals, and humans), there must be some other force or process that accounts for the reproduction of numbers.

The reproduction of nonliving things, of which numbers are an example, is specifically accounted for in relation to the actions implicit in the verb *askhayachiy.* This word has the sense, "to cause something to increase, augment, or multiply through the intervention (or action) of a third party." That is, the multiplicative power of things—such as numbers, commodities, and money—is not inherent within those things themselves; rather, it requires, and is the consequence of, the force(s) of pluralization and/or accumulation exerted by some interested party. In other words, what is required in order for numbers and other nonliving things to "multiply" is an *agent* who acts on the thing(s) in question. This is the role fulfilled by the individual who, for instance, performs the act of multiplying two numbers together, or who accumulates property (thereby becoming wealthy), and so on. I should note one exception to the general principles stated here; this is with the use of the term *miraynin* (ca., "it multiplies itself"), which refers to "profit" gained in a financial transaction and to "interest" earned on the loan of money.

Thus, while the analogy of human reproduction is discernible in metaphors of the reproduction and multiplication of numbers—thereby allowing us, for instance, to formulate the conceit: "the social life of numbers" as the title to this work—there is no confusion (so far as I am aware) in the minds of the Quechua-speaking actors who direct and control this drama-by-analogy as to the agency of the multiplication of numbers; that force is located in human actions—whether those actions be economic, linguistic, symbolic, or otherwise..

Finally, I would note that an analogy for, and an actual synonym of, the multiplicative action of *askhayachiy* is *wiñashan;* this is the third person progressive form of the verb *wiñay* ("to grow"). Whereas *wiñay* generally refers to the steady increase in size of an organism (human, animal, and/or plant), *wiñashan* refers specifically to the accumulation and acquisition of separate, namable and countable objects—such as one bicycle, another bicycle, a burro, a 100 Boliviano note. It is the form of accumulation of quantities of things identified as *askhayachiy* and *wiñashan* that is most directly characteristic of the multiplication of numbers.

To Divide; Division

Divide. 1. *To part asunder (a whole); to sever.* 2. *To cause to be separate; to keep apart by a partition, or by an imaginary line or limit.* 3. *To make partition of among a number; to apportion.* 4. *To make hostile; to set at variance.* 5. *To separate into classes or parts; to classify.* Syn. Separate, Distribute. . . .

Division, n. 1. *Act or process of dividing or state of being divided; separation; distribution* . . . 8. Math. *The process of, or rule for, finding how many times one number or quantity is contained in another.*

Of the four arithmetic operations that we are concerned with here, division is by far the most complex. This is reflected in the large number of terms and grammatical constructions in Quechua that denote one form, or principle, or another of this state or type of activity. The terms and grammatical constructions for divide/division are collectively highly nuanced, defining as they do a semantic domain for this key concept which is broader and richer than those of the other operations that we have considered up to this point. It is instructive to note in this regard that in the mathematics of fifteenth-century Europe, as character-

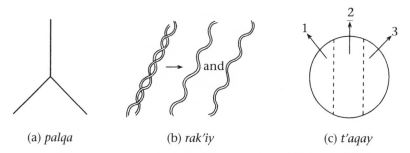

(a) *palqa*   (b) *rak'iy*   (c) *t'aqay*

FIGURE 5.2.   Core terms for "division": (a) *palqa* ("split, branch"); (b) *rak'iy* ("separate, analyze"); (c) *t'aqay* ("divide and apportion").

ized in the *Treviso Arithmetic,* division was also considered to be the most complex of all the arithmetic operations. A knowledge of division was considered to indicate proficiency in the other three operations (Swetz 1989: 212–213).

There are three core terms in Quechua that roughly correspond to different aspects or forms of the English core term "divide." The first of these is *palqay,* which refers to the formation of a division, or fork (as in a road or river). The second form is *rak'iy,* which is glossed in various contemporary Quechua dictionaries as "divide, distribute, separate, dispose." The act of *rak'iy* is essentially realized in the process of dividing or separating one large, complex object or entity into several smaller, simpler ones. A third form of "division" is identified by the verb *t'aqay,* which carries the sense of dividing up and then classifying and (re-)distributing a group or set of things. Figure 5.2 illustrates the three basic types of division outlined here.

In Figure 5.2a, we confront a situation in which, in moving from the top to the bottom of the figure, one encounters a "division," or "separation" of the line. This type of division is referred to as *palqa* (see the discussion of different classes of pitchforks in Chapter 3). An example of the use of this term would be: *Pichus wurruypaj ninrinta* **palqarqapis.** **Palqapacha** *ninrin* ("Who **split** my burro's ear in two so that its parts were left hanging? Its ear looks like a **fork**"). *Palqa* is also used to indicate a fork in a road or a river. Interestingly, *palqa* is not used for a fork in an irrigation canal because (I was told), since irrigation water passes *through* the canal, the canal divides the water only for a short time. This, then, is an episodic, temporary event; the canal will eventually dry up (the "division" of water in an irrigation canal is referred to by the term *rak'iy*).

In Figure 5.2b, we see an example of *rak'iy* based on the "division" of a plied thread. In this case, "division" refers to the "separation" of the component parts (the individual spun yarns) of the piece of thread. In *rak'iy*, a complex whole is "decomposed" into its constituent parts. For instance, combing (or "disentangling") one's hair could be an example of such action: *Qanraj chujchayta* **rak'iway***; chantá noqañataj* **rak'isqayki** ("You **comb** my hair first; then, in turn, I will **comb** yours").

We gain an interesting perspective on the meaning of *rak'i(y)*, as a form or process of division, from Chris Franquemont's comments on the use of this term in its duplicated form *rak'i rak'i*. Talking to a male nonweaver from Chinchero, Peru, about the names and significance of weaving designs, the man said of one fernlike design: "This is obviously *rak'i rak'i* . . . , like the *rak'i rak'i* that exists when a husband is in one land and his wife is in another, or a son is alive and his mother is dead." Franquemont (1986: 332) goes on to state that, "when two things are separate that should be together, they are *rak'i rak'i*."

Finally, Fig. 5.2c illustrates a type of division called *t'aqay*, which involves the partitioning and (re)distribution of the parts of a whole. *T'aqay* is the verb used when the act of "division" in question involves the classification and ordering by categories of different objects that are mixed together into a single group. The objects that are divided in an act of *t'aqa* are considered to be independent entities. For example, if you *separate* two bottles that are standing side by side, this is an act of *t'aqay*; however, if you break (thereby "dividing") one bottle in half, this is an act of *rak'iy*. The following examples will clarify both the independent nature of objects "divided" in the manner of *t'aqay* and the way in which this verb denotes the assignment of the objects that are separated to their appropriate place:

Uwijasninchejta ripunanchejpaj **t'aqana***.* ("Let's **separate** our sheep in order to go to our respective houses.")
Ama yachay wasi ukhupi qhariswan warmiswan chajrukun-qankuchu. Ujnejman qhari wawasta **t'aqanki***, wajnejmantaj warmi wawasta.* ("One should not mix males and females within the school house. Separate the boys and girls, putting the boys in one place and the girls in another.")

Given the variation and complexity of the forms of division illustrated in Fig. 5.2, it should be obvious that the use of "division" as a means of achieving rectification demands an intimate knowledge and a sophisticated understanding of Quechua ideas about the ways things are considered to be structured in their natural, "appropriate" state. That is, is some substance containing various parts composed of different examples of the same type, which can be "separated" (rak'iy)? Or is it composed of distinct types of things that can be classified, set apart from each other, and redistributed (t'aqay)? Clearly, such questions indicate the degree to which the language of arithmetic operations was (and is) an important tool in Quechua cosmological and classificatory practice. As for the antiquity of such ideas and values in Quechua language and culture, I would note that in his early-seventeenth-century dictionary of Quechua, González Holguín basically reproduces the same triadic classification of types, or forms, of "division" that we have outlined above (see Table 5.6).

I should comment on the lack of correspondence between the label for the third group of terms listed above (t'aqay) and the terms that are actually used for that form of division by González Holguín. That is, for the form of "division" that was defined earlier (see Figure 5.2c) as involving both the division *and* the distribution of portions of the thing divided, Holguín gives a verbalized form of the noun *aycha* ("meat"). This reflects the notion that the quintessential form of dividing and redistributing some resource in Quechua society involves not just cooked food, but the highest status type of food—meat. This same idea was repeated by my principal informant, Primitivo Nina, during a conversation in which he stated that the prototypical image of the "divider" in Quechua ideology is the woman/mother (the *"mama"*) who cooks food and then distributes it to the various members of the household, not giving to herself a full portion. This action is clearly expressed in the phrase given by González Holguín *aychani aycharccarini,* which he glosses as "to divide parts, or portions."

Table 5.7 will help us to appreciate the nature and dimensions of the forms and processes of division as conceptualized and articulated in Quechua. These terms could easily accommodate discursive statements about the operation of division in a great variety of arithmetic and mathematical contexts.

Aside from the use of the verb *rak'iy* ("to divide, fragment") to denote

TABLE 5.6

Forms of "Division" from González Holguín (1952 [1608])

Quechua "Division" Words and Forms	Spanish Translation	English Translation
palqay:		
pallca ñan	división de caminos	division of roads
pallcamayu	división de ríos	division of rivers
rak'iy:		
raquini raquir-		
ccayani raquir-ccarini.	dividir distribuir	to divide [in order] to distribute
raquiscca raquir-ccariscca	dividir cosa	to divide a thing
raquinacuni.	dividírselo entre sí	to be divided up among
t'aqay:		
aychani aychar-ccarini	dividir partes, o porciones	to divide parts, or portions
aychani aychacta	dar porciones de carne, o de otra cosa	to give portions of meat, or other thing
aycharcarini	repartir comida a muchos	to divide up food among many
aychanacuni	partir algo entre sí	to divide something up among

the process of dividing a group or set of things into different units, I do not know of specific statements of division using numbers. In my attempts to elicit terms for "quotient," I found that there is no general, technical term for this number; rather, there is only the term *rak'i* for the "equal share of a whole." This is, of course, approximately the sense of quotient. For instance, in a statement such as $12 \div 4 = 3$, what we would call the "quotient" (in this example, 3) is phrased in Quechua by

TABLE 5.7

Word Groups Related to the Three Forms of "Divide/Division"

Word Groups	Translation or Commentary
1. *Palqay*	
"separate/separation"	
jurk'a	(n.) separation; fork
kinsaman	(n.) a division, or separation into three parts
palqay	(v.) to divide, separate, fork
sayay	(v.) to separate, divide; to partition
t'isay	(v.) to "tease apart" wool in preparing it for spinning
2. *Rak'iy*	
"divide/separate/fragment"	
ch'apa ch'apa	(adj.) small pieces of something (e.g., leaves dried and crumbled up)
juch'uyachiy	(v.) to take apart one large/long thing in order to make two or more smaller ones
kinsapi	(adj.) division into three parts
p'itiy	(v.) to separate (esp. threads)
q'asay	(v.) to make a crack, division
rak'iy	(v.) to divide, separate, take apart; to make (an artificial) division
t'unay	(v.) to break into smaller parts; to fragment (e.g., used esp. for making change with currency)
wikhay	(v.) to divide up an entire unit into two or more portions
3. *T'aqay*	
"repartition/distribution"	
achuy	(v.) to distribute, repartition; also refers to the act of placing a weight on a scale; the act whereby a mother cat picks up her kittens by the scruff of the neck and places them where she wants them; to put in a particular place as a part of the act of (re-)distributing things

TABLE 5.7

(*continued*)

Word Groups	Translation or Commentary
chayachiy	(v.) to divide, distribute; to help conduct to a destination; to participate/share in an action
chiqllay	(v.) to select carefully, or to divide into types
ch'ullallaray	(v.) to classify to the point that you achieve "one-for-one" division/classification of a group of objects
iskay ukhu	(prep. phrase) [divide] between two
jap'iy	(v.) to partition the total; to divide a part of a road (each part of which may then be assigned to a particular community for its upkeep); Syn.–*chayaqin*
jawaray	(v.) to hand out, or pass around portions
kinsachay	(v.) to divide among three; or to divide something into three parts
khuchuy	(v.) to part, split, separate, divide; also has the sense of "to count"
kutu kutu	(adj.) group-by-group (division)
laya	(n.) class, type; *layan layan*–the sub-classes; refers to the independence of a group of subclasses
milgay	(v.) to divide a field by making several canal-like divisions, or lines; these divisions may be used to assign parts of the field to people who help in planting (i.e., *ayni,* or *mink'a* laborers)
paskay	(v.) to undo; to take apart
suyu	(n.) a part of the whole (ca., a "fraction"); e.g., a part of a task assigned to a worker, or a group
t'aqay	(v.) to divide, or separate things, putting them in their proper place; refers to things that are independent (e.g., separating two bottles; not breaking a single thing into two parts)
t'aqaray	(v.) to once again separate and classify things, but now to do it in detail
yupapuy	(v.) to divide things up and count them off; to divide things and assign them to their proper place

saying that *kinsa rak'i* ("three shares") results when 12 is divided into four equal parts.

Conclusions

In concluding this discussion of the arithmetic and mathematics of rectification, I want to make clear that the analysis and exposition of this philosophical system derives largely from conversations that I had over a period of several months in 1993–1994 with Primitivo Nina. In addition, while I have recorded everyday uses of about half of the terms in the four tables of arithmetic operations in my fieldnotes, the precise meanings and additional uses of many of these terms were supplied by Nina. Meanings and glosses were also confirmed from consulting several published Quechua–Spanish dictionaries (especially, Cusihuamán 1976; González Holguín 1952 [1608]; Herrero and Sánchez de Lozada 1983; Lara 1991; Lira 1982; Mossi 1860). I also consulted a number of Quechua grammars to confirm and clarify certain points in the grammatical uses of enfixes, suffixes, and other features of the syntactical construction of arithmetic phrases (for example, Santo Tomás 1992 [1560]; González Holguín 1975 [1607]; Huerta 1993 [1616]; and Morató Peña and Morató Lara n.d.). As stated earlier, the sentence-level examples included in the above discussions of the four operations were taken from the [Bolivian] Quechua–Spanish dictionary of Herrero and Sánchez de Lozada (1983). This is an excellent and extremely valuable resource for such uses, allowing the reader not only the ability to refer to a published source for the forms of the verbs given, but also to investigate other nuances and uses of these operations. By way of the addition and (re-)combination of the many suffixes and enfixes used in the formation of Quechua words, Primitivo Nina has stated that each one of the verbs representing a specific form of *yapa* has a total of 102 possible forms (e.g., I have recorded the different definitions and glosses of 52 different forms of the verb *yupay*, "to count").

I do not want to leave the reader with the impression that the analysis and articulation of the philosophy of rectification are recognized and consciously reproduced by Quechua-speaking peoples as they go about their daily affairs. This is no more true of the Quechua than it is of people in our own culture, very few of whom are able to reproduce the philosophical and logical foundations of Western number theory, arithmetic, mathematics, or indeed even to use for everyday purposes the rules and procedures of arithmetic that they learned in school (Lave 1991). Thus, the philosophy underlying the arithmetic procedures discussed in this chapter contains the logical principles according to which everyday practices cohere and make sense, in more general terms. It ought to be the case, therefore, that we can investigate and, one hopes, understand both how Quechua arithmetic is meaningful in relation to Quechua culture and ideology more broadly, and how Quechua arithmetic practices conform to certain standards and patterns of organization over time, in terms of the general principles outlined in this chapter. In the next chapter, we will take up the question of whether or not, in fact, it is possible to identify something similar to the arithmetic and mathematics of rectification at work in the organization of Quechua society and culture in earlier times.

Numbers and Arithmetic in Pre-Hispanic and Colonial Andean Societies

Introduction

The purpose of this chapter is to provide a historical perspective on the ontology of numbers, arithmetic operations, and the philosophy of arithmetic and mathematics discussed in earlier chapters. As is true of all ideas, institutions, and values in Quechua society and culture, the knowledge of, and beliefs about, numbers and arithmetic encountered in communities today—or constructed from the semiotic study of speech and linguistic categories in contemporary Quechua language— are products of history. In fact, it is our ability to say something about continuities and changes in these and other aspects of Quechua culture that distinguishes this case from others in South America and elsewhere (for example, the Iqwaye) for which little or no historical documentation exists. However, while we do have relatively good sources for studying Quechua society and culture through time, these are not entirely satisfactory for trying to understand the nature and meaning of numbers, arithmetic, and mathematics on the part of the population at large. The limitations of the historical sources can be clarified by stating the specific question that I want to address in this chapter; that is: What was the meaning and the experience of numbers and mathematics on the part of Quechua-speaking peoples in the Andes from late pre-Hispanic times through the momentous social, political, economic, and intellectual changes wrought by the European invasion in the sixteenth century? By "experience of numbers," I mean the understanding of numbers and the uses to which they were put in organizing social, political, economic, and other activities and relations in Andean communities.

It is precisely in our attempts to answer such questions as that posed above that the historical sources from any era in the past are shown to be of somewhat dubious value. This is because whether characterizing pre-Hispanic, colonial, or contemporary traditions, most of our sources speak primarily of the knowledge and practices of the record keepers, and the elites whom they serve(d), rather than of urban workers and rural farmers who have made up the vast majority of the Andean population from pre-Hispanic to contemporary times. Nonetheless, it is important to attempt to answer the question raised above, because only by doing so can we gain confidence that the ontology of numbers and the philosophy of arithmetic and mathematics outlined earlier have deep historical, intellectual, and semiological roots in Andean language, culture, and society.

A Historical Perspective on the Ontology of Numbers

If by the phrase "the ontology of numbers" we now understand—in the case of Quechua language and culture as developed in Chapters 2 and 3— several important ideas and values that can be condensed (in one way at least) into a representation based on a hierarchical series of some five entities organized on the model of a mother (*mama*) and her four age-graded offspring (that is, 1 . . . 5, or 1st . . . 5th), then the question that arises is whether or not such a characterization and model finds any confirmation in the historical documentation from late pre-Hispanic and early colonial Andean societies. I will not pretend that my answer to this question here will be exhaustive, as this is a large and complex topic, one that requires its own study. However, I would like to discuss certain data that strongly suggest that the model briefly restated above had considerable salience in pre-Hispanic and early colonial Quechua ideology and numerical ontology. In fact, I think we can argue on the basis of this material that groups of *five* had an importance in Andean cosmology that was comparable, for instance, to the number and groups, or cycles, of *four* in the cosmology and symbolism of Mesoamerican and Southwestern Puebloan societies (see Aveni 1980; Ortiz 1969).

The examples of the pervasiveness of age-graded groups of *five* members that I will discuss come from the so-called Huarochirí document (Salomon and Urioste 1991). This document, a 227-page text written almost entirely in Quechua, was recorded in the early seventeenth century.[1] The document represents the historical, cosmological, and religious beliefs from pre-Hispanic to early colonial times of various ethnic groups that lived in and around the province of Huarochirí, in the central Peruvian Andes. The narrative line of the text goes (roughly) from the origin of gods and humans, to contests among different ethnic groups (often characterized eponymously in the identities of their founding and/or patron deities) for control within the area, through the Inka conquest of these populations, and down to events—both historical and legendary— that apparently occurred not long before the information was recorded (Salomon 1991: 5).

What I want to emphasize here is a series of characterizations of groups, or sets, of entities (both divine and human) that are central to the structures and events organizing the narrative which have as one of their common, shared features a "model of fives" consistent with the numerical ontological model developed here, especially in Chapter 3. I will provide below a number of examples of this "obsession" with sets and series of five(s) as they appear dispersed throughout the early part of the English translation of the Huarochirí text.

Although people did die in those times, they came back to life on the fifth *day exactly. And as for their foodstuffs, they ripened exactly five days after being planted. (Salomon and Urioste 1991: 43)*

Now we'll return to what is said of very early people. The story goes like this. In ancient times, this world wanted to come to an end. A llama buck, aware that the ocean was about to overflow, was behaving like somebody who's deep in sadness. . . . [To his master, who became angry at him for not eating] that llama began speaking like a human being. "You simpleton, whatever could you be thinking about? Soon, in five days, the ocean will overflow. It's a certainty. And the whole world will come to an end," it said. The man got good and scared. "What's going to happen to us? Where can we go to save ourselves?" he said. The llama replied, "Let's go to Villca Coto mountain. . . . There we'll be saved. Take along five *days' food for yourself." (p. 51)*

In ancient times the sun died. Because of his death it was night for five *days. (p. 53)*

These people, the ones who lived in that [ancient] era, used to spend their lives warring on each other and conquering each other. . . . We speak of them as the Purum Runa, "people of desolation." It was at this time that the one called Paria Caca² was born in the form of five *eggs on Condor Coto mountain. (p. 54)*

After Huatya Curi³ finished all these deeds, Paria Caca flew forth from the five *eggs in the shape of* five *falcons. . . . These* five *falcons turned into humans and they began to roam around. (p. 63)*

They say that when Paria Caca set out to defeat Huallollo Caruincho,⁴ the five *persons who composed him whirled hunting* bolas. . . . *(p. 66)*

The names of these five *brothers [who composed Paria Caca] are*
Paria Caca
Churapa
Puncho
Paria Carco
We don't know the name of one of these five *(p. 67). [Later, p. 92, the fifth brother is identified as]*
Sullca Yllapa

The victors' [i.e., Paria Caca's children] names are these, starting from the oldest one:
Choc Payco
Chancha Runa
Huari Runa
Utco Chuco
and Tutay Quiri, with his brother, Sasin Mari. (p. 70–71)

Now we'll tell about the sisters of Chaupi Ñamca⁵ whom we mentioned. Chaupi Ñamca was the oldest of them all.
Her next sister was Llacsa Huato.
Her next-born sibling was Mira Huato.
We don't know about the other one. In all they were five *(p. 78).*
[The fifth *sister is later identified as Añas, Aña Paya, or Caui Llaca (p. 86)]*

The Concha people were born from out of the earth's interior, at Yauri Llancha, as five *persons. Their names, starting from the first [i.e., oldest] one, they were:*
Llacsa Misa
Pauquir Buxi

Llama Tanya
Hualla
Calla (p. 136).

While an assortment of quotations such as that given above does not make an argument, it can be helpful, in this case, in suggesting a kind of emphasis, or "insistence" (Ascher and Ascher 1981: 37 ff), that the people of a culture place on particular ideas, values, and practices (Mendizábal Losack 1989: 84–85 also notes the ubiquity of groups of five in the Huarochirí manuscript). Certainly, for the Huarochirí document, one would be hard put to come up with another number, or sum, that has the prominence and the importance in organizing the narrative that is given to five(s). But our interest goes beyond looking for a particular number that might be significant; for the "model of fives" developed in Chapters 2 and 3 is specifically based on the derivation of a group of this size through processes of reproduction and the relations of siblingship and age-grading. These elements are clearly present in several of the examples cited above (as in the five eggs giving birth to five falcons that are transformed into five brothers; and in the age-graded groupings made up of: the five brothers Paria Caca; the group of Paria Caca's children; Chaupi Ñamca and her sisters; and the five ancestor-founders of the Concha people). Furthermore, many of the same structures and principles of organization emphasizing groups of five in the Huarochirí document are seen elsewhere in colonial sources on the Inka, especially with respect to the Inka age grades and classes (Rowe 1958; Zuidema 1964: 211–218).

The conclusion that I draw from the above examples is that, certainly for the inhabitants of the area of Huarochirí who maintained the oral traditions that were the basis of this document in early colonial times, the model of fives that we arrived at earlier on the basis of contemporary ethnographic and linguistic data seems to have been an important and defining element of their conceptualization and ontology of number(s).

Numeracy and Literacy in the Pre-Columbian Andes

The question of the nature and degree of both numeracy and literacy among late pre-Hispanic populations in the Andes is intimately bound up with the history of the *khipus*. As will be recalled from the brief discussion of them in Chapter 1, these were the knotted-string devices used for record keeping in the Inka empire. As I stated earlier, the *khipus* are said to have been used to record both quantitative data as well as information concerning genealogies, histories, and other types of narrative accounts. The Spaniards, many of whom saw this device in operation and who both talked to, and heard recitations produced from *khipus* by, the "keepers of the *khipus*" (called *khipukamayuqs*), have left us with a rather confusing assortment of opinions as to the nature of the recording units and the general "readability" of the *khipus*. However, with only a few notable exceptions, the opinions we read leave us with the impressions, first, that while capable of retaining complex types and bodies of information, each *khipu* was readable only by the individual who recorded the information on it, or by initiates whom that *khipu*-maker might have instructed in the reading of the *khipu* (see, for example, Cobo 1983 [1653]: 253–254);[6] and second, that the units of information that were recorded primarily took the form of numbers (Garcilaso 1970 [1609]: 330).[7]

From these colonial characterizations, there has developed over the years the view that the *khipu* represented a system of mnemonic record keeping; that is, that the units of information that were recorded on them represented no more than "cues" from which the officials who kept the *khipus* constructed—from memory—narrative accounts of histories, myths, and so on. This notion has not only been taken up into the Andeanist literature (for example, Rappaport 1994; Rowe 1946: 325–326) but has even made its way into general, comparative discussions of types of literacy, in which the *khipu* is characterized as almost a paradigmatic example of "record-keeping without writing" (see Crump 1990; Goody 1977).

As I have argued elsewhere (Urton 1994 and n.d.), I think that there was probably a much higher degree of shared knowledge underlying the *khipu* recording units, and their interpretive values, than is either suggested in most Spanish colonial sources or has been assumed to be the case by most modern commentators. In other words, I think that the information recorded on the *khipus* constituted something much closer to the units recorded in a system of writing than has heretofore been supposed (this more expansive interpretation is shared, to some degree, by Ascher and Ascher 1969: 533; 1981: 78; and Pärssinen 1992: 26–51). However, I would also stress that, whether we are talking about a single system for recording both quantitative and narrative information, or perhaps two different systems (one for quantitative data, another for narratives), the control and manipulation of at least the larger and more complex versions of these devices were probably limited to a relatively small number of bureaucratic officials in the empire (but see below). Although the *khipu* is of great comparative interest in terms of its probable use as an instrument for writing, this is not the time (nor are all the pieces yet in place) for undertaking an analysis of this aspect of the Inka recording system. Rather, I will focus here on how numbers were recorded on *khipus* and what we can learn from this about the probable meaning of numbers and arithmetic operations in pre-Hispanic Andean societies.

From what we can learn about *khipus* from the Spanish documents and chronicles, it is clear that the Inkas used this device to record census data, including information on population, agricultural produce and herd animals, tribute assessments (such as the number of days owed to the state in labor service),[8] and the amount and types of produce stored in local state-owned storehouses, as well as calendrical information pertaining to the scheduling of agricultural and pastoral activities and the celebration of festivals throughout the empire (see Ascher and Ascher 1969, 1981; Espinoza Soriano 1971–1972; Murra 1975, 1982, 1987; Pärssinen 1992; Radicati de Primeglio 1979; and Zuidema 1989). The officials who collected these various types of information, the *khipukamayuqs* ("knot-makers/keepers"), were organized in a hierarchical fashion. Information that was collected from smaller, local groups was passed on through successively higher, more inclusive levels of the state bureaucracy—from overseers of 10 households to those of 50, 100, 500, 1,000 and on up to the lords of 40,000 households. This information was brought together and evaluated for such purposes as the assessment and (re)assignment of tribute, the redistribution of resources during hard times (as when harvests were insufficient to meet local needs), the maintenance of the army, and the coordination of economic and ceremonial activities.

In order to explain how such information was recorded and organized on the *khipus*, it is necessary to say something about how these devices were constructed. *Khipus* are composed of a relatively thick cord (ca. 0.5–1 cm.), made of spun and plied threads, called a primary cord. Attached to the primary cord were a variable number of pendant strings, so called because they hang straight down from the primary cord when it is held up and stretched taut. Some *khipus* also have top strings; these are attached to the primary cord opposite, or 180° from, the pendant strings. Both pendant strings and top strings may have additional strings attached to them; the latter are known as subsidiary strings. Subsidiary strings may also bear subsidiaries, which themselves may bear subsidiaries—and so on.

The classification of information on the *khipus* was signaled by a number of symbolic and structural features produced by variations in the construction, especially of the strings. These included variations in the direction of spinning, plying, and tying knots into the strings (see Urton 1994), as well as differences in the color and placement, or grouping, of the strings and knots (see Ascher and Ascher 1969, 1981). Numerical information was recorded by means of tying knots into the strings in clusters representing successively higher units of value in a base-10 system of place notation. Ones were tied farthest from the point of attachment of the strings to the primary cord; units from 2 to 9 were recorded higher up; next were recorded 10s, then 100s, then 1,000s and on up to 10,000s (see Locke 1923; Radicati de Primeglio 1979; Ascher and Ascher 1981; Mendizábal Losack 1989: 50–54). In addition to differences in their location on the strings, three different types of knots were tied to indicate different classes of numerical values in the *khipus*. Figure-8 knots were tied to indicate ones; long knots (that is, knots tied with the appropriate number of turns of the string within the body of the knot) represented the units from 2 to 9; and single, or "granny," knots were tied for full decimal units (10s, 100s, 1,000s, and 10,000s). The absence of a knot in a place of notation on a string represented zero.

The most important fact to note with regard to the quantitative values recorded on the *khipus* is that they conformed to a decimal system of place notation. As to the question of *why* the decimal principle was so pervasive in Inka/Quechua numerical practices, and what its logical and semantic foundations were, I will attempt to answer these questions in my conclusions (Chapter 7). For the time being, we will continue to explore some of the practical consequences of the application of the decimal principle in Inka social, political, economic, and ritual organization.

Whereas the information recorded on the *khipus* by the various methods discussed above represented a special body of technical knowledge manipulated by the *khipukamayuq* specialists, nonetheless, the recording techniques themselves (the spinning, plying, dyeing, and knotting of strings) were quite common and widely known skills among spinners and weavers in communities throughout the Andes. Thus, there was a continuum of skills in the Inka empire in terms of the manipulation of the materials and techniques used in the production of the *khipus*—from weavers who used many of these techniques on a daily basis to produce textiles, to the *khipukamayuqs* who used these same techniques to record statistical and narrative information. Therefore, the problem of determining the nature and degree of literacy and numeracy in the late pre-Hispanic Andes is considerably more complicated and challenging than, for instance, in Europe at this same time (that is, during the period from the late fifteenth through early sixteenth centuries). In the European tradition, people who could not read or write did not (to my knowledge) spend the better part of every day producing useful objects with the tools and symbols—pen, paper, letters, and number signs—that were otherwise used for reading and writing.

The research undertaken by the Aschers on the *khipus* represents the most systematic body of work available to us concerning the nature of numerical knowledge and mathematical practice among the Inkas (Ascher and Ascher 1981; see also Radicati de Primeglio 1979). However, while the Aschers' investigations have given us a very good general understanding of the types of arithmetic and mathematical calculations that must have been performed by the *khipukamayuqs,* what we cannot derive from these observations is a sense of when and under what conditions the arithmetic operations used in any one of these types of calculations might have been performed. The question that I am leading up to here is whether or not something like a philosophy of the "arithmetic of rectification" existed among Andean populations in pre-Hispanic times. In the next section, I will discuss several examples which suggest that such a philosophy did, in fact, exist in ideas about, and the manipulation of, numbers in the Inka empire.

Pre-Hispanic Arithmetic Operations and Philosophy as Seen through the Colonial Sources

In this section, I will present three case studies that collectively provide strong support for the existence of something akin to an arithmetic of rectification informing numeracy and arithmetic practice in the pre-Hispanic Andean world. These examples also provide the context for taking account of the second principal source of information (the first of which were the *khipus*) available to us for trying to understand the experience of numbers and mathematics on the part of pre-Hispanic populations in the Andes. This involves the information contained in Spanish colonial chronicles, administrative documents, and dictionaries (especially of Quechua and Aymara).

As background for the three case studies to be discussed below, I should identify certain features of the sociopolitical structures and territorial and administrative organizations that were apparently common throughout the Andes in late pre-Hispanic times. The primary structures and forms of organization, our sources tell us, were based on two integrated but ideologically distinct sets of principles. One was based on dualism and elaborations thereof (such as quadripartition); the other was based on a decimal principle. As for the principle of dualism, individuals or groups representing an "upper moiety"—called in Quechua *Hanansaya*—were consistently opposed to others composing a "lower moiety"—*Hurinsaya*. Although their opposition to each other was commonly expressed in terms of complementarity, such dual divisions were also explicitly built around hierarchical and asymmetric relations. However, insofar as the moieties interacted with each other on the basis of an ideology of complementarity, such interactions were perfectly suited to a calculus of relations—as in the distribution of resources, duties, etc.—according to an arithmetics of rectification; that is, in the event that the complementarity and balance between *Hanansaya* and *Hurinsaya* was threatened, balance could be restored through the application of "corrective procedures" (that is, the appropriate form of *yapa*).

Here, we are essentially describing the well-attested Andean principle referred to as *ayni*. This term, which is perhaps best glossed as "reciprocity," refers to the balanced give-and-take of relations over time between individuals, sociopolitical groups (such as *ayllus*), and local groups and the state (at least in Inka times). Such relations continue to play an important role in certain contexts, such as labor exchanges, in communities throughout the Andes to the present day (Mayer 1974; Isbell 1985). The principle of *ayni* is generally consistent with the principles of equilibrium and balance underlying the arithmetic and mathematics of rectitude as described in Chapter 5. However, as I have noted above, the organizational principles and ideological values underlying moiety group-ings were also characterized by asymmetry and hierarchical relations. For instance, it was common for one moiety to take precedence over the other socially and politically, as well as in ritual and ceremonial settings. Thus, our examination of the arithmetics of rectification will need to account not only for the qualities of complementarity and equilibrium in moiety relations, but also for those of hierarchy and inequality.

In addition to dualism, decimal organization was also an important principle for recruiting and organizing social, political, economic, and other groups in the Inka empire (Wedin 1965). For example, in the or-ganization of provincial populations throughout the empire, the Inka predisposition was to group households into standardized decimal units. This is seen, for instance, in the colonial documents, especially from the north-central and southern Andes, in the names that were used for var-ious levels of sociopolitical groupings, such as *chunka* (10), *pachaka* (100) and *waranqa* (1,000; see for example Rostworowski and Remy 1992). It is important to point out here that the Inka system of tribute took the form of labor demands levied on local populations, not on individuals. In addition, the Inkas did not demand the payment of goods or money by their subjects (as was true later in the Spanish system of tribute). For instance, the Inka might require a group of 100 tribute payers to provide 20 people to work for 10 days each year on the upkeep of a road. It was up to the group in question to decide collectively how best to meet its labor assignment. Such decisions, however, were normally arrived at under the direction of the highest authority of the group, the *kuraka*. An ideal province in the empire was composed of a *huno* (10,000 tributaries) or a multiple thereof; *huno* subunits of 1,000 (*waranqa*) and 100 (*pa-chaka*) were established as labor-service units to perform work for the state. It was also common in certain cases, such as the province of Chu-pacho, where the population was composed of 4 *waranqa*s (or 4,000 trib-utaries) to establish a certain percentage of a *waranqa*—such as 1 per-cent, or 40 tributaries—as the standard size for the assignment of groups to perform labor service (Julien 1988; see also discussion of uniformity and fairness, below).

Finally, we should take note of the general range of magnitudes of the numerical units recorded on the *khipus* that represented the num-bers of households that were actually required to perform labor in the fulfillment of tribute obligations. The small amount of explicit testimony that we have regarding such values from pre-Hispanic times comes to us by way of colonial documents that were produced when Spanish scribes recorded the testimony of *khipukamayuqs* who "read" from their *khipus* the tribute that was owed to the Inkas.[9] To generalize, what we find in these documents is that the tributary units—the numbers of workers assigned to perform various tasks—took the form *overwhelmingly* of full decimal units, such as 10, 20, 50, or 100 workers (see below). In fact, I would argue that the organization of labor by, or into, *full decimal units* was a fundamental feature of the "experience of numbers" on the part of native people in local communities throughout the Andes in pre-Hispanic times. Such an emphasis is also evident in the data on Inka age-classes, which were organized by multiples of five and/or ten (Rowe 1958; Zuidema 1964: 211–218). We will see later how radically this experience changed with the Spanish conquest and the imposition of a new system of tribute with its own, decidedly different, logic of numbers.

Achieving Rectitude through Uniformity and Fairness

The first case study that I will summarize which affords us a glimpse of the pre-Hispanic logic and experience of numbers comes to us by way of a brilliant and insightful historical reconstruction focusing on the question of "how Inka decimal administration worked," which appeared in an article of the same title by Catherine Julien (1988). Julien's study involves an analysis of the logical principles guiding Inka decimal administration as reconstructed on the basis of *khipu* accounts containing census records and tribute assessments from late pre-Hispanic through early colonial times.

Julien's arguments center on the question of how Inka tribute was assessed and assigned, or distributed, within a given population. She notes that the process began with a census of the population within the region in question. An assessment was then established, which represented a standing labor assignment that covered all subject households within the population. Finally, certain numbers of households were then assigned to perform a particular labor service. Julien points out that the central government in Cusco, as represented by its record-keepers, the *khipukamayuqs*, was involved at three different times in this process: (a) when the population was organized into accounting units, *or* when adjustments were required in those units; (b) when the assessment of labor service was carried out; and (c) when tribute assignments were actually established (Julien 1988: 266–267). What is particularly notable in this process is the standardization of the procedures for assessment and the uniformity of the size of the groups assigned to different labor-service tasks.

Julien argues that a fundamental feature underlying the standardization and uniformity in the tribute system was the establishment of a relationship between the actual population count of a given tributary group and then the calculation, or abstraction, from that figure of an ideal *decimal* total. From that point, the Inkas then *assessed* tribute on the basis of percentages of the ideal decimal total, while accounting for the difference between the ideal and the actual population count in the *assignment* of tribute duties. For instance, in her study of the *khipu* account transcribed in 1549 detailing the labor obligations assessed and assigned to the 4,108 households of the Chupacho (Huánuco, north-central Andes) under the Inkas, Julien found that the assignments overwhelmingly represented a percentage of the ideal decimal population total of 4,000. The percentages fell within the range of 1 percent (or 40 households) to 12.5 percent (or 500 households; see Table 6.1). After establishing numerous labor groupings on the basis of various percentages of the ideal assessment, the Inka administrators were left with an actual excess of 108 households (i.e., 4,108 − 4,000 = 108). Of this remainder, one regular "ideal" unit of 1 percent (40 households) was extracted, leaving 68 households for some sort of labor assignment. As we see in Table 6.1, this *nondecimal* grouping—the *only* such grouping recorded on the Chupacho *khipu*—was assigned guard duty at the "way-station" (*tambo*) of Huánuco (Julien 1988: 265).

In addition to stressing the values of standardization and uniformity of labor units in the assessment and assignment of tribute, Julien notes that underlying these values was a doctrine of *fairness*. She characterizes "fairness" as follows.

When the assessment adhered to the ideal decimal total of households, fairness between provinces was the result. When the distribution adhered to the actual household total, fairness within a province was the result. . . . Increases or decreases brought about by changes in the birthrate could have been accommodated by the system over a period of time, because those individuals were not part of the class subject to the

TABLE 6.1

Chupacho Labor Assignments

Assignment	Total	Percent of 4,000
Gold miners	120	3.00
Silver miners	60	1.50
Masons in Cuzco	400	10.00
Cultivators in Cuzco	400	10.00
Retainers (*yanaconas*) of Huayna Capac	150	3.75
Guards for the body of Thupa Inca	150	3.75
Guards (*yanaconas*) for the weapons of Thupa Inca	10	0.25
Garrison in Chachapoyas	200	5.00
Garrison in Quito	200	5.00
Guards for the body of Huayna Capac	20	0.50
Feather workers	120	3.00
Honey gatherers	60	1.50
Weavers of tapestry (*cumpi*) cloth	400	10.00
Dye makers	40	1.00
Herders of Inca herds	240	6.00
Guards for corn fields	40	1.00
Cultivators of *ají* fields	40	1.00
Salt miners (variable)	60/ 50/ 40	1.50/ 1.25/ 1.00
Cultivators of coca	60	1.50
Hunters for royal deer hunts	40	1.00
Sole makers	40	1.00
Woodworkers	40	1.00
Potters	40	1.00

TABLE 6.1

(*continued*)

Assignment	Total	Percent of 4,000
Guards for the *tambo* of Huanuco*	68	1.70
Carriers between local *tambos*	80	2.00
Guards for the women of the Inca	40	1.00
Soldiers and carriers	500	12.50
Cultivators of Inca lands	500	12.50
Totals	4,108	112.70

*The nondecimal labor assignment.

SOURCE: From Julien 1988: 265 (Table 4).

standing labor assignment until they had formed their own households. The system appears to have been designed to function optimally under conditions of zero or incremental population growth. . . . The system was meant to be self-regulatory, and assessment and adjustment were carried out from above and outside, by officials [i.e., the khipukamayuqs] *from the central administration who appeared on occasion. (Julian 1988: 270)*

Thus, as reconstructed by Julien, Inka decimal administration was grounded in the values and principles of *standardization, uniformity,* and *fairness.* Corrections were made over time to account and make adjustments for variations in the population that might threaten these principles. In summary, it is clear from Julien's study, first, that what is represented in technical terms in the Inka system of tribute was a strategy for achieving equality and equilibrium in the distribution of service to the state that was based on a *decimal* principle of organization; and second, that what would have been required for the long-term maintenance of such a system of organization was something very much like the procedures and processes (not to mention the philosophy) of the "arithmetic and mathematics of rectification" discussed in Chapter 5.

Significant changes in the population or in the labor-service demands of the state would have necessitated the implementation of techniques of adjustment and accommodation in order to maintain fairness in the relationship between a population and its assessed labor-service duties. Such techniques would have been consistent with the adjustment procedures that are known collectively today as *yapa*—that is: addition, subtraction, multiplication, and division.

Considered in this light, we may find here some faint, and heretofore unrecognized, clues as to how to go about interpreting the numbers and groupings, or number patterns, recorded on the Inka *khipus*. For example, certain *khipus* may constitute records of states of disequilibrium or disharmony (as in the distribution of resources, assignment of tribute, etc.); in such cases, the *khipu* would have served as the "raw material" for the application of procedures of rectification. Other *khipus* may represent idealized versions, or models, of the desired "postrectification" state of affairs (that is, of harmony, balance, and equilibrium) of the circumstance in question.

As we will see in the next example, however, standardization, uniformity, and fairness were not the only values that governed processes of rectification in the Inka world. The case we take up now concerns the organization of the Inka ritual calendar.

Achieving Rectitude through Nonstandardization and Hierarchy

In a series of studies beginning in 1977, Zuidema has worked to construct an interpretation of the Inka calendar system, especially as it pertained to the regulation and coordination of social and political relations, as well as economic and ritual activities, in the valley of Cusco (Zuidema 1977, 1982; see also Aveni 1980: 298–306). While I do not intend to summarize Zuidema's findings here in detail, I do want to point to certain aspects of his reconstruction that afford us a glimpse into a set of principles of rectification that were decidedly different from those of "standardization" and "fairness" governing Inka decimal administration and tribute assessment throughout the empire.

The Inka annual calendar was based on several different astronomical cycles. These included: the solar year (365¼ days); the two periods between successive passages of the sun through zenith, which (at Cusco's latitude of ca. -13°30' south) produced "half years" of 258 and 107 days;

the synodic lunar cycle (29.5 days); the sidereal lunar cycle (27.3 days); and multiples of these various periodicities. These cycles and periods were combined and recombined in various ways with respect to a variety of interests that the Inkas had in the organization of time and public activities in the city and throughout the empire as a whole. Most importantly, the astronomically based calendar was coordinated with another calendar—this one for the regulation of ritual activities—that was composed of an active period of 328 days. Successive runs of the 328-day ritual calendar were separated from each other, and correlated with the solar calendar, by a "liminal" period that coincided with the disappearance of the Pleiades from the night sky for a period of some 37 nights ($328 + 37 = 365$; Zuidema 1977). Such calendrical adjustments would have represented, of course, prime areas for the application of procedures of rectification.

Now, the 328-day ritual calendar was subdivided among the populace of the city of Cusco for the purpose of assigning responsibility for worshipping at, and paying homage to, the various shrines within the valley. The number of days assigned to different groups varied so that the resulting periods were of unequal numbers of days (for example, there were units of from 2 to 10 days; of 30 or 31 days; 41 or 42; 60 or 61; or 178 days; see Zuidema 1977, 1990). This information was recorded on a *khipu*. The *khipu* that recorded this system of sacred places and ritual celebrations in Cusco (which is known in the literature as the "*ceque* system"; see Zuidema 1964), has not, to our knowledge, survived, although we do have preserved in the chronicle of Bernabé Cobo (1990) what appears to be a Spanish transcription of the information that was recorded on that *khipu*. Zuidema (1989) has argued that one *khipu* recovered from the south coastal Peruvian region of Ica represents the record of a similar ritual calendar used by the Inka population in that area.

The point to stress concerning the *ceque* system for our purposes here is that there was *not* a strict standardization of, or uniformity in, the units of time assigned to groups of different (or even the same) sizes. Rather, the lengths of the time periods, as well as their respective location in the ritual calendar, were determined on the basis of a variety of factors, ranging from astronomical observations that might have been made to and from different parts of the city or valley; periodicities that happened to be of interest to the Inkas at certain times of the year; the differential status of groups in the sociopolitical organization of the city and the empire; and mythical/historical characteristics of particular groups, which presumably made them *ideologically* better suited to assume ritual or ceremonial activities at one time of the year rather than another. In other words, what was at issue in the ritual and calendrical organization in the Inka capital was a set of calculations aimed at establishing and maintaining "proper" or appropriate relations in the context of unequal—or at least nonuniform—divisions of time, hierarchical social and political relations, and peculiarities of group identity based on unique mythical and historical associations.

In summary, the calculations organizing the Inka calendar represented a mathematics of rectification by maintaining the *status quo;* however, "rectification" in this case was based on values and principles (such as hierarchy, historical contingency, and the absence of uniformity) that were quite different from those of standardization, uniformity, and fairness that were used in the organization of the decimal administration in the provinces. What becomes clear from this example is that in order to grasp both the dimensions and the character of what I would argue was a generalized "Andean" mathematics of rectification, we have to recognize that the values that called for and directed the process of rectification could vary significantly from one case to the next. That is, understanding the broader theoretical and ideological significance of rectification for the Inkas requires that we understand the particular sets of principles and values that were considered to be *appropriate* for organizing relations between or among individuals or groups in each particular case. The identification of "what is appropriate" cannot be determined and reconstructed today in a mechanical way; rather, it is to be found, or discovered, in the record of Inka ideology and culture that is embedded in (while at the same time, in many cases, transformed and even obliterated by) the documentation produced by the Spaniards in the colonial chronicles, administrative documents, and dictionaries.

In short, whether or not Inka/Quechua arithmetic and mathematics were, or seem to us to be, "logical" when their applications are viewed case by case depends on whether or not *we* are able to evaluate each case from the perspective of the values and principles on which they might have achieved rectification in that setting. In the next example, we will encounter an example of rectification that was based on maintaining a balance between the fairness, uniformity, etc., of the first case discussed above and the hierarchy, historical contingency, etc., of the second.

Achieving Rectification through the Balance of Complementarity and Hierarchy

The last example of variations in pre-Hispanic modes of rectification that I will discuss is drawn from Tristan Platt's (1987) analysis of Aymara political organization, a study focusing on a well-articulated set of ideas and values centering around the concept of "accounting." Much of the material discussed by Platt is drawn from Ludovico Bertonio's early-seventeenth-century Aymara-Spanish dictionary (1984 [1612]). Platt's study is especially important for our interests not only because it deals directly with explicitly arithmetic subject matter, such as accounting, but also because it expands the scope of our inquiry of the pre-Hispanic "Andean" arithmetic and mathematics of rectification, which we have so far seen only from the perspective of Quechua and Inka material, to the powerful kingdoms and confederations of the Aymara-speaking peoples around Lake Titicaca and southward into present-day Bolivia. Platt argues, in fact, that the principles of accounting common to Aymara political organization pertain to traditions and practices that were in force prior to the incorporation of the Aymara polities into the Inka empire.

An appreciation of the key points in Platt's article depends on understanding a few basic principles and practices of the organization of Aymara political, economic, and ritual activities. These I will outline as succinctly as possible below.

First, Aymara political organization was characterized by the grouping of lower level subdivisions, such as *pachaqas* ("one hundreds," or 100 households), into successively more inclusive groupings or alliances, such as *ayllus*, and so on up to the level of the two moieties of a confederation. The moieties, which were called in Aymara *Alasaya* (corresponding to the Quechua *Hanansaya*, "upper moiety") and *Majasaya* (corresponding to the Quechua *Hurinsaya*, "lower moiety"), were related to each other both hierarchically and in terms of an ideology of equality, depending on the circumstances (Platt 1987: 69–71).

The second basic element pertains to accounting practices in the Aymara kingdoms. One of the principal accounting procedures was based on a system of checks and balances in the "recording" of debts and credits. This was done by the exchange of stones signifying one or the other of these conditions. That is, for any particular transaction, a black stone, called *cchaara,* signified a debt, while a white stone, called *hank'o* (or *ch'iyara*), signified the loan that established the debt represented by the black stone. The pairing of black stones and white stones represented a system in which loans and debts were maintained in a reciprocal, balanced state. However, hierarchy was also an important principle in this system of accounting. That is, the person who held a white stone was in a superior position *vis a vis* the person who held the black stone of that transaction (Platt 1987: 86–87).[10]

Finally, the third basic element concerns a form of ritualized competition between individuals or groups that occurred in the form of fights, called *t'inkus.* These events, which were (and still are)[11] held at certain times of the year, could oppose, for example, an *ayllu* of *Alasaya* against an *ayllu* of *Majasaya.* The ideal of the *t'inku* is of a reciprocal, balanced exchange of blows between the two sides. A more devastating and destructive form of fighting, called *ch'axwa* ("cruel war"), also existed as a possible outcome of the escalation of tensions in Aymara political relations. In a *ch'axwa,* each side attempted to dominate completely its opponent—to invade their land, destroy their crops, overturn their boundary markers, and literally to beat them up, or kill them (Platt 1987: 82–85).

Now, in each of the three elements of Aymara political organization outlined above, we see combined two fundamentally different sets of values and types of relations. One set represents conditions and relations of harmony, balance, and equilibrium: the moieties conceived of as equals; the checks and balances of the white and black stones; and the balanced competition of the *t'inkus.* The other set of values and type of relations emphasizes hierarchy, asymmetry, and the dominance of one entity over another: *Alasaya's* superiority to *Majasaya;* the superiority of the creditor with respect to the debtor; and the escalation of a *t'inku* into a *ch'axwa.* Peaceful political relations in Aymara polities required continual efforts at compromise in diffusing the tensions smoldering just beneath the surface in direct proportion to the degree to which asymmetry and inequality became manifest, for one reason or another, in these various forms of interaction. That is to say, there was always the possibility of a "rupture of the balance"—of *Alasaya* to exert its dominance over *Majasaya;* of the creditor to call in all debts; and of the actual escalation of *t'inku* into *ch'axwa.* As Platt notes:

> *The slight disequilibrium between the two poles of a symmetric opposi-*
> *tion represents a fundamental nexus in Aymara thought. It means that*
> *the political* reflexión *will not remain suspended in a state of static*
> *equilibrium, but rather that it will be thrown back for what it is . . . a*
> *continual flux of reordering. It could perhaps be said that a precondition*
> *for continuity in the social order is the constant process of smoothing over*
> *the excesses of a hierarchy in order to achieve once again the sought-*
> *after state of* mokhsa *["sweetness, peace, harmony"]. (1987: 98–99;*
> *my translation)*

For the issues we have been discussing, the relevance of Platt's analysis of the dynamic tension between excess and harmony in Aymara political institutions and relations should be obvious. The ideal of balance and equilibrium in Aymara political, economic, and ritual organization is consistent with the *ideals* of an Andean arithmetic and mathematics of rectification. Furthermore, just as the latter is premised on the understanding that "ruptures of the balance" will inevitably occur and, therefore, that it must maintain in good working order its strategies (the various forms of *yapa*) for rectifying emergent states of disharmony and disequilibrium, so too was Aymara political ideology premised on this same understanding and on what we can suppose to have been similar techniques of adjustment. Thus, I argue again on the basis of this example that in the pre-Hispanic Andes—at least as we understand that world through our Spanish colonial sources—arithmetic and mathematics would not have been conceived of, nor would they have occupied a status, separate from any number of other social and cultural activities. To the degree to which numbers were objects of arithmetic manipulations in different settings in the pre-Hispanic Andes, we have reason to suppose that their values and relationships may have been conceived of in terms of the particular, and potentially variable, principles and values of the arithmetic and mathematics of rectification identified in each of the three case studies summarized above.

In summarizing the experience of numbers on the part of the vast majority of people in their local communities in the pre-Hispanic Andes, I would suggest that this needs to be considered on two levels. The first, which I have not discussed specifically in this chapter but which is basically that represented in the material presented in Chapters 2 through 4, involves everyday uses of cardinal and ordinal numerals to organize, coordinate, and classify the separate, but at the same time interrelated, objects, events, and other phenomena that made up the world of production and experience (such as counting threads in warping and weaving textiles or taking an inventory of one's resources). The second level of the experience of numbers in pre-Hispanic societies occurred in the relationship between the local community and more inclusive regional, or state-level, forms of organization. Judged on the basis of the meager information that we have on this relationship, which comes to us principally in the form of Spanish transcriptions of Inka tribute lists contained in colonial documents, it appears that the nature of the experience of numbers in this case was linked in a profound way to the decimal principle of organization and administration. That is, tributary obligations in the Inka state took the form of demands for labor groups that were organized into, or calculated on the basis of, full decimal units. Thus, I would argue that the meaning and sense of numbers experienced by people in local communities in their interactions with the Inka state centered around the principles of completeness and wholeness represented by even numbers, full decimal units (that is, 10s, 100s, 1,000s), and multiples thereof. As we will see below, these values underlying the public, community experience of numbers in the Andes underwent a profound and dramatic change following the Spanish conquest.

A New World of Numbers

Having recently passed through the intellectual and emotional turmoil of the Columbian quincentenary, the citizens of what has become—largely by virtue of that singular event of the European crossing of the Atlantic in 1492—the "global community" undertook a wide and deep reassessment of the intellectual and historical significance of the European discovery and conquest of the Americas. Innumerable conferences, publications, commemorations, and other events of a celebratory or funereal spirit were observed in 1992, highlighting the importance of a variety of transformations that occurred in Europe and the Americas following the conquest and colonization of the Americas during the fifteenth and sixteenth centuries. It is a notable, but perhaps not at all surprising, matter to note that at least in my own experience and knowledge of the events that transpired in 1992, I was not aware of a single event that focused on the significance of 1492 for the history of numbers and mathematics.

I would argue that the lack of such recognition can be explained according to a few persistent and uncritical ideas about the nature of arithmetic and mathematics. First, as I have argued in Chapter 1, it has generally been thought in the West that there is ultimately only one arithmetic and mathematics, and that while whatever can be stated in normal language about these numerical sciences may perhaps be translated into any number of other languages, nonetheless, the truths of mathematics themselves will not—cannot, by definition—undergo meaningful changes in the process of translation. As Bishop has articulated this general point in an article to be discussed more thoroughly below,

> Up to fifteen years or so ago, the conventional wisdom was that mathematics was culture-free knowledge. After all, the popular argument went, two twos are four, a negative number times a negative number gives a positive number, and all triangles have angles which add up to 180 degrees. These are true statements the world over. They have universal validity. Surely, therefore, it follows that mathematics must be free from the influence of any culture? (1990: 51)

Second, since mathematicians working in the Western tradition have carried mathematical thinking to its greatest heights, it might be thought that there is really nothing to be gained for mathematics in the consideration of any particular non-Western numbering and mathematical system. I must leave it to the reader to evaluate whether or not the present work, in addition to the few others of an ethnographic, linguistic, and philosophical character that touch on non-Western number theory and arithmetic and mathematical philosophy (such as Mimica's study of the Iqwaye numbering system), not to mention the wealth of information on non-Western arithmetic and mathematics presented elsewhere (see, for example, Ascher 1991; Crump 1990; Joseph 1992; Needham 1959), have given the slightest reason for hesitation in fully accepting either one or both of the positions outlined above.

The third explanation that I would give for what I at least experienced at the time as a complete silence on the relevance of the Columbian encounter for the study of numbers and mathematics is actually a corollary to the first reason adduced above. That is, since mathematics is considered, at least by its practitioners, to be concerned with universal, noncultural and non- (or pre-) linguistic truths, there is really no sense in which Western number values and mathematical systems can be thought to have played anything other than perhaps, or at most, a supporting or "instrumental" role in the events and processes of the European conquest and colonization of the Americas (such as in the keeping of census records, or the calculation of tribute).

I should make it clear that I strongly disagree with this latter position. As I will show below, there is a considerable body of evidence and a clear line of reasoning—the latter of which does not depend on the hyperbole of "multiculturalism," nor, I think, is it based on a misguided historical analysis—by which one can argue that much of what was initially imposed and subsequently became embedded as elements of everyday practices of colonial administration in the Americas rode in on the back of a new political arithmetic that gave coherence and authority to the Spanish colonial adventure. The most obvious and active elements of the political arithmetic of colonialism, in the sense that these were the elements that most directly shaped a new experience of numbers in the post-Conquest Andean world, were: first, the (profusion of) written number signs; and second, a new set of values that lay behind the conception of numbers and the manipulation of those numbers in arithmetic and mathematical operations. As we will see, the values alluded to in the latter were quite different from those underlying the arithmetic and mathematics of rectification discussed previously.

Before turning to discussions of the topics raised above, I should note that the basic argument that I will make here is generally in agreement with that put forward (although without the benefit of a historical or ethnographic case study for its support) by Alan Bishop in an article entitled "Western Mathematics: The Secret Weapon of Cultural Imperialism" (1990). Bishop argues that Western mathematics played a key role in the establishment of Western cultural values and disciplinary techniques in colonial regimes worldwide. This influence is especially notable, for instance, in such areas as trade, governmental administration, and education (Bishop 1990: 53–56). But beyond its pivotal role in helping to establish and maintain particular institutions and practices of Western colonialism and state capitalism and their reproduction, Western mathematics influenced non-Western cultures at a deeper, ontological level by inculcating particular values and philosophical principles that were often fundamentally at odds with the "traditional" values that Europeans came into contact with in local communities around the world from the fifteenth through the nineteenth century. Concerning the nature and force of such values, Bishop concludes that

> *In total, then, these values amount to a mathematico-technological cultural force, which is what indeed the imperialist powers generally represented. Mathematics with its clear rationalism, and cold logic, its precision, its so-called "objective" facts (seemingly culture and value free), its lack of human frailty, its power to predict and to control, its encouragement to challenge and to question, and its thrust towards yet more secure knowledge, was a most powerful weapon indeed. When allied to the use of technology, to the development of industry and commerce through scientific applications and to the increasing utility of tangible, commercial products, its status was felt to be indisputable. (1990: 59)*

We will see below that many of the factors in the association between mathematics and colonialism cited by Bishop played a role in the encounter between Europeans and native peoples in the Andes throughout the sixteenth century.

The Transformation of Numbers in the Colonial Andes

Following the initial conquest of the Andes, which began in 1532, the Spaniards set about the process of imposing a variety of institutions and policies for managing relations with, and utilizing to their greatest advantage the labor and wealth of, the native Andean populations (see Rowe 1957: 159–161; Andrien 1991: 121–124). One of the principal institutions for establishing effective control in the colonial Andes and for extracting a surplus (in goods and labor) from the native population was the *encomienda*. An *encomienda* was a grant by the Spanish crown to a Spaniard of responsibility for, as well as rights over, a particular group of Indians. The institution had precedents in the political machinations of the *reconquista* of the Iberian peninsula (Phillips and Phillips 1991:

20). While *encomenderos* (those holding *encomienda* grants) did not have rights to land by virtue of receiving such a grant, they did effectively have complete control over both the productive capacities, or labor, and the production of the natives assigned to the Spaniard by the terms of the *encomienda* grant. Any particular *encomendero*'s ability to exploit the labor and extract wealth from "his" Indians was based on forging an alliance with the native authorities, the *kurakas*. The *kurakas* were instrumental, for instance, in meeting the *encomendero*'s demands for tribute, which primarily came in the form of requests for labor and produce. This was done by the *kurakas* both by appealing to their traditional (pre-Hispanic) positions of authority within the (usually) *ayllu*-based sociopolitical systems of organization within communities, as well as by utilizing traditional strategies and relations of reciprocal exchange between themselves and the *ayllu* members whom they represented (Spalding 1984: 126–128; Stern 1982: 40–43). The specific traits of each *encomendero/kuraka* alliance worked to produce a multitude of different exploitative relations, resulting in a patchwork of different types and levels of tributary arrangements over the some five hundred *encomiendas* that existed in the *Audiencia* of Lima within the first three decades following the conquest (Spalding 1984: 124–125). We will look at an example of one such arrangement below.

In the late 1550s and the early 1560s, the *khipukamayuqs* in service to the *kurakas* of the Huanca peoples of the valley of Jauja, in the south-central Peruvian Andes, gave an accounting of the tribute that the Huanca supplied every year to their *encomendero*, Francisco Pizarro (Espinoza Soriano 1971–1972; Murra 1982). Table 6.2 contains a representative sampling of the items listed in the *kuraka* Jerónimo Guacrapáucar's account in 1558 of what the people under his authority either gave to Francisco Pizarro or what had been "looted" (*rancheado*) from them.[12]

The list in Table 6.2 reflects in numerous ways the significant changes that had taken place in the system of tribute since Inka times. Some of these changes, such as the shift from labor-based tribute, under the Inkas, to demands for money, goods, and labor, in colonial times, have been commented on extensively elsewhere (see Murra 1975, 1987; Pärssinen 1992). I should also note that it was common practice for *encomenderos*, upon receipt of tribute in kind (as with several of the items listed in Table 6.2), to put those goods up for sale in the market. This was potentially an important source of revenue for *encomenderos*. Aside

TABLE 6.2

Selected Tribute Items Given to Pizarro from Jauja*

a) in addition we gave him [Pizarro] 149 *fanegas*** of corn

b) in addition we gave to Capitán Soto by the command of the *marquéz* (i.e., Pizarro) 37 Indian men [and] 45 Indian women . . .

c) in addition we gave him 238 *fanegas* of quinua

d) in addition we gave him 2386 *fanegas* of potatoes

e) in addition we gave him 2983 pots and vases

f) in addition we gave him 209 pairs of sandals

g) in addition we gave him 2386 partridges

h) in addition we gave him 3862 pounds of fish

i) when the *marquéz* left for Cuzco, we gave him 837 Indians as bearers, and 102 Indians were lost . . .

*Cited in Pärssinen 1992: 34–36.

**Fanega* is a grain measure, equaling about one and a half bushels.

from changes in the types of objects that were required as tribute, and the use to which they might be put, what I want to stress is an equally radical shift that had taken place in the ideology and use of numbers, as well as in the principles motivating and directing the practice of arithmetic. These changes can best be appreciated by comparing the quantities of items given to the Spanish by the people of Jauja, as shown in Table 6.2, with the quantities making up the labor groups noted in the earlier list of the tribute that was provided to the Inkas by the Chupacho (see Table 6.1).

In the earlier Chupacho list, we see an expression of numerical values in the assignment of labor service that adheres almost without exception to the practice of recruitment by *full* decimal units. This is very much in keeping with the general principles and values of the ontology of numbers (in which full decimal units are regarded as "whole and complete") that was developed in Chapters 2 and 3. On the other hand, the numbers in the later Jauja list, while also calculated according to a decimal system of numeration (the European Hispanic one), reflect a fundamentally different notion and use of numbers. For these were not, according to pre-Hispanic Andean principles and values, "logical" numbers, or types of units. That is, these quantitative units were not readily identifiable in terms of the "traditional," Inkaic types of tributary values— 10s, 20s, 50s, 100s, etc.—which were themselves compatible with the units of social and political organization found throughout much of the Andes in social groupings identified as *chunka* - "ten," *pachaqa* - "one hundred," and *waranqa* - "one thousand." Rather, these new, Spanish units of accounting were not only very precise, but they were also largely what I would call "interdecimal" values, that is, numbers denoting values between whole decimal units (such as 2,983, or 209, or 2,386). Where did such values come from? How was one to think about such numbers and understand their meaning?

Unfortunately, we do not have in the colonial documentation testimony reflecting the reaction of people, especially not that of the *hatunruna* (the "great people," or commoners), to a set of tribute demands such as those outlined in Table 6.2. In fact, it is unlikely that, in the first few decades following the conquest, "commoners" would have been confronted in any sustained way with such numerical values. For the most part, demands for tribute would have been communicated directly to the *kurakas,* who would have passed them on to the people who were expected to supply either the labor time or goods demanded (see Mayer 1982; Spalding 1984: 131). However, it was only a matter of time until the *comuneros* became deeply involved, both individually and collectively, in activities that demanded, or allowed, them to confront these new numerical values and forms of calculation directly. This occurred, for instance, through their participation in marketing surplus produce and their own "free" labor (see, for example, Harris, Larson, and Tandeter 1987; Larson 1988; Lehmann 1982). It was in such activities as these that a significant and ever-increasing proportion of the population in the colonial Andes began to experience directly the meaning and significance of the political arithmetic that sustained, and served as the means of communicating, the values and relations of mercantile capitalism.

One of the more direct and tangible ways in which the "new" European numbers were encountered in the emerging capitalist economy was in the handling of money. Coins bearing elaborate motifs combining pictorial representations (such as the coat of arms of the ruling house of the Hapsburgs), inscriptions (initially most commonly in Latin), as well as numbers (both Hindu-Arabic and Roman numerals) were struck in Lima and Potosí within a few decades following the conquest; coins were in widespread circulation thereafter (see Bischoff 1989). Although the possession and use of coins by both *kurakas* and *hatunruna* became increasingly common with each passing decade, we have very little information concerning how these objects were conceived of and "consumed" by Andean peoples (for a careful study of one of the few such accounts available to us, see Salomon 1991).

Given the paucity of the sources informing us on what people in local communities might have thought about the changes that were going on all around them, the best course to take here is to examine one remarkable attempt to appropriate the number signs of the new political arithmetic that was imposed and controlled, to an overwhelming degree, by the Europeans. As is true in so many of the spirited, intellectual battles that were waged against the Spaniards by a native Andean for which we have any documentation whatsoever from early colonial Peru, the case in question involves Guaman Poma de Ayala.

The Appropriation of Numbers in *Nueva Corónica y Buen Gobierno*

Guaman Poma de Ayala (ca. 1534–1615) was a descendant, on his father's side, from a line of *kurakas* of the province of Lucanas (in south-central Peru) and, on his mother's side, from an Inka princess, named Curi Ocllo (Porras Barrenechea 1986: 618–623). Very little about the biography of Guaman Poma is certain, neither concerning his ancestry and the dates of his birth or death, nor the period during which he composed his life's work, a chronicle of pre-Hispanic and colonial Peruvian civilization entitled *Nueva Corónica y Buen Gobierno* (ca. 1615). What is clear about Guaman Poma's activities during the 1570s, prior to writing his chronicle, is that he traveled through the central and southern Andes on tours of inspection with the priest Cristóbal de Albornoz, assisting in, or at least attending to, the destruction and burning of idols, the breaking up of *huacas* ("sacred objects/sites") and the persecution of "witches" (Porras Barrenechea 1986: 631). Guaman Poma was also associated later in his life with the priest Martín de Murúa. Although he despised Murúa for a variety of reasons (Adorno 1986: 55), it is possible that it was through his association with Murúa that Guaman Poma was exposed to a wide assortment of historical and ecclesiastical books and documents published in Spanish.

Through a series of personal misfortunes (the nature of which we need not go into here), Guaman Poma began to view in a more critical way both the personalities and the policies of the colonial civil and ecclesiastical administrations in Peru. He became convinced not only of the moral and ethical superiority of native Andeans *vis a vis* their Spanish overlords, but also of the absolute necessity to appeal to the Spanish crown for a halt to the abuses of the colonial system of government in Peru (Adorno 1986: 56 ff). This defense of the natives and appeal to the crown took the form of a 1,179-page letter to the king of Spain, Philip III. Included in the "letter"—which was probably never seen, much less read, by the king—were 397 drawings depicting life in Peru before, during, and after the conquest. I will focus here on a few drawings that depict three of the Inka kings who purportedly ruled in Peru before the Spanish conquest of the Inka empire (see Figure 6.1 a, b, and c).

In the drawings from Guaman Poma illustrated in Figure 6.1, the three kings are shown dressed in three-quarter-length tunics, called *unkus*. The *unkus* bear elaborate designs laid out in small squares arranged in rows and columns. These designs are known as *tucapus*, which González Holguín glosses as "worked pieces of a textile." As we see, many of the *tucapu* designs are rendered as Hindu-Arabic numerals; the numbers depicted are: 2 (=Z?), 3, 4, and 8. Since Hindu-Arabic numerals did not exist in the pre-Hispanic Andes, the question is: Why did Guaman Poma attribute the knowledge of such numbers to the Inka kings— or to the weavers of their tunics—of pre-Hispanic times? Before addressing this question, we should take a moment to familiarize ourselves with what are otherwise the "normal" designs of Inka *tucapus*.

Figure 6.2 is a reproduction of the elaborate *tucapu* designs that adorn an *unku* currently in the pre-Columbian collection at Dumbarton Oaks. This exceptionally diverse collection and complex arrangement of *tucapus* provides us with something on the order of a "sampler" of the range of *tucapu* designs that are found either on *unkus* in museum collections or as depicted in the drawings of Guaman Poma. Obviously we do not— nor would we expect to—see anything resembling Hindu-Arabic numerals in the designs of the Dumbarton Oaks *unku*.

Cummins (1994: 199) notes that *tucapu* designs probably denoted eth-

FIGURE 6.1.   *Unkus* with numerical *tucapus,* drawn by Guaman Poma.

nic, political, and religious status when woven into textiles and worn on ceremonial occasions. On the basis of his study of the *unkus* bearing *tucapus* depicted in the drawings by Guaman Poma, and from a comparison of these with actual Inka-period *unkus* surviving in museum collections, Zuidema (1991) similarly argues that the *tucapus* were used to make distinctions of rank and political organization in the Inka empire.

Now, it is quite likely that Guaman Poma would have been knowledgeable about the *tucapu* designs that actually appeared on Inka *unkus.* Such tunics were still occasionally worn on ceremonial occasions by descendants of Inka nobility in the late-sixteenth century in the two cities, Cusco and Huanuco, in which Guaman Poma lived for much of his life.

FIGURE 6.2. *Tucapus* on the Dumbarton Oaks tunic. Interlocked tapestry, cotton and wool. Each side of the tunic has a different checkerboard of motifs. Dumbarton Oaks Pre-Columbian collection.

Whether or not this was the case, as a highly literate and exceptionally intelligent man, Guaman Poma would undoubtedly have known that Inka *tucapus* did not include Hindu-Arabic numerals and that the Inkas did not, in fact, write numbers in the way that he depicts them in his drawings. So, again, the question arises: Why did Guaman Poma "invent" *tucapus* in the form of numbers? Or, perhaps more appropriately: What did Spanish numbers and Inka *tucapus* represent to Guaman Poma so that he felt compelled, or justified, in rendering *tucapus* as Hindu-Arabic numerals?

My answer to the above questions is premised on the supposition that Guaman Poma understood very well the power and significance of numbers in the colonial Andes. After, perhaps, the God of Christianity, numbers—that is, the symbols that were used by Spanish administrators for keeping census and tribute records—represented one of the most powerful instruments of colonial rule in the Andes. Faced with that knowledge, Guaman Poma had either to concede the unique invention and knowledge of numbers to the Spaniards or, alternatively, he had to appropriate that knowledge on behalf of native Andean peoples. It is clear which course Guaman Poma chose. How are we to interpret the larger significance and meaning of his choice?

There are two factors that should be taken into account in arriving at an interpretation of Guaman Poma's appropriation of Hindu-Arabic numerals for the Inkas. One takes as its point of departure the relationship between these number signs and the Andean numbers, or values, recorded on the *khipu;* the other centers on Guaman Poma's probable understanding of the parallel status of the God of Christianity and European numbers. As for the former, it could be argued that since the Inkas *did,* in fact, have a complex and sophisticated science of numbers in the *khipus,* Guaman Poma did not have to resort to the artifice of giving the knowledge of written number signs to the Inkas. All he had to do in order to demonstrate the comparability of Andean and Iberian numerical sciences was to provide graphic depictions of the *khipus* and then explain (in the drawings or perhaps in the text) their relationship to numbers as Europeans understood them. In fact, Guaman Poma *did* provide several depictions of *khipus* (see the example in Figure 6.3), although he did not go on to explain in any detailed way how these devices were used to record numbers.

It is important to recall here (for Guaman Poma himself never forgot

FIGURE 6.3. Depiction of a *quipucamayoq* by Guaman Poma.

this point for a moment) who his audience was; that is, he was writing for the king of Spain. While Guaman Poma was undoubtedly capable of producing a description of the numerical significance of the *khipus*, there were certain dangers offered by such an approach. Most significantly, Guaman Poma lived at a time when the reliability and integrity of the *khipus* were being called into question for a variety of reasons (Cummins 1994: 213, n. 24; Solórzano y Pereyra 1972 [1736]: 308–309; Urton n.d.). In addition, Guaman Poma would have been acutely aware that in the contest between the use of *khipus* and Spanish written documents for maintaining statistical records, the latter had decisively won out over the former. Thus, he could not afford to rest his case for the comparability of the achievement of Andean civilization *vis a vis* that of the Spaniards on such an arcane device as the *khipu*. He had to appropriate for Andeans the knowledge of "true" numbers.

In order to understand and appreciate Guaman Poma's dilemma and the logic of the tactic that he used for its resolution—the appropriation of the numerical symbols of the "other"—we should look briefly at another area in which he employed a similar tactic: his appropriation of the Christian God for pre-Hispanic Andeans.

Rolena Adorno, in her elegant and incisive study of the *Nueva Corónica y Buen Gobierno,* identifies a number of overarching themes that drove Guaman Poma's polemic against both the Spanish colonial system in Peru and the attitude of the Spaniards in their interactions with native Andeans. One of the central themes is reflected in Guaman Poma's many comments to the effect that, by virtue of their greed, avarice, and immorality in dealing with Andean peoples, the Spaniards had forfeited any claim to moral or ethical superiority (see Adorno 1986: 32–35). In a concomitant rhetorical move, Guaman Poma not only asserted the moral superiority of Andeans over Spaniards but he also claimed specifically that Andean peoples had known the God of Christianity, and had lived according to the Ten Commandments, since long before the European invasion. As Guaman Poma stated the case:

And thus we Indians are Christians, on account of the redemption of Jesus Christ and of his blessed mother, St. Mary, patroness of this kingdom and by the apostles of Jesus Christ, St. Bartholomew, St. James the Greater, and by the holy cross of Jesus Christ, all of which arrived in this kingdom before the Spaniards. Because of them we are Christian and we believe in only one God of the Holy Trinity. (cited in Adorno 1986: 27–29)

What is notable here is that Guaman Poma is not making a claim for a *similarity* between the Christian God and any one of a number of Andean deities, such as Viracocha or Pachacamac, that he might have chosen to cast in a comparable role. Guaman Poma seems to have clearly recognized, and at least partially accepted, the superiority of the Christian God over the native *huacas* and deities. Thus, he could not build an argument—and certainly not one for the benefit of the king of Spain—for the spiritual enlightenment and moral superiority of Andean peoples on the basis of their worship of a non-Christian god. By this line of reasoning, we arrive at an understanding of the necessity of appropriating the God of Christianity for native Andeans that is almost precisely parallel to the suggestion put forward earlier concerning why Guaman Poma must have felt the need to appropriate European numbers (in the form of Hindu-Arabic numerals) for pre-Hispanic Andeans.

In summary, I would argue that Guaman Poma's representation of *tucapus* in the form of Hindu-Arabic numerals is to be explained according to two propositions. First, in his drawing of the number-laden Inka *unkus,* he was implying that there was a correspondence (at some level) between what he understood the *tucapus* to represent for the Inkas and what he knew to be the meaning, use, and power of numbers in the late-sixteenth- and early-seventeenth-century world of colonial Peru. If such interpretations of the use and meaning of *tucapus* as those adduced by Cummins and Zuidema are correct, then we may suppose that Guaman Poma recognized in the two systems of signs similar instruments of representation whereby two different states, the Inkaic and the Spanish, used complex symbols, which were little understood by the people at large, to signify systems of ranking (that is, ordinal sequences) and organization whereby control over political, social, and economic affairs and resources was established and maintained. And second, the instruments of the political arithmetic of the Spaniards—that is, Hindu-Arabic numerals—were on a par, in Guaman Poma's view of the matter, with the God of Christianity as elements that could not be compromised, or translated, into a supposed Andean equivalent if his argument to the king of Spain for the integrity and high level of achievement of Andean civilization was to prove successful.

Conclusions

Given the limitations on our knowledge of the beliefs, attitudes, values, and knowledge of Andean *comuneros* before the present century, and given that we are nearing the end of this study, I must now be explicit about what I think is the historical status of the construction of the ontology of numbers and the philosophy of arithmetic and mathematics developed in Chapters 2 through 5. This is called for at this point for the following reasons.

As we have been concerned in this chapter with the question of the introduction into Andean societies in the mid-sixteenth century of a largely new and wholly "other" world of beliefs, knowledge, technical practices, and cosmology, we are forced to adopt some position with respect to two critical issues; first, what knowledge, beliefs, and values concerning numbers, arithmetic, and mathematics existed at the local level in Andean societies prior to the European invasion? And second, through or into what levels of native pre-Hispanic society can we be confident the new European ideas penetrated, took hold, and either replaced or became mixed with indigenous ideas, practices, and knowledge? These are critical issues to resolve at this juncture because how we answer these questions will to a large degree orient our thinking about the reaction of native Andeans to European ideas and administrative policies in early colonial times. For example, if our construction—from contemporary ethnographic and linguistic data—in Chapters 2 and 3 of a Quechua ontology of numbers, and in Chapter 5 of a mathematics of rectification, had salience in the ideas about numbers and their manipulations held by Quechua-speaking peoples during the colonial era, then we have at least some narrow footing on which to stand in thinking about native perceptions and constructions of the possible meaning and intentions of numbers and mathematical practice in the political economy of the Spanish colonial regime with its tribute in money, produce, and labor; its currency of arcane, nondecimal[13] denominations; and its market transactions promoting the exchange of quantities of produce for coins whose value per unit of produce could change from one year (or day) to the next.

Now, my supposition is that both the ontology of numbers and the philosophy of mathematics articulated earlier in this study would have been understood and shared to a significant degree by Quechua-speaking peoples of the colonial era. Furthermore, I would insist that the values and principles on which the ontology of numbers was based would not have been seriously challenged by the new numbers introduced by the Spaniards. I argue that this was probably the case because I see no reason to think that the logic and values underlying the Quechua formulation of the nature of numbers, and of the ways of explaining their generation and reproduction (see especially Chapter 3), would have been directly confronted by European (Spanish) ideas. One cannot suppose or even, for that matter, imagine that the meaning and logic of the Hispanic number system would have ever been explained to any Quechua-speaking person by a Spaniard. Therefore, the two systems would have functioned in largely—if not absolutely—separate domains.

For instance, when a woman sat and wove a fabric using (subliminally) the logic of *Mama* as the origin of "numbers" (*yupana*), manipulating threads in "pairs" (*ch'ullantin, khalluntin,* etc.) and decimal (whole and complete) units, the routines, thought, and articulation in speech of any one or all of these notions would have had their own sense and logic in that setting. On the other hand, when the household to which that woman belonged turned over its annual tribute to the village *kuraka* of, for example, "five" (*cinco*) *pesos,* "three" (*tres*) measures (*fanegas*) of corn, and "twenty-four" (*veinticuatro*) eggs, both the numbers and the logic organizing these sets of items would have been completely distinct from those organizing the sets of threads and their manipulation in weaving. In short, I see no reason to think, nor do I have any way of constructing a logical argument for the idea that, the "Quechua" and "Spanish" ontologies of numbers would have ever confronted each other and demanded some resolution in settings such as those imagined here. However, it *does* seem likely, as I will explain below, that the matter was different with respect to the possibility or the inevitability of a confrontation arising between a Quechua and a Spanish philosophy and practice of arithmetic and mathematics.

The reason that I suspect that the (hypothetical) pre-Hispanic Quechua mathematics of rectification would have been directly confronted by conflicting Spanish conceptions, whereas the ontology of numbers would not, has to do with the very different "arenas" to which the two referred and in which they functioned. That is, the ontology of numbers had its direct referents in the Quechua cardinal and ordinal numeral series, which, as suggested above, would have been reproduced in myriad settings connected with everyday production and consumption in villages throughout the Andes. The most direct perturbations in this system of naming quantities would have occurred when some entity, such as church or state, wanted to "rename" some well-known object or value—as would happen, for instance, with the devaluation of coinage (see, for example, the excellent studies by Mitre [1986] and Platt [1986a] on the causes and effects of several episodes of debasing and devaluing coinage in Bolivia throughout the mid- to late-nineteenth century). Such manipulations of values would not, however, undermine the *logic* of the system of number names. Such an occurrence would require transposing one number for another—as "one *real* is now worth three bushels of corn, not four"—but it would not threaten the order or under-lying logic of the number series as a whole.

On the other hand, what such an act of the devaluation of currency as that mentioned above *would* have done is to violate the principles of the arithmetic of rectification. That is, when, through an act such as the devaluation of currency the state changed the value of the coinage in circulation, this would violate the *pact* between the bearer of the coins and the state, and, by extension, it would undermine both the eco-nomic and philosophical systems of values on which exchanges were carried out at all levels of society on a daily basis. The point here, of course, is that the primary referents of the arithmetic of rectification were social, political, economic, and other *relationships* that were (ide-ally) maintained in a state of balance, harmony, and equilibrium. In or-der for corrections to be made—by the application of the "corrective procedures" (*yapa*) of addition, subtraction, multiplication, and divi-sion—the need for such corrections should be understood and obvious to both sides in the contractual relationship. For instance, in its obliga-tion to fulfill labor service for the Inka state, a decrease in the popula-tion within a community would have been recognized by both the com-munity and the state and a correction (such as a reduction in the number of laborers required for state projects) would have been made. Similarly, if the state needed additional labor input, it was obliged to increase its reciprocal *largesse.* However, in the political economy of the Spanish colonial state, the crown could decide that it needed to increase produc-tion (and thus needed more labor), or that it needed to sell more of its production in the colonial market (as with the *repartimiento*),[14] and make the needed corrections in its relation with its subjects. In such cases, however, the *comuneros* in Andean towns and villages who were affected by these "corrective procedures" were not a part of the process of decision making, nor did they enjoy any benefits from their imple-mentation; rather, they were merely the recipients of mandates from the state. Such abridgements by the Spanish colonial administration of what we have found to be certain common and essential philosophical principles of the mathematics of rectification—that is, standardization, fairness, equilibrium, and appropriateness—represented, more importantly, violations of the state's relationship with local communities; such actions were met throughout the colonial era with noncompliance, resistance, and, occasionally, outright rebellion (see O'Phelan Godoy 1988).

Thus, I argue, in relation to questions concerning "cultural continuities" in Andean Quechua beliefs, values, and practices that, on one hand, there has probably been a high degree of continuity in the logic and articulation of the ontology of numbers from late pre-Hispanic times to the present day in Quechua-speaking communities throughout the Andes. On the other hand, I suspect that the particular political and economic forces that have been at work transforming attitudes and values about the nature and meaning of exchange have presented far more challenges to maintaining the logic and sense, much less the practical forms of action—the application of "corrective procedures" (yapa)—that were central to the arithmetic and mathematics of rectification.

Conclusions

Introduction

While Chapters 5 and 6 contain an accurate representation of what I have come to understand, and have had explained to me in explicit terms, concerning the motivation and goal of Quechua arithmetic and mathematics today, I do not want to claim that the style of arithmetic practice that I have characterized as an "art of rectification" has *necessarily* always been the nature of arithmetic and mathematical practices in the Andes. For example, I am not convinced that such a view can account for the full range of conceptions of number(s) and the execution of arithmetic and mathematical operations in pre-Hispanic (especially Inkaic) societies in the Andes. Given both the absence of an indigenous system of writing (or at least of our failure to date to recognize and decipher such a system) in the pre-Columbian Andes in which commentary could have been recorded on native conceptions of number, as well as our as yet rudimentary understanding of the full range of calculations that may have gone into the production of the numerical values recorded on the *khipus,* we should be wary of *not* allowing for the possibility that there may have been mathematics *aficionados* in the Inka empire who explored numbers in highly creative and abstract ways—that is, in ways that go far beyond the concrete, utilitarian requirements of the arithmetic of rectification discussed in Chapter 5. While allowing for such a possibility at the theoretical level, we must, nonetheless, note how well what we *do* know about Quechua arithmetic and mathematical practice accords with what I have called the art of rectification.

Having said the above, I must also (in good conscience) state early on in these conclusions that any mathematically sophisticated reader who has stayed with me to this point must be asking: "So, where's the mathematics?" Just so that that reader will not be under the impression that I think that there *is* anything mathematically complex or fancy about the foregoing, I want to state clearly that I do not think that. I leave it to those who are truly mathematically inclined, *and who have a firm grasp of Quechua language and culture as experienced in the Andes,* to expand on the information and issues raised in this study (much more data about which is recoverable from other ethnographic and ethno-historical sources) in order to illuminate and advance our knowledge about what I firmly believe to be a true depth and complexity in Quechua numerical ideas and arithmetic and mathematical practice.

On the other hand, there are several important contributions, I think, that have resulted from the research, analysis, and writing represented by this study. I outline what seem to me to be the most important of these below.

A Hypothesis for the Logic of Quechua Decimal Numeration and Organization

We have examined several types and bodies of data that have allowed us to articulate a reasonably coherent theory of numbers for Quechua-speaking peoples of the Andes, past and present. These primarily linguistic and ethnographic materials have led us along a number of alternative routes to arrive consistently at a view of, in the first place, *cardinal numbers* as a set of well-ordered positions, each of which is composed of a collection of units having (excepting for the initial position, which I will return to in a moment) a cardinality one unit greater (i.e., more) than the preceding position and one unit less than the succeeding position. As for *ordinal numerals,* these are conceptualized in positional and hierarchical-sequential terms, so that any given position—again excepting the "first" (see below)—is "younger" than its predecessor and "older" than its successor.

The above formal statement of the conceptual organization of cardinal numbers and ordinal numerals may be combined and translated in the Quechua ontology of numbers that we have elaborated here in terms of a group composed of five members. The number "one" (*uj*) and "first" (*ñawpa ñaqen/kaq*) position of the group of five is consistently glossed as a mature reproductive female (*mama*). The positions 2 . . . 5, and/or 2d . . . 5th, are the age-graded offspring of *mama*. I argue now, as I suggested in Chapter 3 with respect to the two sets of positive integers 1 . . . 5 and 6 . . . 10 (e.g., as with the hands), that the logic and relations of the "model of fives" can be advanced along *as a set* generating and organizing successively higher/greater/younger number groupings of fives into the infinite series of positive integers (that is, 1 . . . 5; 6 . . . 10; 11 . . . 15; 16 . . . 20; etc.). As will be apparent, any higher set, such as 96 . . . 100, can be reconceptualized internally as a group ordered according to the same principles as the prototypical group: 1 . . . 5 and/or 1st . . . 5th.

But the "model of fives" is only part of the picture we have developed in this study with respect to the Quechua ontology of numbers. Another essential element is the "pairing" principle. According to this principle, which is phrased in Quechua as the relationship, for example, between *ch'ulla* ("odd") and *ch'ullantin* ("even" [i.e., the partner of "odd"]), any single unit must have its pair, or its partner. Now, I need to introduce a symbol to indicate this process of the unification of an odd and an even unit or set. It is virtually impossible to find a symbol that does not already have a well-defined meaning in mathematical (or other) symbolism. Therefore, I will choose a logical symbol for my purposes to express the action of joining, or uniting, one unit, or set, together with its natural pair; this symbol will be **U** (indicating "union"). Thus, for example, 1 **U** 2 = 2; 3 **U** 4 = 4 (see the system of naming fingers presented by Santo Tomás in Table 3.3, which contains this principle of union in its basic form). The basic pattern here is: *ch'ulla* ("odd") **U** *ch'ullantin* ("even/partner") = *ch'ullantin*.

I argue that when we join the "model of fives" together with the principle of "pairing" (**U**), we derive the semantic values, the structural principles, and the logic of the *decimal* system of numeration in Quechua culture and ideology. Now, in the series of groups of "fives" adduced in the second paragraph above, adjacent groups alternate between what I will call "odd collections" (e.g., 1 . . . 5; 11 . . . 15; 21 . . . 25; etc.) and "even collections" (e.g., 6 . . . 10; 16 . . . 20; 26 . . . 30; etc.). These "odd" and "even" collections of fives are related to each other in the natural number series according to the model of the basic odd/even relationship between 1 and 2; that is:

1 and/or (1 . . . 5) = *ch'ulla* ("odd"); 2 or (6 . . . 10) = *ch'ullantin* ("even")

Under the force of the pairing principle *ch'ullantin* (or *yanantin/khalluntin*) each *odd collection* (e.g., 1 . . . 5) becomes "complete" (i.e., even) by coming together with its (successor) *even collection;* that is: 1 . . . 5 **U** 6 . . . 10 = a complete, paired collection. *The result of this coupling of alternate, adjacent, and complementary "odd" and "even" collections gives rise to the decimal series:* (1 . . . 5) **U** (6 . . . 10) = *10;* (11 . . . 15) **U** (16 . . . 20) = *20;* . . . (91 . . . 95) **U** (96 . . . 100) = *100;* etc. I also argue for the theoretical possibility that, depending on the circumstances, the unity (91 . . . 95) **U** (96 . . . 100) = 100 can be (re-)conceptualized as the pairing: (1 . . . 50) **U** (51 . . . 100) = 100.

This hypothesis for the logic and semantics of decimal numeration in Quechua allows us to move from the typical kinds of vague arguments often adduced to explain decimal numeration, such as: "this relates to the number of fingers of the hands" (an argument that leaves us wondering how there could be anything *but* decimal numeration), to an explanation that is built up on the basis of well-attested logical principles and semantic categories in Quechua language and practice.

In summary, the basic elements of this hypothesis for the logical and semantic categories underlying and motivating the decimal series in Quechua ideology and numerical-arithmetic ontology are illustrated in Table 7.1.

Thus, according to the principles laid out in Table 7.1, we see that dual organization and the decimal system of numeration, which as we saw in Chapter 6 were central principles in Inkaic (Quechua) administrative organization, are seen to have been not only compatible but complementary principles of organization. For example, in a numerical context, what we could call the "moiety" of the odd set (1 . . . 5) is linked to and complemented by the "moiety" of the even set (6 . . . 10) to produce an overall decimal grouping, which I argue became an organizational archetype of Inka political administration.

It is important to note that we have arrived at this hypothesis for the logic underlying Inka political, administrative, and numerical organiza-

TABLE 7.1

The Generation of Decimal Numeration

(odd) **U** (even) = complete set

(*ch'ulla*) **U** (*ch'ullantin*) = *ch'ullantin*

(1) **U** (2) = 2

(1 . . . 5) **U** (6 . . . 10) = 10

(11 . . . 15) **U** (16 . . . 20) = 20

(91 . . . 95) **U** (96 . . . 100) = 100

and/or

(1 . . . 50) **U** (51 . . . 100) = 100

(1 . . . 500) **U** (501 . . . 1,000) = 1,000

etc.

tion on the basis of ontological numerical principles and semantic constructions defining symbolic characteristics of various types of sets and collections that are present in contemporary Quechua language and culture. That is, it is the material analyzed in Chapters 2 and 3 that has allowed us to articulate (for the first time, I believe) a theory of the foundation of decimal organization in the Andes.

Culture and the Art of Rectification

The second contribution of this study is what I must still characterize as a hypothesis for Quechua arithmetic and mathematical practice as an "art of rectification." I have analyzed the logical principles and semantic categories of this art in Chapter 5. In Chapter 6, I have brought together and analyzed several diverse bodies of data and examples that I think allow us to assert with some confidence that these views on, and uses of, arithmetic and mathematics were shared in late pre-Hispanic and early colonial times in the Andes.

Now, it might be argued that, when stated in general terms, *every* system of arithmetic and mathematics is, in the end, an "art of rectification." That is, every system of number manipulation utilizing the arithmetic operations of addition, subtraction, multiplication, and division could be said to have as an actual or potential goal the derivation of equations displaying harmonic number relations. In practice—that is, as the practitioners of the numerical sciences in any particular culture ply their trade—it may or may not be the case that what is *sought after* are expressions of equilibrium, balance, and harmony in relations between and among number sets, groupings, and collections. Whether or not this potential is realized in any given culture is a matter to be investigated and determined on the basis of empirical analysis.

The point to stress here is that in Quechua society and culture, past and present, the goal and purpose of arithmetic and mathematical practice seems to have been the establishment and maintenance of such states *in the real world* (as in the distribution of resources and in human actions). Such a goal is, I think, quite distinct from what we find, for instance, in both the theory and practice of arithmetic and mathematics in the Western tradition. That is, in the West, the performance as well as the results of the operations of addition, subtraction, etc., are not considered to have moral or ethical value; they may, however, have aesthetic value (as is often expressed in terms of the "elegance" of mathematical theorems and equations).

A Unified View: Dualism, the Model of Fives, Decimal Organization, and the Art of Rectification

Finally, at a general conceptual level, there can be made, I think, a convergence of the ontology of numbers and the arithmetic and mathematics of rectification elaborated in this study. However, this possibility will be recognized only after we have successfully arrived at a coupling of the "model of fives" with the logic of dualism and decimal organization (see above discussion of such logic). That is, the union of alternate and adjacent groups of fives—the first set of which is *odd* (1 . . . 5), the second of which is *even* (6 . . . 10)—to produce full decimal units is essentially, I argue, a process of seeking "rectification" (i.e., "completeness" = even numbers = balance and equilibrium) from a state of disequilibrium (i.e., "incompleteness" = odd numbers = imbalance). In the union of the two broad values and sets of principles underlying and organizing the ontology of numbers and the arithmetic and mathematics of rectification, Quechua people have worked to achieve a numerical science grounded in the sensible, logical, and lived categories, relations, and experiences of social life. The latter are virtually never simple, harmonic, or conflict-free—but they are always seeking to be.

At the beginning of this study, I stated that I originally took up the investigation of Quechua numbers and arithmetic from an interest in two problems; the first was the study of the *khipus;* the second was a curiosity about what we might find if, for the first time, we undertook a serious study of Quechua knowledge of, and ideas about, numbers. As I stated earlier, my initially greater interest in the former problem soon gave way to a fascination with the latter. Having now completed the latter, we may now return to the question of the *khipus* and ask: How does what we have learned about the Quechua ontology of numbers and the arithmetic and mathematics of rectification provide us with new ideas and strategies for investigating the quantitative and narrative components of the *khipus?* This question should be addressed in the near future—a task to which I hope to make a contribution.

Appendix:
Quechua Number Symbols and Metaphors

(0)

ch'usaq: "empty" (in terms of weight or contents); *ch'usaq* also shares a part of its meaning with the phrase *mana qallarisqasaqisqa* ("vacant").

jusq'un: zero; hole (specifically in reference to the number sign "0").

muyu: "circle, round."

q'ala: "all/nothing"; e.g., if you give away *all* of your coca, now there is *nothing*. If used to say "that's all," *q'ala* indicates that there is absolutely no more; the term *tuquy* can also be used to say "that's all," but it implies that there may, in fact, be a little bit more.

qhasi: "nothing/all," or "never/always"; e.g., if you want to say that you went to look for someone *all day long* and they were *never* there (if they were *always* gone), *qhasi* is the appropriate term.

Uj (1)

ch'ulla: "one alone"; (odd number) left over after counting a group of things two by two; related usages include:
  ch'ulla ñawi: "one-eyed";
  ch'ulla q'uruta: a person with only one testicle;
  ñuk'u: "odd/uneven," e.g., in relation to hands (i.e., someone with only one hand or arm = *ñuk'u*);
  pichilu: erect penis (= 1).

khallu: "one/alone/only"; related usages include:
  khallun: "its (one's) pair/mate" (when the two are separate);
  khalluntin: "pair";

uj yanantin: "one pair";

yuntayki: "your pair/mate; used for a pair of bulls yoked together, but also for people, things, etc., that always go
together.

uj: 1; 100 things (= 1); iconographically speaking, 1 is:

    aysa(na): "needle of a scale," or *gancho:* "hook";

    chhulu: "the (a) beak";

    chuku: something firmly planted (syn. *chutu*);

    chuta: "one," and a stick for measuring;

    chutu: something firmly planted (syn. *chuku);*

    uj k'aspi: "stick."

uj jach'i: "one handful," but with the hand *under* the quantity, rather
than around it (SEE *uj maki* below); the following are related
usages:

    jachillikuy: "I pick up a handful and taste it";

    uj puqtuy: "a double handful"—of the *uj jach'i* type—offered to
    someone.

uj kaq: "first"; in ordinal sequences, "one" (i.e., the "first") can also be
referred to as *ñawpa,* or *ñawpaqtaqa,* or *mama,* or *uj kaq.*

uj maki: "one hand"; something you can hold in one hand; i.e., the
hand goes all the way around the quantity in question; *uj maki*
also can be used to indicate:

    "all together";

    "five" (of something; e.g., the fingers of one hand all forming a
    unit);

    to help someone ("lend a hand") in a violent, or vigorous,
    manner.

ujninta: "one of a variety of groups."

ujpi: "one time."

uj puchun: the "remainder, or left over" after counting by pairs, or by
larger sets; i.e., *puchu* is not restricted to the characteristic of

ch'ulla ("odd, uneven") if, for instance, you are counting by *fives* and have *four* left over.

uj wiñay: "one century."

yuparay: "to count one by one" (not two by two, etc.) in any order; related usage:

> *suk'api yuparay,* or *sinrupi yuparay:* "to count things in their proper order, one by one."

Iskay (2)

chipiq chipiq: "two times" (twice).

chipiq chipiq ñawisitu: "to wink *two times*" (this phrase is also used for the eyelashes).

ch'ullantin: "pair" (literally, "the odd one together with its natural complement"), composed of two "odds" that complement each other; related usage:

> *ch'ulla ch'ulla:* "odd (one) odd (one)"; things that are unequal (different) in various ways.

iskay (2): iconographically speaking, 2 is *pili:* "duck."

iskaychay: "to take apart," as to take apart 3 *atus* (agricultural terraces) and make 2 of them; or, to divide one *atu* into two (SEE ALSO *iskayman raki*); related usages:

> *iskayman chhikachaqkama raki:* to divide something into two *equal* parts (here, -*kama* = "between");
>
> *iskayman raki:* "divide into two," as to divide one *atu* into two (this usage indicates that one part is smaller than the other);
>
> *juch'uyachiy:* to take apart one large/long thing to make two smaller/ shorter ones;
>
> *pisiyachiy:* to put the contents of one large container into two smaller ones;
>
> *wikhay:* to divide up an entire unit into two or more portions.

iskaykuna: "twos" (-*kuna* = pluralizer); however, one should not say *iskaykuna* for "two"; if you do say this, it means "two or more,"

but not just "two." This conforms to the rule that *-kuna* should
not be used with even numbers.

iskay maki, or *maki maki:* "to weigh something with your two hands."

iskay ukhu: "between two."

khallun: "its, or the, pair" (when the two members of a natural pair are
separate); related usages:

> *iskaynintin:* "two independent things together" (e.g., two bot-
> tles of beer are *separate* things);

> *khalluntin:* "pair"; two things bound/sewn together;

> *ujnintin:* "two together" (used when referring to things com-
> posed of two *parts*);

> *uj yanantin:* "a/one pair."

ñuñu ñuñu: "two breasts together (i.e., a natural pair of things).

pañantin: "two things together that are of the same type, or lineage" (also,
pañapura).

pañapura. SEE *pañantin.*

patampi patampi: "one above/on top of the other."

pataray: "to double, fold."

phishqayunta ch'ullayuq: $(5 \times 2) + 1 = 11.$

puqtuy or *iskay maki:* "two handsful."

purachiy: "to make two things equal; to equalize"; related usage:

> *purarachiy:* "to make a variety of things equal."

puraqpis: "both"; related usage:

> *puraqninchis patapis:* "between both of us (equally)."

puraq uya: "inconsistent"; e.g., a person who acts "two-faced"; related
usages:

> *puraq uyachiy:* "to compare"; "to separate out equivalent
> things"; as the two hands turned back-to-back against
> each other.

> *uya purachiy:* "to justify, or adjust something(s); equity, impar-
> tiality, face-to-face"; as hands placed face-to-face con-
> fronting each other, but separated.

Kinsa (3)

iskaypaq chaupin: "the center/middle of (sets of) twos"; used to refer to
the central member of a group of five (i.e., the third).

kinsa (3): iconographically speaking, 3 is:

    iskay aysana/iskay qichana: "double puller/double opener";

3

    uquti: "anus."

3

kinsa: three; considered a "pivotal" number in counting by dozens.
kinsa ayllu:

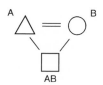

    "three *ayllus*" (social, territorial, and ritual groups); synonyms
        of *kinsa ayllu* include: *kinsa ñan* ("three roads"), *kinsa
        palqa* ("three branches"), *kinsantin palqa* ("three inter-
        connected branches"), and *palqantinkama* ("branching
        together").
kinsa k'uchu: "triangle"; "three angles/corners in/around the same
    place."

kinsaman: "fracture, fragment, divide or separate into three parts"; e.g.,
    division of the year into three parts or the life cycle into three
    parts; these two three-part divisions (of the year and the life
    cycle) are classified as follows:
    1. *tarpuy (muju):* "to plant (seed)";
    2. *puquchiy (wiñay):* "to nurture (to grow)";
    3. *uqhariy:* "to give forth (bear fruit)."
kinsanchay: "(repeat) three times."

kinsa sayayuq: "three partitions."

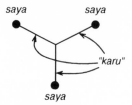

uj yunta ch'ullayuq: "one pair, possessor of one standing alone" (2 + 1 = 3).

Tawa (4)

midiya dusinapaq iskay faltan: four; literally, "two less than half a dozen."
muyu muyu: "(a)round (a)round"; a children's game (also called *t'ullku-
 nakuy,* and *q'iwinakuy*):

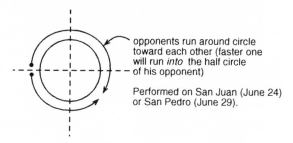

taqllu: indicates four fingers held up for measurement.
tawakana, or *tawqana:* "four-footed" (literally, "fourer").
tawa k'uchuyuq, or *tawa makiyuq,* or *tawa jap'iyniyuq:* "square."
tawantinman: "four all together toward" (i.e., from four different points
 of reference, all merging to point toward another, fifth, point).

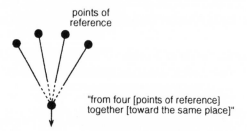

tawantinta: "from four different points all together pointing to the same place."

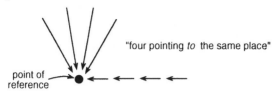

tawa palqa,

or *tawantin:* "four branches, or four (parts) all together"; *tawa palqa,* or *tawantin,* is the basic framework for the widely shared cosmological representation shown below:

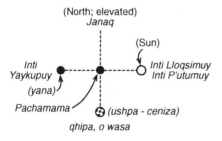

tawa qara: "thick skin"; e.g., skin of testicles. Derived from the expression that one can make love four times, as if having four testicles. (This is something of an insult, like saying *saco largo* ["big bag," "big balls"] in Peru.)

tawas: "four things"; here *-s* is the Spanish pluralizer. One usually does not say "*tawakuna,*" as in *kinsakuna* ("threes"); the Quechua pluralizer *-kuna* is usually used only with odd numbers (i.e., 1, 3, 5, . . .).

tawa tawa: "four (by) four"; refers to a quadrilateral shape, but one that is more rectangular than square.

tawa tawa: "four (by) four; direct, or in one direction."

taway tawa: "four plus four" (here, *-y* = plus).

Phishqa (5)

chunkaq chawpin: "in the middle, or half of, ten" (referring specifically to the two hands together).

isqonpa kuskanin: "half of nine" (= 5); illustrated on the hands:

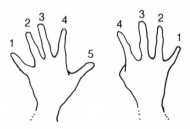

phishqa (5): iconographically speaking, 5 = *jusi* ("sickle").

phishqa phishqa: "five five" (= 10).

suqtaq qhipan: "of six, the previous one" (= 5).

suqta sullk'an: "the younger (sibling) of six" (= 5).

tawaq kuraqnin: "the elder (sibling) of four" (= 5).

tawaq ujnin: "of four, one more" (five); i.e., 4 fingers + 1 thumb; the thumb is called "the senior/elder of four."

ujpa tawan: "the one belonging to four" (= 5).

uj phishqa: "some five"; "around, or in the range of, five" (but not exactly five).

Suqta (6)

allin kawsa: "the good/proper way" (= six); i.e., six is the appropriate number of children to have.

chunka iskayniyuq kuskanin: "half of twelve" (= six).

iskay cuarta: "two sets of three" (= 6); *cuarta,* in relation to clothing, cloth, etc., is a set composed of *three* things/pieces.

iskay kinsa: "two [times] three" (= six).

kinsa kinsa: "three [plus] three" (= six).

llasa kuruta: "heavy testicles," "three sets of testicles" (= six).

Qanchis (7)

chupa sapa: indicates the negative character of a group of seven; indicates bad luck.

pusaqpa qhipan: "of eight, the previous one" (= 7).

qanchis (negative associations): *qanchis* has many negative associations; it is: *qincha* ("adulterous"), *millay* ("ugly"), *saqra* ("devil"), *supay* ("devil"), *pantasqa* ("confounder; the confuser"). Also, for example, *Iskay kinsaqpaq kuraqnin, millay* ("the elder/next higher number of two times six is ugly"). And, it is believed that the month of August is bad, but August 7th is *very* bad (although it is also the day to seek protection against bad influences and bad luck).

"*qanchis, qanchis, qanchis*": sound made by a braying burro.

qanchis uya: "seven faces"; with respect to potatoes, one with "seven faces" is bad, and bad luck; toss it out; related usage:

> *qanchis chuchu:* "destruction; calamity"; when a potato has this form (i.e., "seven faces"), or when a dog is born with seven teats, these are bad auguries.

q'ara ullitu: "little skin penis."

$$7$$

q'ara ullitu: also the name for "dice." In playing the dice game *mayores y menores,* a dice total of more than 7 is *mayor* ("major"); below 7 is classified as *menor* ("minor"); the player does not pay if the number 7 itself comes up.

Pusaq (8)

iskay tawa: "two [times] four" (= 8).

iskay t'aqlu: t'aqlu indicates the measure of the four fingers of the hand held together; thus, *iskay t'aqlu* = 8.

pusaq (8): iconographically speaking, 8 is:

chhuqula: 8; related to the dress of certain groups (e.g., *gauchos*) in which the trunk and legs make a rectangular shape.

ch'uwi: "lasso"; actually, it seems that *ch'uwi ch'uwi* ("two lassos") = 8;

llama ñawi: "llama eye"; figure-eight; also related directly to astronomy, as Alpha and Beta Centauri are called this;

palqa ñawi, or *ñawi palqa:* "branching/bifurcated eyes";

puraq uya: "two-faced," one above the other (= 8);

q'apila: "press the flesh"; also has the sense of "shake hands," and "two vaginas," one placed above the other;

yarabola: indicates a slow, heavy movement, as when the testicles throb and move slightly. Related to comparison of testicles to the number eight (OO) sideways.

Isqon (9)

isqon (9): iconographically speaking, 9 is:

> *uma sapa:* "one/single headed";
>
> *uray millchu:* the posture of someone with upper trunk bent over, frontwards; *uray millchu* also indicates the "character" of 9 as: *zonzo* ("foolish"), and *cosa(s) sin orden* ("a thing without order").

pusaq ñawpaqin: "that which follows eight."

isqun rirun: "nine-fingered"; said of someone who lacks one thumb; related usages:

> *ch'ulla riru:* "odd-fingered"; indicates that one of person's three largest fingers (1st, 2d, or 3d) is missing;
>
> *muru riru:* "spotted-fingered"; said of someone whose little finger is missing; also used to indicate "when almost all the hair is cut off."

Chunka (10)

chunka (10): the implication of things complete, or rounded off, is an important aspect of 10, as in the following:

> *chunkachay:* "round off to 10";
>
> *chunkanchay:* repeat some activity until you do it 10 times;
>
> *chunkata jamun:* to come *more than* ten times, or more than 10,000 times;
>
> *chunkatani:* to say 10 times, or 10,000 times;
>
> *chunkay chunkita:* of the total number present, reduce to two sides of 10 each (as in a fight between two groups);
>
> *q'alay q'alita:* everyone against everyone.

chunka maki: "ten-hand(-ed)"; a capable person; one who can do things very rapidly.

chunkata munaniy: "I want ten"; if 10 is the number wanted but a lesser quantity is given, the term *chunkamuy* ("up to 10 it"; i.e., increase it up to ten) is used.

phishqa phishqa: "five five" (= 10).

Pacha (100)

cien (100) *cosas:* "a hundred things" (= 1).

pachaq chaki: "100 leg"; centipede; used in the conundrum: "The centipede lives 100 years. How does it do this? By changing its skin *[ch'utku]*."

pachaqchu: "having 100"; carries the sense of something done *three times* (three is the number of completion).

pachaq maki: "I have sold to you about a hundred times."

pachaq tian!: "you're a hundred!" (you are very intelligent!).

uj waka: "one cow," or *uj sara* "one ear of corn" = 100 *Bolivianos;* now (i.e., with inflation) *uj waka* = 1,000 *Bolivianos*.

wiñay: "100 years" (i.e., a century).

Phishqa Pachaq (500)

kuskan suk'a: "half a complete unit of money"; SEE *suk'a,* below).

phishqa pachaq: "five one-hundred" (= 500).

Waranqa (1,000)

chunkatani: this form of "10" has the sense of saying or doing something "a thousand times"; syn. *waranqa waranqa* ("1,000 1,000").

suk'a: a "complete" quantity of money, in the amount: 10 x 100 (= 1,000 Bolivianos); kept in a special bag, called a *waqaycha,* where only complete *suk'a* units are kept;

q'asa: ca. "broken, split" = less than 1,000 Bolivianos.

uj waka: "a cow"; 1,000 Bolivianos (or, as is commonly said in Peru, 1,000 *Intis* is *un loco* ("a crazy").

waranqa: "1,000"; often used by campesinos in referring to *1 Boliviano*. This is the old peso equivalent, in centavos, of the *Boliviano* (*1,000 pesos* was changed to *100 centavos,* which equaled *1 Boliviano,* which is now called "*waranqa*").

waranqa waranqa waranqata, or *waranqakuna:* "millions of times."

waranqa waranqa wata: "millions of years"; the three ages of the world.

Multiplicity/Infinity

ch'ipa: an "agglomeration."

mana tukukuyniyuq: "unlimited in its dimensions/borders."

mana willay atina: "you can't say all there is" (to say).

mana yupayta atina: "what cannot be counted."

puraq jusk'u: said of a woman who has intercourse with many different men.

puraq ullu: said of a man who has intercourse with many different women.

yupa: "much, many"; has the sense of the immense quantity of things in the world, which cannot be counted.

Notes

Chapter 1

1. This statement, which I mean to apply to studies of numbers, arithmetic, and mathematics among contemporary Quechua-speaking peoples of the Andes, requires some qualification. The one work published to date whose subject matter bears a resemblance to that addressed herein is Mendizábal Losack's *Estructura y Función en la Cultura Andina (Fase Inka)* (1989). While Mendizábal's study includes some accounts (with little ethnographic context) of the meaning and uses of numbers in contemporary communities in the central Peruvian Andes, most of the data he discusses pertain to the use of numbers as described in the Spanish chronicles, in reference to late Inkaic and early colonial Peru. Mendizábal provides quite novel etymological analyses of Quechua number words, as well as idiosyncratic and often unsubstantiated attributions of symbolic values to particular numerical units (e.g., *chunka* [10] and *pachaq* [100]) in his interpretations of the meaning and significance of these units in colonial documents. Nonetheless, I will make reference, especially in Chapter 4, to relevant materials discussed by Mendizábal. The one other study of numbers published to date is an article by Solís F. and Chacón S. (1990). This short work contains a useful overview of the primary lexemes for numbers in Quechua and discusses some of the basic rules and principles of the formation of compound numbers.

2. Crump characterizes the three traditions of mathematical philosophy in the West as follows. The "*constructivist,*" or *Intuitionist,* view is that "in mathematics nothing can be accepted as meaningful, or even be recognised as existing, unless it can be derived by a finite process whose starting point is the natural numbers." The *logicist,* or *Platonic,* view is that "mathematical objects are real, and their existence an objective fact, quite independent of our knowledge of them. (We can also be content with a subjective variant, attributed to Kant, according to which "the truths of [. . .] arithmetic are forced upon us by the way our minds work; this explains why they are supposedly true and independent of experience. The intuitions of time and space [. . .] are objective in the sense that they are universally valid for all human minds.") And finally, the *Formalist* view argues that "mathematics is a game, with rules made up of symbols and formu-

lae . . . [M]an makes the rules of the game, but the powers then given to numbers are outside his control" (Crump 1990: 5–6; for a stimulating overview of these various traditions, see Barrow 1992). As Rotman notes (1993: 18–19), by far the majority of mathematicians accept the Platonic view of mathematical philosophy and the nature of mathematical truths.

3. As I was preparing the final manuscript of this book for publication, I encountered Brian Rotman's recent book *Ad Infinitum* (1993). This work, whose subject matter is characterized in one of its three subtitles as, "Taking God out of Mathematics and Putting the Body Back In," contains a critique of mathematical Platonism that is, in all of its essential features, identical to that contained in his 1988 article, on which I rely in my discussion in the text.

4. Fieldwork in Pacariqtambo, Peru, was carried out in 1981–1982 with the support of a grant provided by the National Science Foundation (No. BNS 9106254). Support for the fieldwork in 1987–1988 was provided by a Picker Research Fellowship and a sabbatical leave from Colgate University. I express my deep appreciation to the N.S.F. and Colgate University for their support of this research.

5. For a detailed and highly readable account of my fieldwork in Pacariqtambo, see Meyerson 1993.

6. There were several reasons for my decision to carry out this research in central Bolivia rather than in my more familiar research site of south-central Peru. First, I was concerned (especially in traveling with my family) about what was, at the time I wrote my proposal for fieldwork (in 1992), lingering political unrest and occasional acts of terrorism in Peru caused by Sendero Luminoso and the government's counter-insurgency campaign. Also, after having carried out some four years of fieldwork around Cusco, I was interested in, and curious about, life in the Andes *outside* the Cusco area. However, I did not want to lose the use of my knowledge of Southern Peruvian Quechua. As I have explained, there is a high degree of mutual intelligibility between Southern Peruvian and Bolivian Quechua. Therefore, central Bolivia seemed a likely and attractive region for fieldwork. We selected Sucre after visiting the city at the beginning of fieldwork, in 1993, on the recommendation of my Bolivianist anthropologist colleague, Tom Abercrombie.

7. My fieldwork in Misminay, Peru, in 1975–1976 was made possible by the support of a predissertation fellowship from the Organization of American States. I express my appreciation to the O.A.S. for its support.

Chapter 2

1. I should clarify at this point that, unless otherwise noted, what I say herein with regard to "Quechua" numbers and arithmetic is characteristic (in my

experience) of both the Bolivian and the Southern Peruvian varieties. As for the orthography used in this work, I have generally used Jesús Lara's dictionary of Bolivian Quechua (1991) as a guide. For Southern Peruvian Quechua of the Cusco region, I have generally followed the orthographic system utilized in Antonio Cusihuamán's *Diccionario Quechua Cuzco-Collao* (1976). I have tried to be consistent in my use of these two sources as guides; however, the reader will, no doubt, encounter some exceptions. Quechua orthography is a notoriously complex, highly politically charged, messy business. My aim here has been to try to achieve a balance of accuracy in the representation of speech sounds, consistency, and common sense.

2. It may be relevant to note that the "cantankerousness" of seven, as recognized in Quechua number symbolism, coincides with the status of this number as the upper limit of what development psychologists refer to as "subitizing." This is the phenomenon whereby the number of objects present in a set can be correctly grasped at the moment of perception, without having to count them (Crump 1992: 282; see also Hurford 1987: 93; Miller 1956).

3. For comparative purposes, I give below the primary lexemes for number names in Puquina and Uru (based on LaBarre 1941), two languages spoken in the zone of contact between Quechua and Aymara, in present-day north-central Bolivia:

No.	Puquina	Uru
1	pesc	ci
2	so	bisk
3	capa	cek
4	sper	ba'bi
5	tacpa	ta'snuku
6	chichun	taxcuku
7	stu	doko
8	quina	onko
9	checa	san'gu
10	scata	kalo
11		kalosi
12		kalo-piske
13		kalo-chep
100		kalo-kalo/pac
1,000		kalo-pac

4. In one tradition of the conception of numbers in Chinese philosophy, *three* is considered to be the first "true" number. The reason for this, as stated by the noted eighteenth-century Chinese historian and epigrapher Wang Chung is that: "One is odd; two is even. [Therefore] 1 and 2 cannot be regarded as numbers. If 1 is added to 2, the sum is 3. Therefore, 3 is the achievement (perfection)

of number" (Solomon 1954: 244; see also the discussion by Mimica (1992) on the foundation of the Iqwaye counting system in the distinction between "odd" and "even").

Chapter 3

1. The literature on the *ayllus*—the (often, but not always) kin-based, land-holding, communal labor, and ritual groups of community organization in the Andes—is quite extensive; see for example, Isbell 1985; Platt 1987; Urton 1990, 1992, 1993; and Zuidema 1964, 1990.

2. The object referred to here as *Sara Mama* appears to be the same thing that Gifford (1986: 3) labels *sarakuti:* "Quechua *sarakuti* is a corncob which is thought to have special healing powers, for it is one from which a secondary, new cob has sprouted at the time of harvest. The cob has returned to sprout anew, and the two cobs now grow simultaneously."

3. This being said, it is important to note that, while in a single (primary) rainbow, the color continuum goes from red at the bottom to violet at the top, in a double rainbow one rainbow will have the "normal" arrangement of colors while the *additional* rainbow will reverse the usual order of colors (Minnaert 1954: 180 ff.).

4. The term *pachatira* is composed of the Quechua (*pacha*) and Spanish (*tierra*) terms for "earth" (see Urton 1988: 174–177).

5. The role of *mama* as progenitrix extends to the classification of metals. Gold (*quri*) is commonly referred to as "*mama,*" as well as "*ñaupa.*" Precious metals are thought "to grow" (like plants) inside the earth in the sequence: gold, silver, copper, lead, and mercury (Salazár-Soler 1993).

Chapter 4

1. The language known as Yunga, spoken on the north coast of Peru at the time of Spanish contact, contained a distinction in counting different types or classes of things similar to that noted for Quechua by González Holguín. That is, in counting money, the term "*nassop*" was used for the number "10." However, "*napong*" was used for counting 10 when the reference was to people, horses, goats, cane reeds, "and everything else that was not money or fruit" (Carrera 1880 [1644]: 84). These are the few examples that I am aware of in South American languages of what are referred to more generally as "numeral classifiers" (see Ascher 1991: 10–14, 28; Hurford 1987: 165, 214). These usually take the form of

numeral affixes used to indicate the *kind* of object being enumerated. For instance, Friar Beltrán de la Rosa's dictionary of the Maya language, published in 1746, notes the use of *seventy-five* different affixes, forming as many numeral classes (see Nuttall 1903).

2. For suggestions concerning the possible structure of narrative story "lines," or "paths," recorded on *khipus*, see (respectively) Arnold and Yapita 1992, and Abercrombie n.d.

3. Thanks to Elayne Zorn for calling to my attention the work by Rita Prochaska.

4. In fact, as Hornberger's studies (see especially Hornberger 1987) of rural schools in Peru make clear, children will be fortunate if they receive *any* instruction in arithmetic (in either Quechua *or* Spanish) in school. Hornberger found in her studies of rural schools in Puno, Peru, that the majority of students' time is taken up with such activities as maintaining the school building and grounds; lessons in morals, patriotism, and hygiene; and sports. I would also note that the Bolivian Department of Education is currently in the process of introducing arithmetic textbooks written largely in Quechua into the elementary school curriculum in selected schools around Sucre and in the Norte de Potosí (Lic. Adrián Montalbo, personal communication, 1995). From examples of these textbooks that I have had the opportunity to study, it appears that they are Quechua translations of Aymara originals, the latter of which have been used for a few years in selected Aymara-speaking communities in northern Bolivia.

5. Many of the *Mamas* in Candelaria weave *axsus* (elaborate half-skirts) and other fabrics for sale to ASUR. For a very fine *axsu*, which requires for its completion a couple of months of fairly concentrated weaving effort (with constant interruptions for child care and household duties), a woman is paid some 400 to 500 *bolivianos* (ca. $100), depending on the size and quality of the weaving. This is somewhat more than a man can earn during a comparable period of time in more strenuous forms of wage labor, such as harvesting coca or lumbering, away from the village. It is clear—at least from anecdotal evidence, as well as from my own observations and conversations with people—that the women's opportunity to earn money at this rate is precipitating changes in the "traditional" gender relations in communities like Candelaria. This is an area of social and economic change that deserves much more explicit study than it has received to date (for an example, see Zorn 1987).

6. From informal observations I have made on rates of weaving, I have found that an expert weaver (a *Mama*) can weave a complete run across a fairly complex *axsu* in about two- to two-and-a-half minutes. This, however, is working very quickly and without interruptions, a set of conditions unusual for any woman to experience for any length of time.

Chapter 6

1. The "Huarochirí Manuscript" has traditionally been attributed to Father Francisco de Avila, a Jesuit priest born in Cusco around 1573. Avila was probably not, in fact, the author but rather was, as Salomon concludes, "a key figure in the local conjuncture that forced the manuscript into being" (Salomon and Urioste 1991: 24–25); see Salomon's introduction to *The Huarochirí Manuscript* (ibid.: 1–38) for an excellent overview of the themes addressed in this important work and of the redaction of the document.

2. Paria Caca, a five-fold being associated with the high mountaintops, was the principal deity of the Checa ethnic group, whose ceremonial center was at the site of Llacsa Tambo (Salomon and Urioste 1991: 5–6).

3. Huatya Curi ("potato-eater") was a poor Checa man who was the first to view the deity of Paria Caca (Salomon and Urioste 1991: 54).

4. An aboriginal cannibal and fire-monster deity who was banished from the highlands by Paria Caca. Huallollo Caruincho later came to dominate the lowlands and was the principal deity of the Yunca and/or Huanca ethnic group (Salomon and Urioste 1991: 5–6).

5. Chaupi Ñamca was a female land and river deity whose temple was at Mama, on the lower Rimac river; she was the wife of Pacha Camac (Salomon and Urioste 1991: 9).

6. Concerning the *khipus,* Bernabé Cobo noted that:

> not all of the Indians were capable of understanding the *quipos;* only those dedicated to this job could do it; and those who did not study *quipos* failed to understand them. Even among the *quipo camayos* themselves, one was unable to understand the registers and recording devices of others. Each one understood the *quipos* that he made and what the others told him. There were different *quipos* for different kinds of things, such as for paying tribute, lands, ceremonies, and all kinds of matters pertaining to peace and war. And the *quipo camayos* customarily passed their knowledge on to those who entered their ranks from one generation to the next. (1983 [1653]: 254)

7. Garcilaso de la Vega has the following to say concerning the nature of the *khipu* recording units:

> they may be said to have recorded on their knots everything that could be counted, even mentioning battles and fights, all the embassies that had come to visit the Inca, and all the speeches and arguments the king uttered. But the purpose of the embassies or the contents of the speeches, or any other descriptive matter could not be recorded on the knots, consist-

ing as it did of continuous spoken or written prose, which cannot be expressed by means of knots, since these can give only numbers and not words. To supply this want they used signs that indicated historical events or facts or the existence of any embassy, speech, or discussion in time of peace or war. Such speeches were preserved by the *quipucamayus* by memory in a summarized form of a few words: they were committed to memory and taught by tradition to their successors and descendants from father to son. (1970 [1609]: 331–332)

8. The Inkas demanded of their subject population tribute in the form of labor service on state projects (see Murra 1982, 1987).

9. For published examples of Spanish transcriptions of *khipu* accounts, see Murra 1975, 1982, 1987; Pärssinen 1992; and Espinoza Soriano 1971–1972. I have discussed material from these and other transcriptions in Urton n.d.

10. See Mendizábal Losack's (1989: 46–50) discussion of the numerical arrangement of black and white circles (representing stones?) on a supposed Inka "counting board" (*yupana*) in a drawing by Guaman Poma de Ayala.

11. *T'inkus* still occur with some regularity during Catholic saints' day festivals in various communities in the Norte de Potosí of Bolivia (see Platt 1987). Colin Gomez documented a *ch'axwa* in progress in the northern part of the territory of Tinquipaya, pitting *ayllus* of Tinquipaya against some southern *ayllus* of Macha, in 1993 (personal communication, 1993).

12. For more complete discussions of the context in which this *khipu* transcription was drawn up, see Espinoza Soriano 1971–1972, and Murra 1975, 1982.

13. For a discussion of units of currency and the processes and effects of the devaluation of currency in the central and southern Andes in colonial and early Republican times, see Mitre 1986; Platt 1986a; and Bischoff 1989.

14. *Repartimiento* here refers to the forced sale to Andean peoples of goods that were produced primarily in Spain. The practice, aimed at creating a market for Spanish goods and expanding the internal market in the Andes, began in the late-seventeenth century. Resentment toward this practice led, by the 1780s, to a number of both local and large-scale, regional rebellions.

Bibliography

Abercrombie, Thomas A. n.d. *Pathways of Memory and Power: Ethnography and History among an Andean People.* Madison: University of Wisconsin Press (in press).

Adorno, Rolena. 1986. *Guaman Poma: Writing and Resistance in Colonial Peru.* Austin: University of Texas Press.

Alberti, Giorgio, and Enrique Mayer. 1974. "Reciprocidad andina: Ayer y hoy." In *Reciprocidad e intercambio en los Andes peruanos,* pp. 18–33. Lima: Instituto de Estudios Peruanos.

Altschuler, Milton. 1965. *The Cayapa: A Study in Legal Behavior.* Ph.D. dissertation, University of Minnesota.

Andrien, Kenneth J. 1991. "Spaniards, Andeans, and the Early Colonial State in Peru." In *Transatlantic Encounters: Europeans and Andeans in the Sixteenth Century,* edited by K. J. Andrien and R. Adorno, pp. 121–150. Berkeley: University of California Press.

Arnold, Denise Y., and Juan de Dios Yapita. 1992. "*Sallqa:* Dirigirse a las bestias silvestres en los Andes meridionales." In *Hacia un Orden Andino de las Cosas,* edited by D. Y. Arnold, D. Jiménez A., and J. de Dios Yapita, pp. 175–212. La Paz: HISBOL.

Ascher, Marcia. 1991. *Ethnomathematics: A Multicultural View of Mathematical Ideas.* Pacific Grove, California: Brooks/Cole Publishing Co.

Ascher, Marcia, and Robert Ascher. 1969. "Code of Ancient Peruvian Knotted Cords (Quipus)." *Nature* 222: 529–533.

———. 1975. "The Quipu as a Visible Language." *Visible Language* 9: 329–356.

———. 1978. *Code of the Quipu: Databook.* Ann Arbor: University of Michigan Press.

———. 1981. *Code of the Quipu: A Study in Media, Mathematics and Culture.* Ann Arbor: University of Michigan Press.

Aveni, Anthony F. 1980. *Skywatchers of Ancient Mexico.* Austin: University of Texas Press.

Barnes, Monica. 1992. "Catechisms and Confessionarios: Distorting Mirrors of Andean Societies." In *Andean Cosmologies through Time: Persistence and Emergence,* edited by R. V. H. Dover, K. E. Seibold, and J. H. McDowell; pp. 67–94. Bloomington: Indiana University Press.

Barrow, John D. 1992. *Pi in the Sky: Counting, Thinking and Being.* Oxford: Clarendon Press.

Bertonio, Ludovico. 1984. *Vocabulario de la Lengua Aymará* [1612]. Cochabamba, Bolivia: Ediciones CERES.

Biersack, Aletta. 1982. "The Logic of Misplaced Concreteness: Paiela Body Counting and the Nature of the Primitive Mind." *American Anthropologist* 84: 811–829.

Bischoff, William L. (ed.). 1989. *The Coinage of El Perú*. New York: American Numismatic Society.

Bishop, Alan J. 1990. "Western Mathematics: The Secret Weapon of Cultural Imperialism." *Race and Class* 32 (2): 51–65.

Boone, Elizabeth Hill, and Walter D. Mignolo (eds.). 1994. *Writing without Words: Alternative Literacies in Mesoamerica and the Andes*. Durham: Duke University Press.

Bourdieu, Pierre. 1979. *Outline of a Theory of Practice*. Cambridge: Cambridge University Press.

Boyer, C. B. 1968. *A History of Mathematics*. New York: Wiley.

Briggs, Lucy Therina. 1993. *El Idioma Aymará: Variantes Regionales y Sociales*. La Paz: Ediciones ILCA.

Brown, Donald E. 1991. *Human Universals*. Philadelphia: Temple University Press.

Carrera, D. Fernando de la. 1880. *Arte de la Lengua Yunga* [1644]. Lima: Imp. Liberal.

Cereceda, Verónica. 1987. "Aproximaciones a una estética andina: De la belleza al *tinku*." In *Tres Reflexiones sobre el Pensamiento Andino,* edited by T. Bouysse-Cassagne et al., pp. 133–231. La Paz: HISBOL.

———. 1990. "A partir de los colores de un pájaro . . . " *Boletín del Museo Chileno de Arte Precolombino* 4: 57–104.

Chadwick, John. 1958. *The Decipherment of Linear B*. New York: Vintage Books.

Classen, Constance. 1993. *Inka Cosmology and the Human Body*. Salt Lake City: University of Utah Press.

Closs, Michael P. (ed.). 1986. *Native American Mathematics*. Austin: University of Texas Press.

Cobo, Bernabé. 1983. *History of the Inca Empire* [1653]. Translated and edited by Roland Hamilton. Austin: University of Texas Press.

———. 1990. *Inca Religion and Customs* [1653]. Translated and edited by Roland Hamilton. Austin: University of Texas Press.

Conklin, William J. n.d. "Structure as Meaning in Ancient Andean Textiles." Ms. on file with the author.

Connerton, Paul. 1989. *How Societies Remember*. Cambridge: Cambridge University Press.

Crump, Thomas. 1990. *The Anthropology of Numbers*. Cambridge: Cambridge University Press.

Crystal, David. 1987. *The Cambridge Encyclopedia of Language*. Cambridge: Cambridge University Press.

Cummins, Tom. 1994. "Representation in the Sixteenth Century and the Colonial Image of the Inca." In *Writing without Words: Alternative Literacies in Mesoamerica and the Andes,* edited by Elizabeth H. Boone and Walter Mignolo, pp. 188–219. Durham: Duke University Press.

Cusihuamán G., Antonio. 1976. *Diccionario Quechua Cuzco-Collao.* Lima: Ministerio de Educación, Instituto de Estudios Peruanos.

Dantzig, Tobias. 1954. *Number, The Language of Science.* New York: The Free Press.

Dávalos, Johnny, Verónica Cereceda, and Gabriel Martínez. 1992. *Textiles Tarabuco.* Sucre, Bolivia: Ediciones ASUR 2.

Desrosiers, Sophie. 1992. "Las técnicas del tejido: Tienen un sentido? Una propuesta de lectura de los tejidos andinos." *Revista Andina* 10 (1): 7–34.

Dixon, R. M. W. 1977. "Where Have All the Adjectives Gone?" *Studies in Language* 1: 19–80.

Dummett, Michael. 1991. *Frege: Philosophy of Mathematics.* Cambridge: Harvard University Press.

Earls, John. 1972. *Andean Continuum Cosmology.* Ph.D. dissertation, University of Illinois at Urbana-Champaign.

Emery, Irene. 1994. *The Primary Structures of Fabrics* [1966]. The Textile Museum, Washington, D.C.: Watson-Guptill Publications/Whitney Library of Design.

Espinoza Soriano, Waldemar. 1971–1972. "Los huancas aliados de la conquista." *Anales Científicos* 1: 9–407.

Femenias, Blenda. 1987. "Design Principles in Andean Textiles." In *Andean Aesthetics: Textiles of Peru and Bolivia,* edited by B. Femenias, pp. 9–45. University of Wisconsin at Madison: Elvehjem Museum of Art.

Forbes, David. 1870. "On the Aymara Indians of Bolivia and Peru." *Ethnological Society of London, Journal,* n.s., 2: 193–305.

Franquemont, Christine R. 1986. "Chinchero Pallays: An Ethnic Code." In *The Junius B. Bird Textile Conference on Andean Textiles,* edited by A. Rowe, pp. 331–338. Washington, D.C.: The Textile Museum.

Franquemont, Edward M., Christine Franquemont, and Billie Jean Isbell. 1992. "*Awaq Ñawin:* El ojo del tejedor. La práctica de la cultura en el tejido." *Revista Andina* 10 (1): 47–80.

Garcilaso de la Vega, El Inca. 1970. *Royal Commentaries of the Incas* [1609]. Translated with an Introduction by H. V. Livermore. 2 vols. Austin: University of Texas Press.

Gelb, I. J. 1963. *A Study of Writing* [1952]. Chicago: University of Chicago Press.

Gifford, Douglas. 1986. "Time Metaphors in Aymara and Quechua." University of St. Andrews Centre for Latin American Linguistic Studies, Working Paper No. 16. St. Andrews.

Gillings, R. J. 1978. "The Mathematics of Ancient Egypt." In *Dictionary of Scientific Biography* 154, supplement 1. Edited by Roger Adams and Ludwik Zejszner, pp. 681–705. New York: Charles Scribner's Sons.

González Holguín, Diego de. 1975. *Gramática y arte nueva de la lengua general de todo el Perú llamada lengua Qquichua o del Inca* [1607]. Vaduz-Georgetown: Cabildo.

———. 1952. *Vocabulario de la lengua general de todo el Perú llamada lengua Qquichua o del Inca* [1608]. Lima: Universidad Nacional Mayor de San Marcos.

Goody, Jack. 1978. *The Domestication of the Savage Mind.* Cambridge: Cambridge University Press.

Goody, Jack, and I. P. Watt. 1968. "The Consequences of Literacy" [1963]. In *Literacy in Traditional Societies,* edited by Jack Goody, pp. 27–68. Cambridge: Cambridge University Press.

Gough, Kathleen. 1968. "Implications of Literacy in Traditional China and India." In *Literacy in Traditional Societies,* edited by Jack Goody, pp. 69–84. Cambridge: Cambridge University Press.

Green, M. W. 1991. "Early Cuneiform." In *The Origins of Writing,* edited by Wayne M. Senner, pp. 43–58. Lincoln: University of Nebraska Press.

Guaman Poma de Ayala, Felipe. 1980. *El primer nueva corónica y buen gobierno* [1615]. Critical edition by J. V. Murra and Rolena Adorno; translation and textual analysis by Jorge L. Urioste. 3 vols. Mexico City: Siglo Veintiuno.

Gusinde, Martín. 1931. "The Fireland Indians." In *The Selk'nam: On the Life and Thought of a Hunting People of the Great Island of Tierra del Fuego* 1: 1106–1110. Modling bei Wien: Verlag der International en Zeitschrift, "Anthropos."

Hallpike, C. R. 1979. *The Foundations of Primitive Thought.* Oxford: Clarendon Press.

Halverson, John. 1992. "Goody and the Implosion of the Literacy Thesis." *Man* 27 (2): 301–317.

Hardman-de-Bautista, Martha J. 1985. "Quechua and Aymara: Languages in Contact." In *South American Indian Languages: Retrospect and Prospect,* edited by Harriet E. Manelis Klein and Louisa R. Stark, pp. 617–643. Austin: University of Texas Press.

Hardy, G. H. 1993. *A Mathematician's Apology* [1940]. Cambridge: Cambridge University Press.

Harris, Olivia. 1987. *Economía Étnica.* Breve Biblioteca de Bolsillo, No. 3. La Paz: HISBOL.

Harris, Olivia, Brooke Larson, and Enrique Tandeter (eds.). 1987. *La Participación Indígena en los Mercados Surandinos.* La Paz: Centro de Estudios de la Realidad Económica y Social.

Herrero, Joaquín, and Federico Sánchez de Lozada. 1983. *Diccionario Quechua-Español.* 2 vols. Sucre, Bolivia: Talleres Gráficos "Qori Llama."

Hickman, John M. 1963. *The Aymara of Chinchera, Peru: Persistence and Change in a Bicultural Context.* Ph.D. dissertation, Cornell University.

Holmberg, Allan R. 1985. *Nomads of the Long Bow: The Siriono of Eastern Bolivia* [1950]. Prospect Heights, Ill.: Waveland Press.

Hornberger, Nancy H. 1987. "Schooltime, Classtime and Academic Learning Time in Rural Highland Puno, Peru." *Anthropology and Education Quarterly* 18: 207–221.

Huerta, Alonso de. 1993. *Arte Breve de la Lengua Quechua* [1616]. Quito: Corporación Editora Nacional.

Hurford, James R. 1987. *Language and Number: The Emergence of a Cognitive System.* Oxford: Basil Blackwell.

Isbell, Billie Jean. 1985. *To Defend Ourselves: Ecology and Ritual in an Andean Village* [1978]. Prospect Heights, Ill.: Waveland Press.

Isbell, Billie Jean, and Fredy Amilcar Roncalla Fernandez. 1977. "The Ontogenesis of Metaphor: Riddle Games among Quechua Speakers Seen as Cognitive Discovery Procedures." *Journal of Latin American Lore* 3 (1): 19–49.

Izko, Xavier. 1992. *La Doble Frontera: Ecología, política y ritual en el altiplano central.* La Paz: HISBOL.

James, Glen, and Robert C. James. 1976. *Mathematics Dictionary.* New York: Van Nostrand Reinhold.

Joseph, George Gheverghese. 1991. *The Crest of the Peacock: Non-European Roots of Mathematics.* London: Penguin Books.

Julien, Catherine J. 1988. "How Inca Decimal Administration Worked." *Ethnohistory* 35 (3): 357–379.

Karsten, Rafael. 1930. *Ceremonial Games of the South American Indians.* Societas Scientiarum Fennica. Commentationes Humanarum Litterarum 3 (2). Leipzig: Otto Harrasowitz.

———. 1935. *The Head-Hunters of Western Amazonas.* Helsingfors: Centraltryckeriet.

Kitcher, Philip. 1983. *The Nature of Mathematical Knowledge.* New York and Oxford: Oxford University Press.

LaBarre, Weston. 1941. "The Uru of the Rio Desaguadero." *American Anthropologist,* n.s., 43: 493–522.

———. 1948. *The Aymara Indians of the Lake Titicaca Plateau, Bolivia.* Menasha: American Anthropological Association.

Langer, Erick D. 1989. *Economic Change and Rural Resistance in Southern Bolivia, 1880–1930.* Stanford: Stanford University Press.

Lara, Jesús. 1991. *Diccionario Qheshwa-Castellano/Castellano-Qheshwa.* Cochabamba, Bolivia: Editorial "Los Amigos del Libro."

Larson, Brooke. 1988. *Colonialism and Agrarian Transformation in Bolivia: Cochabamba, 1550–1900.* Princeton: Princeton University Press.

Lave, Jean. 1991. *Cognition in Practice: Mind, Mathematics and Culture in Everyday Life.* Cambridge: Cambridge University Press.

Lechtman, Heather N. 1980. "The Central Andes: Metallurgy without Iron." In *The Coming of the Age of Iron,* edited by T. A. Wertime and J. D. Muhly, pp. 267–334. New Haven: Yale University Press.

Lehmann, David (ed.). 1982. *Ecology and Exchange in the Andes*. Cambridge: Cambridge University Press.

Lira, Jorge A. 1982. *Diccionario Kkechuwa-Español*. Cuadernos Culturales Andinos, No. 5. Bogotá: Editora Guadalupe Ltda.

Locke, L. Leland. 1923. *The Ancient Quipu, or Peruvian Knot Record*. New York: American Museum of Natural History.

López-Baralt, Mercedes. 1987. *El Retorno del Inca Rey: Mito y profecía en el mundo andino*. Madrid: Editorial Playor.

Mackey, Carol, Hugo Pereyra, Carlos Radicati, Humberto Rodríguez, and Oscar Valverde. 1990. *Quipu y Yupana: Colección de escritos*. Lima: Consejo Nacional de Ciencia y Tecnología.

Mannheim, Bruce. 1991. *The Language of the Inka since the European Invasion*. Austin: University of Texas Press.

Matienzo, Juan de. 1967. *Gobierno del Perú* [1567]. Travaux de L'Institut Français D'Études Andines 11. Paris: Pierre André.

Mauss, Marcel. 1967. *The Gift* [1925]. New York: W. W. Norton.

Mayer, Enrique. 1974. "Las reglas del juego en la reciprocidad andina." In *Reciprocidad e intercambio en los Andes peruanos*, edited by G. Alberti and E. Mayer, pp. 37–65. Lima: Instituto de Estudios Peruanos.

————. 1982. *A Tribute to the Household: Domestic Economy and the Encomienda in Colonial Peru*. Working Paper, Institute of Latin American Studies. University of Texas at Austin.

Meisch, Lynn A. 1986. "Weaving Styles in Tarabuco, Bolivia." In *The Junius B. Bird Conference on Andean Textiles*, edited by A. Rowe, pp. 243–274. Washington, D.C.: The Textile Museum.

————. 1987. "The Living Textiles of Tarabuco, Bolivia." In *Andean Aesthetics: Textiles of Peru and Bolivia*, by Blenda Femenias et al., pp. 46–59. University of Wisconsin at Madison: Elvehjem Museum of Art.

Mendizábal Losack, Emilio. 1989. *Estructura y Función en La Cultura Andina (Fase Inka)*. Lima: Editorial de la Universidad Nacional Mayor de San Marcos.

Menninger, Karl. 1969. *Number Words and Number Symbols: A Cultural History of Numbers*. Cambridge: MIT Press.

Meyerson, Julia. 1993. *'Tambo: Life in an Andean Village*. Austin: University of Texas Press.

Mignolo, Walter D. 1995. *The Darker Side of the Renaissance: Literacy, Territoriality, and Colonization*. Ann Arbor: University of Michigan Press.

Miller, George A. 1956. "The Magical Number Seven, Plus or Minus Two: Some Limits on Our Capacity for Processing Information." *The Psychological Review* 63: 81–97.

Mimica, Jadran. 1992. *Intimations of Infinity: The Cultural Meanings of the Iqwaye Counting and Number System*. Oxford: Berg.

Minnaert, M. G. J. 1954. *The Nature of Light and Colour in the Open Air*. New York: Dover.

Mitre, Antonio. 1986. *El Monedero de los Andes: Región económico y moneda boliviana en el siglo XIX*. La Paz: HISBOL.

Morató Peña, Luis, and Luis Morató Lara. n.d. *Quechua Boliviano Trilingüe* (Intermediate Level). Mimeograph.

Mossi, Honorio. 1860. *Diccionario Castellano–Quichua*. Sucre, Bolivia: Imprenta Boliviana.

Murra, John V. 1962. "Cloth and Its Functions in the Inca State." *American Anthropologist* 64 (4): 710–727.

———. 1975. "Las etno-categorías de un *khipu* estatal" [1973]. In *Formaciones económicas y políticas del mundo andino*, pp. 244–254. Lima: Instituto de Estudios Peruanos.

———. 1982. "The *Mit'a* Obligations of Ethnic Groups to the Inka State." In *The Inca and Aztec States, 1400–1800*, edited by G. A. Collier, R. I. Rosaldo, and J. D. Wirth, pp. 237–262. New York: Academic Press.

———. 1987. "Existieron el tributo y los mercados antes de la invasión europea?" In *La Participación Indígena en los Mercados Surandinos*, edited by O. Harris, B. Larson, and E. Tandeter, pp. 51–61. La Paz: CERES.

Musters, George C. 1873. *At Home with the Patagonians*. London: John Murray.

Nakayama, Shigeru. 1978. "Japanese Scientific Thought." In *Dictionary of Scientific Biography* 15, supplement 1, edited by Roger Adams and Ludwik Zejszner, pp. 728–758. New York: Charles Scribner's Sons.

Needham, Joseph. 1959. *Science and Civilisation in China*. Vol. 3: *Mathematics and the Sciences of the Heavens and the Earth*. Cambridge: Cambridge University Press.

Nuttall, Zelia. 1903. "A Suggestion to Maya Scholars." *American Anthropologist* 5: 667– 678.

O'Phelan Godoy, Scarlett. 1988. *Un siglo de rebeliones anticoloniales: Perú y Bolivia, 1700–1783*. Cusco, Peru: Centro de Estudios Rurales Andinos Bartolomé de las Casas.

Ortiz, Alfonso. 1969. *The Tewa World: Space, Time, Being and Becoming in a Pueblo Society*. Chicago: University of Chicago Press.

Parker, Gary J. 1963. "La clasificación genética de los dialectos quechuas." *Revista del Museo Nacional* 32: 241–252.

Parsons, Elsie W. C. 1945. *Peguche, Canton of Otavalo, Province of Imbabura, Ecuador: A Study of Andean Indians*. Chicago: University of Chicago Press.

Pärssinen, Martti. 1992. *Tawantinsuyu: The Inca State and Its Political Organization*. Studia Historica, 43. Helsinki: Societas Historica Finlandiae.

Phillips, William D., Jr., and Carla R. Phillips. 1991. "Spain in the Fifteenth Century." In *Transatlantic Encounters: Europeans and Andeans in the Sixteenth Century*, edited by K. J. Andrien and R. Adorno, pp. 11–39. Berkeley: University of California Press.

Piaget, Jean. 1969. *The Child's Conception of Number* [1941]. London: Routledge & Kegan Paul.

————. 1972. *Psychology and Epistemology.* Harmondsworth: Penguin.

Platt, Tristan. 1986a. *Estado Tributario y Librecambio en Potosí (Siglo XIX).* La Paz: HISBOL.

————. 1986b. "Mirrors and Maize: The Concept of *yanantin* among the Macha of Bolivia." In *Anthropological History of Andean Polities,* edited by J. V. Murra, N. Watchel, and J. Revel, pp. 228–259. Cambridge: Cambridge University Press.

————. 1987. "Entre *Ch'axwa* y *Muxsa.* Para una historia del pensamiento político Aymara." In *Tres Reflexiones sobre el Pensamiento Andino,* edited by T. Bouysse-Cassagne et al., pp. 61–132. La Paz: HISBOL.

Polo de Ondegardo, Juan. 1916. *Informaciones Acerca de la Religión y Gobierno de los Incas* [1571]. Colección de Libros y Documentos Referentes a la Historia del Perú 3. Lima: Imprenta y Librería Sanmarti y Ca.

Porras Barrenechea, Raúl. 1986. *Los Cronistas del Perú (1528–1650) y Otros Ensayos.* Biblioteca Clásicos del Perú, No. 2. Lima: Banco de Crédito del Perú.

Posner, Jill K. 1982. "The Development of Mathematical Knowledge in Two West African Societies." *Child Development* 53: 200–208.

Prochaska, Rita. 1988. *Taquile: Tejiendo un mundo mágico / Weavers of a magic world.* Lima: Arius.

Protzen, Jean-Pierre. 1993. *Inca Architecture and Construction at Ollantaytambo.* New York and Oxford: Oxford University Press.

Radicati di Primeglio, Carlos. 1979. *El Sistema contable de los Incas.* Lima: Librería Studium, SA.

Rappaport, Joanne. 1994. "Object and Alphabet: Andean Indians and Documents in the Colonial Period." In *Writing without Words,* edited by E. H. Boone and W. D. Mignolo, pp. 271–292. Durham: Duke University Press.

Rivière, Gilles. 1983. "Quadripartition et idéologie dans les communautés aymaras de Carangas (Bolivie)." *Boletín del Instituto Francés de Estudios Andinos* 12 (3–4): 41–62.

Rostworowski, María, and Pilar Remy. 1992. *Las Visitas a Cajamarca, 1571–72/ 1578.* Lima: Instituto de Estudios Peruanos.

Rotman, Brian. 1987. *Signifying Nothing: The Semiotics of Zero.* London: Macmillan.

————. 1988. "Toward a Semiotics of Mathematics." *Semiotica* 72: 1–35.

————. 1993. *Ad Infinitum: The Ghost in Turing's Machine; Taking God Out of Mathematics and Putting the Body Back In; An Essay in Corporeal Semiotics.* Stanford: Stanford University Press.

Rowe, John H. 1957. "The Incas Under Spanish Colonial Institutions." *Hispanic American Historical Review* 37: 155–199.

————. 1958. "The Age-Grades of the Inca Census." *Miscellanea Paul Rivet Octogenario dicata* 2: 499–522. XXXI Congreso Internacional de Americanistas. Mexico City: Univ. Nac. Aut. de México.

————. 1982. "Inca Policies and Institutions Relating to the Cultural Unification of the Empire." In *The Inca and Aztec States, 1400–1800,* edited by G. A. Collier, R. I. Rosaldo, and J. D. Wirth, pp. 93–118. New York: Academic Press.

Russell, Bertrand. 1980. *Principles of Mathematics* [1903]. New York: W. W. Norton.

Salazár-Soler, Carmen. 1993. "Magia y modernidad en las minas andinas: Mitos sobre el origen de los metales y el trabajo minero." In *Tradición y Modernidad en los Andes,* edited by Henrique Urbano, pp. 197–219. Cusco: Centro de Estudios Regionales Andinos "Bartolomé de las Casas."

Salomon, Frank. 1991. "La moneda que a Don Cristóbal se le cayó: El dinero como elemento simbólico en el texto runa yndio ñiscap machoncuna." In *Reproducción y Transformación de las Sociedades Andinas, Siglos XVI–XX,* edited by Segundo Moreno Y. and Frank Salomon, pp. 481–586. Quito: Ediciones ABYA-YALA.

———. 1995. "'The Beautiful Grandparents': Andean Ancestor Shrines and Mortuary Ritual as Seen Through Colonial Records." In *Tombs for the Living: Andean Mortuary Practices,* edited by Tom D. Dillehay, pp. 315–354. Washington, D.C.: Dumbarton Oaks Research Library and Collection.

Salomon, Frank, and George L. Urioste. 1991. *The Huarochirí Manuscript: A Testament of Ancient and Colonial Andean Religion.* Austin: University of Texas Press.

Santo Tomás, Fray Domingo de. 1951. *Lexicón, o vocabulario de la lengua general del Perú* [1560]. Lima: Edición facsimilar Raúl Porras Barranechea.

———. 1992. *Gramática Quichua* [1560]. Quito, Ecuador: Corporación Editora Nacional.

Sawyer, Alan R. 1967. "Tiahuanaco Tapestry Design." In *Peruvian Archaeology: Selected Readings,* edited by John. H. Rowe and Dorothy Menzel, pp. 165–176. Palo Alto: Peek Publications.

Schmandt-Besserat, Denise. 1978. "The Earliest Precursor of Writing." *Scientific American* (June 1978): 50–59.

———. 1991. "Two Precursors of Writing: Plain and Complex Tokens." In *The Origins of Writing,* edited by Wayne M. Senner, pp. 27–42. Lincoln: University of Nebraska Press.

Shimada, Izumi, Stephen M. Epstein, and Alan K. Craig. 1983. "The Metallurgical Process in Ancient North Peru." *Archaeology* 36 (5): 38–45.

Solís F., Gustavo, and Jorge Chacón S. 1990. "La gramática de la numeración quechua." In *Quipu y Yupana,* edited by Carol Mackey et al., pp. 287–294. Lima: Consejo Nacional de Ciencia y Tecnología.

Solomon, Bernard S. 1954. "'One Is No Number' in China and the West." *Harvard Journal of Asiatic Studies* 17: 253–260.

Solórzano y Pereyra, Juan de. 1972. *Política Indiana* [1736]. Vol. 2. Biblioteca de Autores Españoles. Madrid: Lope de Vega.

Spalding, Karen. 1984. *Huarochirí: An Andean Society Under Inca and Spanish Rule.* Stanford: Stanford University Press.

Starn, Orin. 1991. "Missing the Revolution: Anthropologists and the War in Peru." *Cultural Anthropology* 6 (1): 63–91.

Stern, Steve J. 1982. *Peru's Indian Peoples and the Challenge of Spanish Conquest: Huamanga to 1640.* Madison: University of Wisconsin Press.

Sullivan, Lawrence E. 1985. "Above, Below, or Far Away: Andean Cosmogony and Ethical Order." In *Cosmogony and Ethical Order,* edited by R. W. Lovin and F. E. Reynolds, pp. 98–132. Chicago: University of Chicago Press.

Swetz, Frank J. 1989. *Capitalism and Arithmetic: The New Math of the 15th Century.* La Salle, Ill.: Open Court.

Torero, Alfredo. 1964. "Los dialectos quechuas." *Anales Científicos de la Universidad Agraria* 2: 446–478.

———. 1974. *El Quechua y la Historia Social Andina.* Lima: Universidad Ricardo Palma.

Tschopik, Harry, Jr. 1951. *The Aymara of Chucuito, Peru.* New York: American Museum of Natural History.

Turner, Mark. 1987. *Death Is the Mother of Beauty: Mind, Metaphor, Criticism.* Chicago: University of Chicago Press.

Urton, Gary. 1984. "*Chuta:* El espacio de la práctica social en Pacariqtambo, Perú." *Revista Andina* 2 (1): 7–56.

———. 1986. "Calendrical Cycles and Their Projections in Pacariqtambo, Perú." *Journal of Latin American Lore* 12 (1): 45–64.

———. 1988. *At the Crossroads of the Earth and the Sky: An Andean Cosmology* [1981]. Austin: University of Texas Press.

———. 1990. *The History of a Myth: Pacariqtambo and the Origin of the Inkas.* Austin: University of Texas Press.

———. 1992. "Communalism and Differentiation in an Andean Community." In *Andean Cosmologies through Time,* edited by R. V. H. Dover, K. E. Seibold, and J. H. McDowell, pp. 229–266. Bloomington: Indiana University Press.

———. 1993. "Contesting the Past in the Peruvian Andes." In *Mémoire de la Tradition,* edited by A. Becquelin and A. Molinie, pp. 107–144. Nanterre: Societé d'ethnologie.

———. 1994. "A New Twist in an Old Yarn: Variation in Knot Directionality in the Inka Khipus." *Baessler-Archiv* Neue Folge, Band 42: 271–305.

———. n.d. "From Knots to Narratives: Reconstructing the Art of Historical Record-Keeping in the Andes from Spanish Transcriptions of Inka *Khipu*s." Ms. in files of the author.

Valencia Espinoza, Abraham. 1979. "Nombres del maíz y su uso ritual por los K'anas." *Antropología Andina* 3: 75–88.

Van der Ploeg, Jan Douwe. 1993. "Potatoes and Knowledge." In *An Anthropological Critique of Development,* edited by Mark Hobart, pp. 209–227. London: Routledge.

Van der Waerden, B. L. 1978. "Mathematics and Astronomy in Mesopotamia." In *Dictionary of Scientific Biography.* Vol. 15, Supplement 1, edited by Roger Adams and Ludwik Zejszner, pp. 667–680. New York: Charles Scribner's Sons.

Wachtel, Nathan. 1982. "The *mitimas* of the Cochabamba Valley: The Colonization Policy of Huayna Capac." In *The Inca and Aztec States, 1400–1800,* edited by George A. Collier, Renato I. Rosaldo, and John D. Wirth, pp. 199–235. New York: Academic Press.

Wedin, Ake. 1965. *El sistema decimal en el imperio incaico.* Madrid: Insula.

Wittgenstein, Ludwig. 1978. *Remarks on the Foundations of Mathematics.* Edited by G. H. von Wright, R. Rhees, and G. E. M. Anscombe. Translated by G. E. M. Anscombe. Cambridge: MIT Press.

Zaslavsky, Claudia. 1990. *Africa Counts: Number and Pattern in African Culture* [1973]. Brooklyn: Lawrence Hill Books.

Zorn, Elayne. 1987. "Encircling Meaning: Economics and Aesthetics in Taquile, Peru." In *Andean Aesthetics: Textiles of Peru and Bolivia,* by Blenda Femenias et al., pp. 67–79. University of Wisconsin at Madison: Elvehjem Museum of Art.

Zuidema, R. Tom. 1964. *The Ceque System of Cuzco: The Social Organization of the Capital of the Inca.* Leiden: E. J. Brill.

———. 1977. "The Inca Calendar." In *Native American Astronomy,* edited by A. F. Aveni, pp. 219–259. Austin: University of Texas Press.

———. 1982. "Bureaucracy and Systematic Knowledge in Andean Civilization." In *The Inca and Aztec States, 1400–1800,* edited by G. A. Collier, R. I. Rosaldo, and J. D. Wirth, pp. 419–458. New York: Academic Press.

———. 1989. "A Quipu Calendar from Ica, Peru, with a Comparison to the Ceque Calendar from Cuzco." In *World Archaeoastronomy,* edited by A. F. Aveni, pp. 341–351. Cambridge: Cambridge University Press.

———. 1990. *Inca Civilization in Cuzco.* Austin: University of Texas Press.

———. 1991. "Guaman Poma and the Art of Empire: Toward an Iconography of Inca Royal Dress." In *Transatlantic Encounters: Europeans and Andeans in the Sixteenth Century,* edited by K. J. Andrien and Rolena Adorno, pp. 151–202. Berkeley: University of California Press.

Index

Page numbers in italics indicate illustrations